Field Guide to
acadia national park, maine

Field Guide to
acadia national park, maine

Revised Edition

RUSSELL D. BUTCHER

TAYLOR TRADE PUBLISHING
Lanham • New York • Dallas • Boulder • Toronto • Oxford

Published by Taylor Trade Publishing
An imprint of The Rowman & Littlefield Publishing Group, Inc.
4501 Forbes Boulevard, Suite 200
Lanham, Maryland 20706

Distributed by National Book Network

Library of Congress Cataloging-in-Publication Data
Butcher, Russell D.
    Field guide to Acadia National Park, Maine / Russell D. Butcher.—
Rev. ed.,
1st Taylor trade pub. ed.
        p. cm.
    Includes bibliographical references and index.
    ISBN 1-58979-184-3 (pbk. : alk. paper)
1. Acadia National Park (Me.)—Guidebooks. 2. Natural history—Maine—
Acadia National Park—Guidebooks. 3. Trails—Maine—Acadia National
Park—Guidebooks.
I. Title.
F27.M9B86 2005
917.41'4504—dc22   2004021662

♾ The paper used in this publication meets the minimum requirements of American National Standard for Information Sciences—Permanence of Paper for Printed Library Materials, ANSI/NISO Z39.48–1992.
Manufactured in the United States of America.

TO

All of the employees, researchers, interns, volunteers, and donors
who are helping to protectively manage Acadia National Park
as one of the Crown Jewels of America's
National Park System.

Contents

Contents

Acknowledgments

In 1976, after completing the first edition of this field guide to Acadia National Park, I expressed in the Acknowledgments my gratitude "to my friend Vernon C. Gray for his invaluable help and advice on the Rocks and Landforms and Intertidal Life sections. For helpful suggestions thanks also to Dr. Harold W. Borns Jr., of the Department of Geological Sciences and Institute for Quaternary Studies, and Associate Professor of Botany Richard L. Homola, both of the University of Maine at Orono." I also expressed special thanks to Keith E. Miller, then Acadia National Park's superintendent; and to Robert Rothe, then the park's ranger-naturalist.

For assistance with this revised second edition, I am extremely grateful to the national park staff: Wanda Moran, Keith Johnston, Gary Stellpflug, Marc Neidig, Kate Petrie, and Superintendent Sheridan Steele; and again to Keith Miller. My thanks to Rick Rinehart of Roberts Rinehart Publishers and to Stephen Driver at the Rowman & Littlefield Publishing Group for publishing this updated edition of the Acadia field guide. Thanks also to Barbara Werden and Beth Easter for their work on the book. Thanks also to my parents, Mary and Devereux Butcher, who deeply loved Mount Desert Island, for encouraging me to see and cherish the wonders and beauty of nature. I am lovingly grateful to my wife, Karen, for her supportive encouragement in revising this enjoyable project.

—RUSS BUTCHER

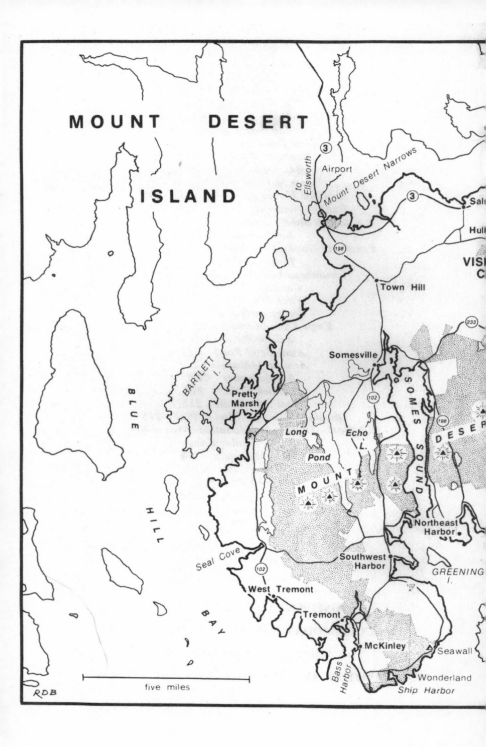

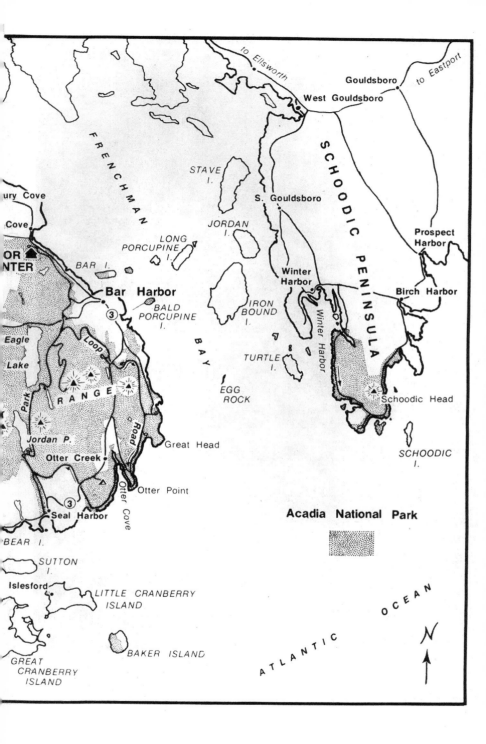

Acadia National Park

MOUNT DESERT ISLAND

Two-thirds of the way "down east"
along the rugged coast of Maine lies
a unique and special place called
Mount Desert. It is the largest of the
many hundreds of land fragments
that rise out of the cold sea between
Kittery and Eastport. The island's
108 square miles embrace some of
the most varied and charming
scenery of any area of comparable
size in America.

Just on this single island . . .

- A spectacular range of glacially
  carved granite mountains rises
  boldly out of the Atlantic Ocean,
  seven summits of which exceed a
  thousand feet in elevation.
- More than a score of lakes and
  ponds are magnificently framed by
  mountains and forest, many of
  them filling basins that were
  scoured out thousands of years ago
  by glacial ice.
- A 5-mile-long arm of the sea, Somes
  Sound, the only fjord on the United
  States Atlantic coast, slices between

the mountains and nearly cuts the
island in half.

- Forests contain a rich blend of nee-
  dled and broad-leaved trees that
  provide varied habitats for an abundance of wildlife.
- Well over a hundred kinds of wildflowers and flowering shrubs put
  on a continual parade of color from
  April to October.
- Clear brooks flow down the mountainsides and sheltered valleys,
  bubbling and chattering along boulder-strewn courses and producing
  occasional waterfalls.
- Carpets of miniature gray lichens
  and lush green mosses cover exposed ledges and the ground in
  deeply shaded spruce woods.
- Fragile, Arctic-like peat bogs,
  ringed around by slender spruces
  and tamaracks, offer ideal conditions for tiny rare orchids, insectiv-
  orous plants, and springy mats of
  water-storing sphagnum moss.
- An abundance of wildlife inhabits
  the island, including such resident
  species as white-tailed deer, red fox,

raccoon, and beaver; and such migratory birds as thrushes, flycatchers, and warblers.

- Numerous coves and harbors indent the shoreline—some secluded and wild, while others that are bordered by many of the island's villages have long been safe havens for lobster-fishing boats and sailboats.

- Widely fluctuating ocean tides along rocky shores have created a broad intertidal zone that is an ancient and primitive link between marine and terrestrial life.

- Offshore clusters of smaller spruce-covered islands and barren surf-washed reefs dot the surrounding bays and open ocean.

HISTORICAL BACKGROUND

Long before the first European explorers arrived, Native Americans—possibly the ancestors of the present day Penobscots and Passamaquoddies—paddled down the rivers and along the coast of Maine in their birch-bark canoes. They established camps at choice spots, such as Northeast Harbor and the mouth of Somes Sound on Mount Desert. Here they gathered supplies of finfish and shellfish, wild animal meat, and berries. Much of this food they dried in the sun or smoked, for use during the long winter months.

One of the earliest European explorers to sail by this island was the Frenchman, Samuel de Champlain, who was subsequently called the Father of New France. In September 1604, he described this island as "very high, and cleft into seven or eight mountains, all in a line. The summits of most of them are bare of trees, nothing but rock. I named it *l'Isle des Monts-déserts.*" He was also the first person to accurately describe Mount Desert as an island, separated as it is from the mainland by only about 300 feet at the Narrows, between Frenchman and Blue Hill bays.

Just nine years later, after France had laid claim to the northeastern part of North America, a small group of French Jesuits became the first Europeans attempting to establish a permanent colony on Mount Desert. At the invitation of local Native Americans, under Chief Asticou, these forty or so individuals, led by Father Pierre Biard, began building their community of St. Sauveur near the mouth of Somes Sound.

Within less than a month, however, disaster struck. A British warship from Virginia, under orders to obliterate all French outposts in the region, attacked and destroyed the fledgling settlement and captured the French settlers.

There followed 150 years of conflict between Great Britain and France for possession of this region of North America. Warships of both nations patrolled the coastline. Here at Mount Desert, the sheltered waters of Frenchman Bay were frequently used as a staging area for French ships preparing to do battle with the British. The protected waters behind the Cranberry Islands, leading into Somes Sound, were also used by the British warships.

While there was no permanent European settlement on the island during this period of international conflict, in 1688, Mount Desert, as well as some of the adjacent mainland and smaller islands, was given by the governor of Canada to a Frenchman, Antoine de la Mothe Cadillac—a land grant that was subsequently approved by France's King Louis XIV. Cadillac, with his bride, resided for part of the summer at a spot overlooking Frenchman Bay, before heading west to found the city of Detroit and serving as governor of French Louisiana. Today, the island's highest mountain is named in his honor.

With the defeat of the French military forces at Québec in 1759, some of the British subjects in the American colonies began turning their attention to the settlement and development of the Maine coast. At the urging of Sir Francis Bernard, governor of the Massachusetts Bay Colony, a Gloucester barrel-maker by the name of Abraham Somes moved to the head of Somes Sound in 1761 and founded the island's first permanent community. It was initially called "Betwixt the Hills," but is now the classic New England village of Somesville. Additional settlements soon sprang up around other sheltered harbors. These became

centers for building all kinds of sailing craft to meet the demands of a rapidly growing fishing industry and coastal trade in such products as lumber and granite.

After American independence was declared on July 4, 1776, another territorial dispute arose—this time between the United States of America and Canada—as to exactly where to establish the international boundary. Two alternatives would have given Mount Desert and eastern Maine to Canada. But a third plan, drawing the line farther east, along the St. Croix River, was finally approved in 1783.

Artists, writers, and scientists began discovering Mount Desert in the 1840s, their paintings and words conveying to the nation and the world some of the island's incomparable natural beauty. In the subsequent decades of the 19th century, Mount Desert developed rapidly into one of America's foremost summer resorts, attracting many of the country's wealthiest families, such as the Astors, Carnegies, Fords, Morgans, Pulitzers, Rockefellers, and Vanderbilts.

To accommodate the influx of vacationers, progressively larger and fancier summer hotels were built in a number of the villages, especially Bar Harbor. Scores of summer "cottages"—many of them actually large and elaborate mansions—were built overlooking the bays and harbors. Only two historic hotels remain. The Claremont Hotel, overlooking the mouth of Somes Sound, near Southwest Harbor, dates from 1884; and the Asticou Inn was founded in 1883 and its main building, overlooking Northeast Harbor, was opened to guests in 1901.

For many years, coastal steamboats, such as the *Mount Desert* and the *J.T. Morse*, provided the main transportation link for visitors from the major eastern cities. Horse-drawn carriages, surreys, and buckboards, including the famed Tallyho, offered most of the island's mobility. Also, for just a few years in the 1880s, a narrow-gauge railway took sightseers from a steamboat landing on the eastern shore of Eagle Lake to the rocky summit of Cadillac (then called Green) Mountain.

In 1901, a few prominent summer residents, under the leadership of Harvard College's president Charles W. Eliot, began to work toward the dream of saving the island's most scenic places, setting them beyond the reach of commercial developers, and establishing a nature reserve for the inspiration of future generations. Consequently, the Hancock County Trustees of Public Reservations was founded as a tax-exempt, land-acquiring organization. After an initially discouraging lack of progress, a few gifts of land were finally received from private individuals. By 1913, the Trustees held title to more than 5,000 acres, including Sieur de Monts Spring, The Beehive, The

Bowl, and the 1,530-foot-high summit of Cadillac Mountain.

In 1916, President Woodrow Wilson accepted these lands as a gift from the Trustees and by presidential proclamation established Sieur de Monts National Monument (named for the Frenchman who had led the expedition, on which Samuel de Champlain described Mount Desert Island). George B. Dorr, who had been executive director of the Trustees and the organization's chief advocate of a national monument, was appointed as the monument's caretaker.

In 1919, Congress authorized the renaming and re-designation of the monument as Lafayette National Park, thus establishing the first such park east of the Mississippi River. Finally, in 1929, the name was changed to Acadia, derived from the early French name for much of this region of North America.

On October 17, 1947, sparks from a smoldering refuse dump near the northern end of Mount Desert Island were suddenly whipped into tinder-dry vegetation by strong northwest winds. For nearly two weeks, wind-driven flames roared out of control on the East Side of Mount Desert Island. The ferocious wildfire burned southeastward along much of the Frenchman Bay shore, between Hulls Cove and Great Head. Witnesses have described the gigantic flames that torched the dense forest on Great Head as appearing like an enormous blow-torch extending out over the ocean.

The wildfire blackened a large expanse of Acadia's forests. It burned furiously over Champlain Mountain and The Beehive, along Ocean Drive to the neck of Otter Point, across Dorr Mountain and over the eastern slope of Cadillac Mountain, around the north end and east side of Eagle Lake, across the northern flank of Sargent Mountain, and over the Bubbles to the north end of Jordan Pond. It also destroyed many homes and other structures in and around Bar Harbor, including more than 60 of the once-grand summer mansions.

When the fire was finally out, its fury had consumed more than 17,000 acres, of which nearly 9,000 acres were in the national park. Seeing the charred and blackened scenes not quite two years later, this writer was among those who assumed the forest would not be restored for at least a century. But the rich nutrients that were released by the fire brought about a remarkably rapid rebirth and renewal of the forest ecosystem. Initially, there has been a natural re-vegetation with deciduous trees, such as aspens, birches, maples, and oaks. In recent decades, these predominantly deciduous woodlands have grown lushly, providing a beautiful and valuable habitat for a tremendous diversity of wildlife, including a multitude of spring and summer songbirds. Most of today's park visitors are likely un-

aware of the horrendous mid-20th-century wildfire, even though there is still a predominance of deciduous forest that contrasts with the areas of old-growth conifer and mixed woodlands that were untouched by the conflagration.

In recent decades, too, the national park has gradually continued to grow, most of it with generous private gifts of land. More than 10,000 acres of the park, on the island's East Side, were generously donated by the philanthropist, John D. Rockefeller Jr., who was a longtime summer resident of Seal Harbor.

In 1986, Congress authorized the establishment of a master boundary for Acadia and gave the National Park Service authority to protect additional lands within that boundary, either by fee acquisition or by conservation easements. As of this writing in 2004, the national park contains more than 35,000 acres of federally owned lands, plus roughly 12,000 additional acres that have been given protection under the terms of voluntary conservation easements with private property owners.

From 1915 to the early 1930s, Mr. Rockefeller also created a 57-mile network of graveled carriage roads, 44 miles of which are within the park, on the island's East Side. These peaceful routes, which wind through forested valleys, loop around lakes and ponds, and cross over or under 16 beautifully designed granite-faced bridges, offer Acadia's visitors magnificent opportunities for walking, carriage tours from Wildwood Stables near Jordan Pond, horseback riding, and bicycling (certain stretches are closed to the latter two activities). In winter, when there is sufficient snow, the carriage roads are transformed into ideal cross-country ski routes. Acadia also offers more than 120 miles of delightful woodland, shore, and mountain hiking trails that invite exploration into virtually every part of the park.

MOUNT DESERT TODAY

It was a cold, invigorating mid-November. Heavy rains had earlier brought the lakes and ponds full to the brim and sent streams dashing down their rocky courses to the sea. When the temperature suddenly dropped below freezing, great masses of glistening icicles formed at all the waterfalls, on sheer mountain cliffs, and along road cuts. An initial, delicately patterned skim of ice formed around the edges of the lakes and ponds, while expanses of open water continued a while longer to reflect the mountains in the crystal calm of early morning.

As the hours of daylight diminished, the sun rose only a little way above the southern horizon at sea, casting long shadows behind every rock and shrub. Seen from the summit of Penobscot Mountain, the ocean was glistening silver, against

which the clustered Cranberry Islands contrasted as black silhouettes. Mount Desert now seemed wilder and more rugged without the summer's broad-leaved lushness. The dark-green pines and spruces were now more prominent against the grays and browns of the leafless maples, birches, oaks, and aspens. The rockiness of the mountains' cliffs and summits now seemed more obvious.

It would not be long before the first real snowfall would cover Acadia, crowning the exposed ridges and mountaintops with gleaming white and emphasizing the elegant symmetry of spruces and firs. It would soon be time to get out the cross-country skis and once again glide along the miles of carriage roads. One of my personal favorite routes begins at the Brown Mountain Gatehouse just north of Northeast Harbor and winds through Upper Hadlock Valley and back through the Amphitheater. Another starts near the Jordan Pond House and heads north, offering spectacular views of Jordan Pond, below, and Penobscot Mountain's sheer Jordan Cliffs, above.

Although most bird species either migrate south to warmer regions or are less evident in winter, a spectacular influx of ducks often provides a great show around the shores of the island. Common eiders flock in large numbers, in some years gathering by many thousands just beyond the surf, as between Great Head and Otter Point. Large flocks of black ducks and several species of scoters congregate in Frenchman and Blue Hill bays. Long-tailed ducks (formerly called old-squaws) come in small numbers to such sheltered waters as Somes Sound, Northeast Harbor, and Southwest Harbor. Perky little bufflehead ducks—the males with prominent white facial markings—at first may gather in small flocks on the lakes and ponds, before moving down to the harbors and coves when the surface of freshwater has frozen over. You will likely seldom see the elegant harlequin duck, but once in awhile one or a few will ride the rollers just beyond the surf near such places as Otter Point or will seek the more sheltered waters of Somes Sound.

You can walk the Shore Path between Sand Beach and Otter Point, as a winter storm unleashes its fury. Again and again, gigantic waves crash against the sloping pink granite cliffs and thunder into narrow crevices. At places such as Otter Cliffs, the powerful surf "erupts" high into the air, resembling awesome Yellowstone geysers. Such phenomenal battering power as this might make you wonder how all the animal and plant life of the intertidal zone along the shore can possibly survive. But miraculously, most of the seaweeds, periwinkles, barnacles, mussels, sea-stars, and all the other inhabitants not only survive but thrive in this restless, challenging environment that is twice-daily exposed to the air by the ebbing tides.

By late March, you finally begin to detect the first faint hints that winter may soon release its grip. Little chickadees begin to sing a few of their clear notes—a cheerful sound, like the voice of a long-lost friend, that lifts the human spirit toward the anticipation of a reluctant but certain springtime.

By early April, or occasionally as early as late March, just slightly milder temperatures take the ice out and open expanses of rippling lake water. Almost immediately, the buffleheads return and perform a preliminary period of cavorting courtship, before winging away to their breeding territory far to the north. Common loons return from the saltwater, too, and prepare to raise their young at secluded places around the lakeshores.

April and May are a lot like the opening petals of a flower . . . slow and modest at first, then spreading quickly to a showy climax. Although there are many ways to measure the advancing pace of spring, one of the most exciting is the increasing concert of bird songs and calls. In early April, for instance, song sparrows, robins, and red-winged blackbirds begin singing; and occasional long V's and lines of Canada geese go honking by overhead.

Before mid-April, tree swallows return from Mexico and coastal southern United States, endlessly swooping and circling over lakes and ponds in graceful pursuit of insects, while chattering their high-pitched calls. Jaunty little brown winter wrens begin singing their rapid, breathless trills of high, tinkling songs that seem to echo through the deepest, darkest spruce forests.

By mid- or late-April, fuzzy gray pussy willow buds appear in damp roadside thickets. Red maples suddenly burst forth with masses of tiny reddish flowers; while on the ground, clusters of the delicate, fragrant, pink-and-white blossoms of trailing arbutus suddenly appear among their patches of evergreen leaves.

May on Mount Desert Island brings the flowering of blue and white violets, early saxifrage, wild strawberry, hobblebush, and shadbush. The latter small tree or shrub is briefly smothered, like a dusting of new snow, as small flowers with long white petals appear usually just before the leaves unfurl.

Tiny colorful warblers arrive from the tropics in an ever-increasing torrent, flooding the forests with their varied musical trills. White-throated sparrows throw back their heads to sing long clear notes that seem to say, *"Old Sam Peabody, Peabody, Peabody."* Thrushes return to the shady woodlands and suddenly begin singing their flute-like solos—the hermit, wood, Swainson's, and veery, holding you entranced with their reedy, liquid ascending and descending notes. Bright rose-breasted grosbeaks and

scarlet tanagers add their robin-like melodies to the chorus.

Each day brings some new kinds of birds back to Acadia. All the while the broad-leaved trees are slowly opening their new foliage, spreading a canopy of varying shades of a vibrant light-green across the valleys and mountainsides and contrasting with the darker green conifers. The last deciduous trees to unfurl their leaves are the red oaks. Groves of them can be seen along the western shore of Eagle Lake and elsewhere, initially taking on a pale greenish-yellow color that darkens as the leaves expand.

Late spring is one of the most enjoyable seasons for canoeing on Acadia's lakes and ponds, especially Long (Great) Pond, Echo Lake, Eagle Lake, and Jordan Pond. To hear the gentle lapping of water and feel the silent surge of the paddles as you glide by a forested shore and into a secluded cove is surely one of the greatest pleasures of the northern lake country. You can drift close to loons and mergansers, and later in the season watch the parent birds with their families of tiny young. One of nature's most comical sights is a young loon enjoying a free ride on its mother's back.

When the dozens of sailboats return to the ocean waters around Mount Desert Island and the harbors are once again full of yachts from near and far, you know that summer has finally arrived. One of the highlights of a Mount Desert summer is a boat excursion, preferably under sail. There is simply nothing to quite compare with the sensation of being swept effortlessly around the Porcupine Islands in Frenchman Bay, a stiff northwest breeze heeling the boat over as you tack back and forth. Equally memorable is a sail out of Southwest Harbor, down Western Way between Great Cranberry Island and Seawall Point, and on across the expanse of ocean to the Ducks. Little Duck Island is a wildlife sanctuary, and as you pass close by the rocky shore, harbor seals may be lounging about on some of the lower ledges or swimming just offshore. The higher cliffs are typically populated with eiders, gulls, and cormorants.

On a clear day, the view of Mount Desert northward from out on the ocean is impressive. As Champlain observed so aptly, the series of mountain summits provides a grand panorama. But there are also summer days when you see no panoramas at all—days when a thick bank of cool, damp fog moves in along the Maine coast, obscuring everything to within a few hundred yards or less. Acadia is then an even more intimate place that is full of mystery and the muffled boom of distant foghorns.

Sometimes you can drive to the top of 1,530-foot-high Cadillac Mountain, or climb Champlain Mountain or Dorr Mountain, and look down on slow-moving arms and wisps of fog extending far into Frenchman Bay and creeping gracefully up and over the Porcupine Islands. On other days, the atmosphere is so clear that you can see Mount Desert Rock, southward 20 miles at sea; eastward beyond Schoodic Peninsula, for miles across the irregular coastline of bays and peninsulas; and northward across the mainland forest.

Evening is one of the best times to observe some of Acadia's animal life. Beavers come out of their conical stick-and-mud lodges at dusk and begin their nocturnal logging operations. Aspens offer them leaves and tender twigs for food and branches for constructing or repairing their lodges and the dams that create ponds that are necessary for their way of life. As daylight fades, a striped skunk may be seen hunting for grubs in a meadow; a lone porcupine shuffles out of the woods and across a clearing; and a red fox barks somewhere in the forest.

White-tailed deer are plentiful on Mount Desert, but they lead secretive lives, often hiding far back in cedar swamps or up in mountain ravines. Usually your only view of a deer is a fleeting one—the white "flag" of its tail raised as it bounds off through the forest, after letting out a loud snort. But there are those magic moments when you may happen upon a doe and her two spotted fawns drinking silently at a lakeshore in a misty dawn; or a young buck standing in a clearing—his fur and rack of antlers backlighted by the slanting sunshine.

No summer on Mount Desert Island is complete without a taste of mouth-watering blueberries, raspberries, or blackberries. From about mid-July through early August, as you climb the mountain trails or follow the carriage roads through more open terrain, a tasty *hors d'oeuvre* of low blueberries picked along the way is an irresistible delicacy. Or in brushy thickets, where tall spruces have been blown down, you may discover an abundance of juicy red raspberries.

Another Epicurean delight of Acadia National Park can be enjoyed from late spring through early autumn at the Jordan Pond House, located in a meadow near the south end of Jordan Pond. After hiking one of the nearby mountain trails, looping around Jordan Pond on the shore path, taking a stroll on a stretch of carriage road; or pausing for a while on the drive around the Park Loop Road, what a pleasure it is to stop here for luncheon, afternoon tea-and-popovers, or dinner.

The pond and restaurant are named for brothers, George and John Jordan, who built a modest little farmhouse in 1847 at the south end of the pond. In 1884, the Melvan Tibbetts family bought the Jordan Farm and soon offered "a full line of first class boats and canoes" for rent on the pond, as well as "good stabling and feed for horses. . . . Parties crossing from Eagle Lake to Jordan's Pond can have boats come for them by raising a signal which will be found on reaching the pond...." Four years later, *Chisolm's Mount Desert Guide* said that "the lonely and weather-beaten little farmhouse" is where "one or a score can get a good rural lunch [often a bowl of homemade fish chowder] for a small rural price, or a pitcher of rich milk, or various cold and refreshing beverages . . . or confectionary for the children." By 1890, a small dining room had been added to the farmhouse; and in 1895, Seal Harbor summer residents, Mr. and Mrs. Thomas A. McIntire, acquired the property.

The McIntires were so pleased with their first summer of forty-four dinner guests that they began expanding the building, ultimately including a series of rooms and covered verandas. Mr. McIntire also originated what has become a long tradition at Jordan Pond: the delicious golden-brown popovers. The local newspaper reported that "Almost from the start, the fame of his chicken and popover dinners attracted parties from the summer colonies on different parts of the island." In 1910, broiled live lobster was added to the menu.

In 1928, John D. Rockefeller Jr., who by then had already completed most of the carriage roads, purchased the Jordan Pond House for addition to the national park, retaining Mr. McIntire as proprietor. In 1945, The Acadia Corporation, a national-park concessionaire, took over the restaurant's management and continued offering the ever-popular afternoon tea-and-popovers on the tea lawn, as well as luncheons and dinners in the birch bark-paneled dining rooms and on the verandas.

In 1979, a raging "Tinder-Box Blaze" erupted and the roaring flames quickly burned the historic, rustic structure to the ground, leaving only tall chimneys rising above the ashes. Sad though this loss was to those of us who knew the ambiance of the original structure, a new, more spacious Jordan Pond House was soon built and today continues offering the tradition of good food and genial hospitality from early May to October, in view of mountain-framed Jordan Pond. (For information and reservations, telephone: (207) 276-3316.)

As summer tilts all too quickly toward autumn, the meadows, clearings, and grassy roadsides everywhere are aglow with the many species of goldenrod—from those that are large and gracefully spreading to delicate smaller ones and the rigid seaside variety. These are soon joined by some of the early asters, notably the tall, white-rayed flat tops that are prolific along sunny trails.

At regular intervals through the warmer season, there come those rainy, cooler days that put a damper on camping, hiking, sailing, and the other outdoor pursuits. But it is then that you see why Acadia has so many mosses, lichens, and mushrooms, and why many of the woodlands, with their rich, damp fragrances, seem like a miniature version of the Pacific Northwest rain forest.

There are other distinctive Acadian scents that you will never forget: the gentle fragrance of white pine needles, accentuated by warm sunshine; a pinch of the pungent leaves of sweetfern, bayberry, and sweetgale; or a seaside patch of crowberry, its delicate sweet aroma blending with the salty sea air. One of the most typical of all the north-country fragrances is the balsam fir. It perfumes the air along many a mile of forest trails and exudes a spicy scent when you crush a few needles.

The visual climax of an Acadia year begins after mid- or late-September, with the first small splashes of autumn-foliage color—here the bright yellow of birch, there a blazing red branch of a maple, contrasting with the predominant green. As the hours of sunlight diminish and a nip of frost filters through the night air, the vibrant colors spread. Red maples turn crimson in swampy places around lakes and ponds; birch, ash, and aspen trees sweep their shades of golden yellow across the valleys and mountainsides; and sugar maples display a magnificent blending of yellow, orange, and red.

The grand show of foliage-color generally reaches its climax during the first half of October. Climb the mountains then and gaze across the vast patchwork of multicolored landscapes. Canoe the lakes and ponds, and marvel at the scenes reflected in the calm of early morning or evening. Walk the woodland paths and see how the vibrant hues glow through the forest.

Then come the colors of late berries that are so conspicuous after the leaves have fallen. There are clusters of bright-red berries of the hawthorn and the perfectly round little red fruits of winterberry, an otherwise nondescript shrub in wet thickets around some of the lakeshores. Finally, the island returns to the subdued brown, gray, and dark-green tones that set the stage for the long, cold winter stretching ahead.

SCHOODIC PENINSULA

Across Frenchman Bay from Mount Desert Island lies the 2,000-acre mainland unit of Acadia National Park. Encompassing most of the outer end of Schoodic Peninsula, this area offers some of the park's most picturesque spruce- and crowberry-bordered pink-and-gray cliffs. Beaches and seawalls of smoothly rounded cobblestones line sheltered little coves. Fragrant forests of spruce and jack pine, and miniature mountain summits convey a special feeling of intimacy and delicate beauty—a feeling heightened by the remoteness of the peninsula, combined with the awesome vastness of the open sea. Among Schoodic's special spots are Mosquito Harbor, West Pond Cove, Little Moose Island, the

sloping surf-pounded pink granite at the tip of the peninsula, and the sweeping panoramas from Schoodic Head and The Anvil.

In 2002, the U.S. Navy closed its base near the tip of Schoodic Peninsula, and the land reverted back to the National Park Service. The Schoodic Education and Research Center has been established there to facilitate education and research consistent with the mission of the National Park System.

ISLE AU HAUT

A 3,000-acre unit of Acadia National Park encompasses roughly two-thirds of Isle au Haut (High Island)—a beautiful outer coastal bit of land that rises out of the sea about 15 miles to the southwest of Mount Desert Island. The island measures roughly 6 miles long by 3 miles across at its widest point.

A forested ridge runs along most of Isle au Haut's length, reaching the highest elevation atop 543-foot Mount Champlain. Near the eastern shore, a long narrow pond extends nearly 1.5 miles. All around the island are picturesque little coves, harbors, pebble and cobblestone beaches, and bold rocky cliffs. A few smaller islands and ledges lie offshore. Much of the island's forest consists of old-growth spruces, pitch pines, and balsam firs, while other areas are covered with young stands of birches, maples, and oaks.

Other parts of Acadia National

Park are located on Thompson Island, in Mount Desert Narrows; Bar Island, Sheep Porcupine Island, and Bald Porcupine Island, in Frenchman Bay; Bear Island, at the mouth of Northeast Harbor; Bar Island, in upper Somes Sound; Baker Island; the Islesford Historical Museum on Little Cranberry Island; and Little Moose Island, Schoodic Island, and Rolling Island, just off Schoodic Peninsula.

ACADIA'S VOLUNTEERS

Volunteers annually contribute more than 30,000 hours of service to Acadia National Park. In cooperation with the National Park Service and the nonprofit organization, Friends of Acadia, hundreds of individuals that include park visitors, island residents, families, school groups, scouts, clubs, and businesses help to maintain and care for Acadia's trails, carriage roads, campgrounds, vistas, summits, shores, and islands.

As the Friends of Acadia says, "Meet Tuesday, Thursday, and Saturday mornings, the first of June through Columbus Day, at the flagpole at Park Headquarters [about 4 miles west of the village of Bar Harbor on State Route 233], 8:30 a.m. Work until 12:00 noon. Many volunteers bring a bag lunch. Call 288-3934 for a recorded message of work projects and site locations." What to bring: "Water. Snack. Lunch. Insect repellent. Stout footgear with covered toes. Appropriate clothing to accommodate changeable Maine weather, often much cooler at higher elevations. A generous spirit. Tools, gloves, and training will be provided." Special volunteer events are held on National Trails Day—the first Saturday in June, National Public Lands Day—September 20, and Take Pride in Acadia Day—the first Saturday in November. Volunteers in groups of six or more persons are asked to please contact the Friends of Acadia ahead of time. Special efforts are made to match each group with an appropriate project.

In addition to organizing volunteer work crews in cooperation with the National Park Service, the Friends of Acadia raises funds for park projects and is an advocacy organization on behalf of park users and against threats to Acadia National Park. For further information: Friends of Acadia, 43 Cottage Street, P.O. Box 45, Bar Harbor, ME 04609; telephone: (207) 288-3340; and web site: www.friendsofacadia.org.

THE NATIONAL PARK SYSTEM

Acadia is part of the National Park System, of which there are approximately 390 national parks, monuments, lakeshores, seashores, recreation areas, and numerous pre-Columbian and historical parks, monuments, and sites throughout the United States. Yellowstone became the world's first national park in 1872. Other spectacular places in the American West were also soon given this protective management status, including Yosemite and Sequoia (1890), Mount Rainier (1899), Crater Lake (1902), Wind Cave (1903), Mesa Verde (1906), Petrified Forest (1906, initially a national monument), Grand Canyon (1908, initially a national monument), Olympic and Zion (1909, both initially national monuments), Glacier (1910), Rocky Mountain (1915), Lassen Volcanic (1916), Hawaii Volcanoes and Haleakala (1916, initially established as a single national park), and Denali (1917, initially named Mt. McKinley).

Wild places, such as Acadia, are havens for people as well as for wildlife. Extractive resource uses, such as commercial timber harvesting and mining are not permitted. Instead, these irreplaceable and magical parts of the American heritage will continue to inspire future generations of visitors. And they offer an opportunity to gain a meaningful perspective on the *interconnectedness* of all life on Earth.

Rocks and Landforms

Acadia is one of the few places in the eastern United States where you can actually see much of the face of the land and in doing so, glimpse something of the phenomenal geological events that have produced the beautiful landscapes we now enjoy. While most of the topography in the eastern United States contains a lush cover of vegetation, many of Acadia's mountain summits and ridges of granite lie largely bare and exposed. Sheer cliffs rise boldly. Lakes, ponds, and arms of the sea occupy ice-scoured valleys.

Coastal cliffs exhibit the persistent power of the sea, as it inexorably wears away the edge of the land. The varied composition and texture of the region's bedrock hint at the complexity of events that resulted in its formation through eons of the Earth's history. Eroded sediments were deposited beneath a shallow sea. In time, this sedimentary material was transformed by intense heat and immense pressure within the earth into molten rock that brought about fundamental changes to this part of the planet.

Over these long ages of geologic time, the one constant has been never-ending change. "Our" world is not a static landscape of everlasting hills, but the tiniest instant in a dynamic, on-flowing evolution of land forms and climatic variations. To give a bit of perspective to the contemporary scenes of Acadia, here are a few of the major events of geological history, with indications of where some major rock types and landforms relating to these events can be found.

ACADIA'S OLDEST ROCKS

When you cross Mount Desert Narrows on State Highway 3's short bridge from the mainland, you can catch a glimpse of rocks exposed along the shore that geologists tell us are the oldest on the island. Known as the Ellsworth Schist, these rocks consist of thinly layered sediments of sand, silt, mud, and volcanic ash that were significantly altered by heat and pressure. Geological research has indicated that these formations are at least 500 million years old.

The forces that metamorphosed these sediments into tightly compressed, folded, and foliated rocks are believed to have been associated with the movements of continents. Thus, as North America was just beginning to move on a collision course with Europe and Africa, the light greenish-gray, mica-rich **schist** was being formed. Much of this formation was laid down beneath an ancient sea, during a time when primitive fish were the only known vertebrate animals in the world, and when seaweeds were the highest form of plant life.

VOLCANIC ERUPTIONS

Nearly as ancient as the schist is a complex and varied set of volcanic rock formations, known as the Cranberry Island Series. These rocks are composed of volcanic ash and other ejected materials that were distributed widely across this region, around 420 million years ago. Geologists believe that the source of these materials was a chain of long-vanished volcanic islands that lay just to the east of the present coast of Maine. As the ash and volcanic fragments fell and accumulated, they became solidly welded into rock known as **volcanic tuff**; and where these fragments were of considerable size,

the rock is called **volcanic breccia**. The volcanic materials that comprise the Cranberry Island Series may have accumulated on the floor of a shallow sea, for they are well sorted, highly stratified, and vary in color from green and purple to brownish-red and black.

As the name implies, these volcanic formations are the bedrock of Great and Little Cranberry islands, where rough, predominantly grayish ledges are best viewed around the shore of some of the points jutting into the sea. This series shows up again on the opposite side of Western Way, where a few ledges crop up along the cobblestone seawall, at the Seawall Picnic Area. Here the rough, fractured, grayish rocks are volcanic tuff that is patterned with angular pieces of rock. Farther south, this rock forms grayish outcrops along the trail around the inner shore of Ship Harbor.

RENEWED SEDIMENTATION

Next in the geological sequence, there came a time of gradual erosion and deposition of sediments beneath a shallow sea. This process created a conglomeration of sand and gravel, inter-bedded with thickly layered silt. Subsequent pressures and cementing eventually produced various **siltstones**, **sandstones**, and **conglomerates** in a new set of strata, known as the Bar Harbor Formation.

This predominantly gray or pale-purplish formation, often containing brown iron oxide staining, typically breaks sharply along small cleavage planes that create a jagged surface. This formation is found along the Bar Harbor shore of Frenchman Bay and comprises the lowest strata of the high, south-facing cliffs of the Porcupine Islands and Bar Island. It also crops out as the rugged, dark shore cliffs extending away from the mouth of Northeast Harbor and on nearby Bear Island.

VOLCANIC INTRUSIONS

Following the gradual changes resulting from metamorphism, deposition of ejected volcanic materials, and deposition of sediments, a radical change began to affect the region. First, there was a preliminary period in which several invasions of molten **dioritic magma**, under intense pressure deep within the earth, squeezed upward into fractures and other openings in and between some of the overlying surface strata—in some places forming extensive masses of liquid rock that cooled very gradually.

The resulting **diorite**, formed deep within the earth, was ultimately exposed at the earth's surface, after long periods of erosion. Most of the resistant rock that forms a protective cap on the Porcupine Islands in Frenchman Bay, as well as prominent outcrops on Great Head, date from this time of early igneous intrusion. This formation also forms the

jagged medium-grained, black-and-white-speckled ledges at Compass Harbor's Dorr Point, a short distance south of Bar Harbor. The diorite contains crystals of whitish **plagioclase feldspar** and black **hornblende**.

Accompanying this interval of intrusive volcanic activity was an invasion of **granitic magma**. Subsequent erosion has exposed this **fine-grained granite** as pale-pinkish or "sugary" outcropping ledges along Seawall, opposite Seawall Pond; along the shore at Wonderland; at the narrow mouth of Ship Harbor; and as high cliffs at Bass Harbor Head. Some of the most spectacular ledges and cliffs of this fine-grained granite crop out on much of mainland Schoodic Peninsula, 6 miles east across Frenchman Bay from Mount Desert Island.

These and other intrusions of volcanic material were merely the prelude, however, to an even more dramatic geological event. A huge pool of molten granitic magma, welling up from deep within the earth's interior, now pushed toward the surface strata. As the fiery liquid created enormous heat and pressure, a gigantic section of crustal rock separated from the overlying rock and began to sink into the molten magma. The latter, in turn, was forced around the sinking rock and was squeezed upward into a huge dome-like cavity. Still thousands of feet below the earth's surface, the magma within this cavity slowly cooled to form what eventually became the basic core rock of Mount Desert Island—a **coarse-grained granite**. This pinkish granite is now exposed at the surface and provides much of the beauty of Acadia's mountains, as well as the scenic shore along Ocean Drive, between Great Head and Otter Point. More than half of this crystalline granite contains pink **orthoclase feldspar**, identified by its flat, lustrous cleavage surfaces; while the rest is made up of whitish **quartz** and tiny particles of black hornblende.

Surrounding and in direct contact with the island's central core of coarse-grained granite is a narrow zone of rock, the origin and appearance of which help to relate it to the formation of the granite. Known as the **shatter zone**, much of the rock here consists of large angular fragments of diorite, the Bar Harbor Formation, and Ellsworth Schist. These rocks were separated from their own formations when that enormous section of the earth's crust sank into the subterranean pool of upward invading magma. The molten lava filled the areas in and around fragments of these and other formations and provided a matrix in which they lie today.

This relatively narrow contact zone forms a great arc that is readily seen around much of Mount Desert Island. Starting at Town Hill, it curves around to Hulls Cove; extends southward behind the downtown section of Bar Harbor; and comprises the bedrock of Schooner Head, much of Great Head, and some outer ledges on Otter Point. The contact zone then swings around to the cliffs at Little Hunters Beach and Hunters Beach Head; continues westward across the outermost ledges at the mouth of Seal Harbor, and the entrances of Northeast Harbor and Somes Sound; and finally dips into Blue Hill Bay, along the shore of Seal Cove.

Shatter-zone rocks contrast sharply with adjacent granite ledges. They are finer-grained, fracturing and weathering into brittle, small, sharp-edged surfaces that give cliffs and ledges a more severe and jagged appearance than those of granite. Usually the shatter-zone rocks are dark-gray, taking their color from the diorite and the Bar Harbor Series sedimentary rocks. But an outstanding exception is the conspicuous whitish band of metamorphosed **quartzite** on the shore ledges at the tip of Otter Point. This is a remnant of the Bar Harbor Formation that was altered by the intense heat of the invading magma.

Besides the basic core rock of Acadia, there were several other intrusions of granitic magmas. Whitish **medium-grained granite** constitutes the bedrock of Baker Island. The ledges on the outer shore of that island are a fantastic jumble of giant granite slabs that have been tossed by the sea. It is amazing how the wave-forced air pressure of the surf has been able to move such huge pieces of rock upward onto the beach.

At numerous places across the granite surfaces of Acadia, bands of varying widths, textures, and colors create contrasting patterns. Many are fined-grained, dark-gray volcanic **basalt dikes** that are comprised of **diabase**—an intrusive form of basalt that filled fractures in the granite. The massive dikes in the granite at Schoodic Peninsula are especially impressive.

This period of volcanic intrusions, which ended roughly 350 million years ago, generally coincided with major mountain-building activity in eastern North America, occurring as this continent crunched against Europe and Africa to form a single super-continent. Vast periods of time followed, in which a huge thickness of overlying rock layers was gradually eroded away. This erosion ultimately left the once deeply buried dome of coarse-grained, resistant granite elevated above the surrounding landscape—forming a continuous, roughly east-to-west mountain ridge across what is now Mount Desert Island. V-shaped stream valleys were gradually cut into and even through this ridge, and the stage was basically set for the most recent major topographical change—grand sculpturing by continental glaciation.

GLACIATION

At least four major **continental glaciers** have covered northeastern North America during the past 1 to 2 million years. Each cold period lasted from about 15,000 to 20,000 years, with milder interglacial stages ranging from roughly 20,000 to over 100,000 years.

The most recent major glacial advance occurred during the Wisconsin Stage, which geologists now believe began around 100,000 years ago and reached a maximum here about 18,000 years ago. The main part of this vast continental expanse of glacial ice, called the Laurentide Ice Sheet, spread southward from north-central Canada, covering New England, New York, parts of Pennsylvania, Ohio, and the Great Lakes region.

As this huge mass of ice moved southeastward toward the coast of Maine, its flow was impeded at right angles by the Mount Desert Range. The glacier initially piled up behind and flowed around the ends of the range, but it then crept up and over the crest of the mountain range. As an increasing volume of ice poured from the north, the glacial ice thickened to hundreds of feet and then to several thousand feet—perhaps even as much as 2 miles thick. As this powerful, grinding, scouring force moved slowly along, it gradually molded and smoothed the mountain range's granite into gently rounded contours. An important part of the scouring, contouring, grooving, and polishing process was performed by the sand, gravel, rocks, and boulders that were picked up and carried along beneath the weight of the ice. The results of this massive abrasive force are most evident on the northern and northwestern flanks of all the major mountain ridges, where they slope relatively gently, becoming slightly arched or rounded near the top.

In contrast, the southern and southeastern mountain slopes often show a sharply cut, step-like profile that was caused by "glacial plucking." As the ice and its load of abrasive sediments spilled over the mountain summits, some of the materials were forced into a circular motion, similar to a back eddy in a stream. The plucking phenomenon was facilitated by numerous horizontal and vertical fractures that are typical of Acadia's outcropping granite. Prominent profiles can be seen at the sheer cliffs of Champlain Mountain, The Beehive, the Bubbles, Penobscot Mountain's Jordan Cliffs, St. Sauveur Mountain's Eagle Cliff, and Beech and Canada cliffs above the south end of Echo Lake.

The ice also flowed through shallow passes in the crest of the range and squeezed through narrow stream valleys. These V-shaped valleys were gradually widened and deepened by the scouring power of the ice, until this once-continuous, east-west-trending mountain range was divided into a series of smaller,

north-south-trending ridges that were now separated from each other by deep, glacially carved U-shaped valleys.

After the return of a milder climate and the retreat of the sprawling glacier, most of the deeper parts of these valleys became filled with lakes and ponds. One valley, scoured deeper than the others, became Somes Sound—the only fjord on the east coast of the United States. Other especially prominent U-shaped valleys can be seen at The Tarn, between Huguenot Head and Dorr Mountain; at Bubble Pond, between Cadillac and Pemetic mountains; and at the southern end of Long (Great) Pond, between Beech and Western mountains.

As the glacial ice melted, the great quantities of sand, gravel, rocks, and boulders that had been transported considerable distances were deposited at the outer edges of the glacier. The levels of both Jordan Pond and Long (Great) Pond, for instance, are at a higher level because of **moraines** consisting of gravel barriers deposited at the southern end of their valleys as the ice melted.

Large boulders, known as **glacial erratics**, were also dropped where the ice melted. The largest and most visible erratic is perched on the South Bubble. Other prominent erratics can be seen along the exposed South Ridge of Cadillac Mountain and on the shore ledges near the end of Otter Point. Most of the granite of these erratics—a very coarse-grained **granite pegmatite**—is distinctly different from the rock on which they are sitting, and some are believed to have been carried by the glacial ice from granite hills on the mainland, at least twenty miles to the northwest.

REBOUNDING LAND AND FLUCTUATING SEA LEVEL

Continental glaciation brought about two other major changes: down-warping and subsequent rebounding of the land; and fluctuations of the sea level. Try to imagine: The awesome weight of the 4,000 to 10,000-foot-thick glacier was so great that it actually pressed down the crustal rock strata of the earth by at least 600 feet below their present level. Also during this period of maximum glaciation, a huge quantity of the world's water was converted to ice. As a result, the level of the sea is believed to have dropped at least 300 feet below its current level.

According to calculations by geologists at the University of Maine, the receding margin of the glacier retreated from what is now the coast of Maine a little over 13,000 years ago. As the ice melted, thinned, and its edge withdrew northward, the land began slowly to rebound from its down-warped level.

In the meantime, while the land was still substantially depressed and the sea level was still at a low level, the coast extended much farther seaward than it does today. Looking

at the myriad of islands, peninsulas, points, bays, harbors, and coves, you can perhaps visualize a geologically distant time when there were long stream valleys that are now bays and when there were ridges and hills that are now narrow peninsulas and islands.

The sea's level rose steadily higher on the still substantially down-warped land, as increasing quantities of water flowed to the sea from the melting continental ice. This rise brought the sea's level to roughly 300 feet above today's sea level on Mount Desert Island. Numerous old sea beaches and stream deltas on the island are evidence of this post-glacial relationship of the sea to the land. The submergence of coastal lands that are now above sea level is believed to have begun about 12,900 years ago. By about 800 years later, the rebounding crust of the earth re-emerged from the sea. By about 9,000 years ago, the land was essentially stabilized near its present elevation. And during the past 3,000 years, the sea has risen about 12 feet, generally at a decreasing rate (although scientific research is revealing that this rate has recently been increasing, as the result of global warming).

So, now the surf incessantly pounds away at the land, breaking off pieces of the rocky shore and smoothing the ledges within its grasp. In many coves, it has created beaches of sand, pebbles, and cobblestones. At a few places, it has built up high barriers of smoothly rounded stones, such as between Seawall and Ship Harbor; Bracy Cove at the south end of Little Long Pond, and along stretches of outer shore on Great and Little Cranberry islands.

With each passing day, the mountains of Acadia are very gradually being eroded down by winter's ice, fracturing the rocks apart, and by rainstorms washing down particles of the rocks. The mantle of vegetation also helps to tear down the mountains—from encrusting lichens, whose acid breaks down the minerals in the rocks; to the shrubs and trees, whose roots work their way into cracks and crevices.

Acadia's mountains will ultimately be worn away and new geological events will bring changes to this land. But for now, at least, we can enjoy the great beauty that the millennia have created.

Birds

All through the years, there is a pattern of ever-changing seasonal activity of Acadia's birdlife. Like a great tide sweeping back and forth, there comes the springtime flood of migratory songbirds that suddenly appear overnight from wintering in warmer insect-rich regions to the south. In the autumn, another influx of waterfowl and other birds arrive from northern breeding grounds and spend the winter here. Still others, such as many shorebirds, only pause as they pass through on their way to and from breeding grounds farther north. And there are those birds that reside year-round along the coast of Maine.

As soon as the surface freshwater freezes over in the autumn, the **Common Loon** moves from Acadia's lakes and ponds and spends the winter on the ocean waters around Mount Desert Island. The little **Horned Grebe** comes here after summering in northern Canada and Alaska. Small numbers of **Bufflehead**, **Common Goldeneye**, and

Red-breasted and Common Mergansers are often seen in sheltered coves and harbors. Flocks of the **White-winged Scoter** and a scattered few of the **Long-tailed Duck** (formerly called Old-squaw) favor such places as Somes Sound and Frenchman Bay. Congregations of **Black Duck** and **Greater Scaup** can be seen in the upper reaches of Blue Hill Bay and Frenchman Bay, while flocks of **Common Eider** gather along the outer coastal shores. In some years, eiders come down from their Arctic breeding grounds in tremendous numbers— thousands of them riding the gray-green ocean swells just beyond the crashing surf, as along Ocean Drive.

On a cold winter day, an occasional **Great Cormorant** may fly by offshore, and the fortunate birdwatcher may catch sight of one or two of the beautifully patterned **Harlequin Duck**. It seems surprising to find a shorebird in this frigid season, but the **Purple Sandpiper** spends the winter along the coast of Maine,

Pileated Woodpecker

Long-tailed Duck

foraging for food among surf-pounded seaweed-covered rocks and cliffs.

Land birds of winter are somewhat less obvious, even though there are many species. **Black-capped Chickadee, Blue Jay, White-throated Sparrow, White-breasted and Red-breasted Nuthatches,** and **Downy and Hairy Woodpeckers** are among the most noticeable. The striking yellow, black, and white **Evening Grosbeak** is usually a winter visitor. In some years, flocks of grosbeaks are so numerous that you seem to hear their raucous ringing chirps almost everywhere. The **Pine Grosbeak** winters at Acadia, but is often much harder to find, since it tends to forage for seeds more quietly and singly or in pairs. **Red and White-winged Crossbills** are often but not always present on Mount Desert Island in great numbers. Their harsh, almost metallic *"jeep-jeep-jeep"* or *"jip-jip-jip"* calls are a familiar sound, as they perch in the top of cone-laden spruce trees or fly from one tree to another.

One of the winter birdwatcher's biggest thrills is to catch sight of a **Snowy Owl**. Once every few years, a few of these large and predominantly white-plumaged predatory birds, which breed on the Arctic tundra of Canada's far northern mainland and islands, suddenly appear this far south in search of food.

Late February can often seem the most depressing part of a long

Maine winter. But just as you think the cold and snow will never relent, you may hear the first tentative two-note song of the **Black-capped Chickadee**—a sign that even though a few more weeks of wintry weather stretch ahead, spring has suddenly begun.

In early March, the **Mourning Dove** begins its mournful cooing. And then, without warning, flocks of the **Red-winged Blackbird** arrive from the south. The males return a couple of weeks ahead of their mates and display their yellow-tipped bright red shoulder patches. In addition to the various marshes around the island, there is a place in the village of Seal Harbor where you can usually rely on hearing the red-wings' first cheerful liquid *"konk-ka-ree,"* in mid- or even early March. By the end of the month, the secretive little **Dark-eyed Junco** begins its musical even-pitched little trills. The prehistoric-looking **Great Blue Heron** silently stalks for prey at marshy areas and tidal flats.

In early spring, Acadia's resource managers begin looking for the return of the **Peregrine Falcon,** a species that had nested on Mount Desert Island "at least as long ago as 1936: the last known nesting pair was reported in 1956," according to the National Park Service. "By the mid-1960s, researchers determined peregrines were no longer a breeding species in the eastern United States. Nest robbing, trapping, and shooting first contributed to their

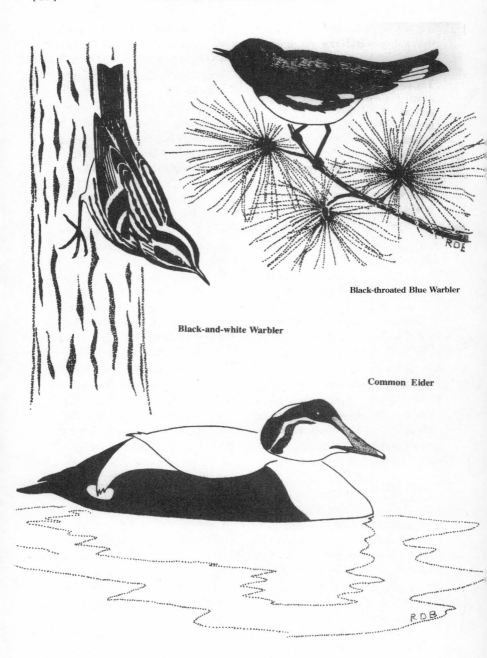

Black-throated Blue Warbler

Black-and-white Warbler

Common Eider

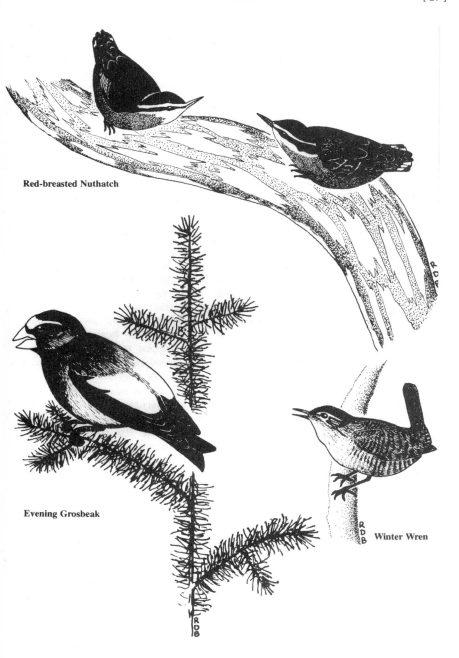

Red-breasted Nuthatch

Evening Grosbeak

Winter Wren

downfall, followed in the 1950s by ingestion of chemical pesticides and industrial pollutants.... When Congress passed the Endangered Species Act in 1973, mandating all federal agencies to protect endangered species and their habitats, Acadia National Park responded enthusiastically by participating in a cooperative management plan to restore a self-sustaining population of peregrines.... The method used to increase falcon populations is the reintroduction of captive-reared chicks into the wild. This process is termed 'hacking.' Acadia first participated in 1984.... From 1984 until 1986, 22 peregrine chicks were successfully hacked in Acadia National Park from a high cliff face overlooking Jordan Pond.... From 1987 to 1990 adult peregrines returned to Acadia but did not produce young. [The year] 1991 marked the first successful nesting at Acadia in 35 years. Peregrines have fledged young at this site each succeeding year...." The National Park Service notes that when mating and nesting activities are observed, certain trails will be temporarily closed to avoid disturbing the nesting area. Peregrine courtship occurs from March to mid-April, nesting takes place from mid-April through May, young peregrines hatch out in early June and take their initial flights by late June or early July.

By about the first of April, flocks of the **American Robin** are caroling their rich musical two- or three-note phrases. Joining in with its exuberant notes is the little brown **Song Sparrow**. The slightly milder rainy days of early April usher in from overhead the deep honking sound of the **Canada Goose**. Flocks of them pause to rest and feed at Mount Desert Narrows and other tidal shallows, on their way north to breeding grounds in northeastern Canada.

When the ice goes off the lakes and ponds—from late March to late April—loons and buffleheads quickly return to the lakes and ponds. Small flocks of buffleheads are a comical sight as the males bob their heads back and forth and dash about in a lively courtship display. But suddenly they are gone, heading for their Canadian breeding grounds near Hudson Bay or beyond.

In the vicinity of Sieur de Monts Spring, the **American Woodcock** prepares to breed and raise its young. If you walk cautiously, you may hear their nasal "*peent-peent*" calls or you may be startled when one of these inconspicuous squat little birds explodes into flight. The common **Ruffed Grouse** also leaps suddenly into flight, and when the males are courting their mates, the rapid beating of their wings creates a muffled drumming that carries through the forest.

By mid-April, flocks of the **Tree Swallow** are once again swooping gracefully for insects over the Breakneck Ponds. A solitary russet-tailed **Hermit Thrush** flies silently from perch to perch in the dark spruce forest. Toward the end of the month, the secretive little **Winter Wren** begins flooding deeply shaded conifer forests with its enthusiastic long jumbles of rapidly tinkling notes and trills. It is soon joined by the **White-throated Sparrow**. The white-throats' clear sweet notes are suggestive of the phrase, *"old Sam Peabody, Peabody, Peabody"*—one of the most characteristic songs of the northern forest. **Eastern Towhee, Brown Thrasher,** and **Catbird** return to their sunny haunts in more open brushy habitat, especially in some of the areas that burned during the 1947 wildfire.

The month of May brings the climax of new avian arrivals to Mount Desert Island. This full orchestration of songs is highlighted by the high-pitched musical arrangements of the little wood-warblers and the flute-like solos and duets of the thrushes. By around the first of the month, the **Hermit Thrush** begins singing its variously pitched liquid phrases. The hermit's is a serene ethereal song that starts on a long clear note, followed by a rising and falling jumble of tones. It is especially magical when heard in the peaceful early and late hours of the day.

Almost precisely on the 12th or 13th of May, the **Wood Thrush** returns overnight to such places as Stanley Brook valley, near Seal Harbor. Until just a few years ago, this species did not breed and spend the summer as far north as the central coast of Maine. Now the woods ring

with its endlessly repeated decisive flute-like phrases that sound like *"ee-oh-lee,"* *"ee-oh-lay,"* each followed by a short soft trill. The **Swainson's Thrush**, with its reedy upward-spiraling song; and the less common thrush, the **Veery**, with its downward-spiraling cascade of notes, also return at about this time.

Wood-warblers provide the greatest variety of color and songs. Many species of these cheerful-seeming little birds flood back to Acadia's woodlands, after wintering in the insect-rich West Indies, Mexico, and/or Central and South America. A few species winter in the southeastern United States. The eastern phase of the common **Yellow-rumped Warbler** (formerly called the Myrtle) and the bobbing-tailed **Palm Warbler** arrive first, usually around or just past mid-April. The latter species is infrequently seen and favors hidden sphagnum bogs, where it breeds. In early May, the **Black-and-white Warbler** begins singing its extremely high-pitched, almost squeaky song—a two-note *"weezee"* that is repeated at least seven times in rapid succession, as it scurries, nuthatch-like, up and down tree trunks and branches in search of insects.

Arriving from winter in South Florida, the West Indies, Mexico, and Central America is the abundant **Black-throated Green Warbler**, the male brightly patterned with an olive-green back, yellow face, and black-throat. Its slow wheezy musical phrases, suggestive of *"pines, pines, murmuring pines,"* seem to capture the very essence of warm lazy days in a northern conifer forest.

About the middle of May, the quantity of songbirds suddenly increases, literally overnight, in a climactic rush. Just as the leaves of the aspen, birch, and maple are beginning to unfurl, the woodlands are filled with their songs and activities. Of the increasing numbers of warblers, there are the colorful **Nashville, Yellow, Chestnut-sided, Magnolia, Cape May, Black-throated Blue, Blackburnian, American Redstart, Common Yellowthroat,** and **Canada**. It is sometimes possible to identify a half-dozen or more warbler species in just a single tree!

The **Ovenbird**, which looks more like a thrush than a warbler, builds its nest among dry leaves on the forest floor. Its emphatic song, sounding like *"teacher, teacher, teacher,"* steadily increases in volume with each of the 8 to 10 repeated phrases that resound loudly in deciduous woodlands. And then there is the yellow-throated and bluish-backed **Northern Parula Warbler,** singing its buzzy ascending trills that snap off at the end. This species, which winters mainly in the West Indies, builds its nest among hanging wisps of Beard Lichen (*Usnea barbada*) that is common on the branches and trunks of

spruce trees near the ocean.

Various flycatchers arrive, beginning in early April with the **Eastern Phoebe**; and in May, such others as the **Eastern Kingbird, Least Flycatcher,** and the larger **Olive-sided Flycatcher**. The latter typically sounds off from the top of a tall spruce tree with a loud call that sounds like *"whip-three-beers."*

Two of the most stunning songbirds now returning from wintering as far away as northeastern South America are the **Rose-breasted Grosbeak** and the dazzling red-and-black **Scarlet Tanager**. By about the third week in May, both species are caroling in rich old-growth deciduous and mixed woodlands, by the shores of Long (Great) Pond, Eagle Lake, and elsewhere. Their melodious songs are suggestive of the robin's musical phrases. But the grosbeak's is higher pitched and faster paced, with more frequent changes of pitch; and the tanager's has a distinctly hoarse or burred quality, with only three or four deliberate phrases. Both are a special thrill to hear, especially if you happen to be canoeing and the melodies drift across a lake's expanse of calm water.

One of the most common birds of the rich deciduous woods is the hard-to-spot little olive-gray **Red-eyed Vireo**. Its short, high-pitched phrases are monotonously repeated for long stretches of the day.

All through June, as the great

Belted Kingfisher

chorus of songs fills the island's woodlands, the lush deciduous foliage, which has fully unfurled by now, makes visual identification of birds much more difficult. But out on the lakes and ponds, in early morning and early evening, the yodeling calls of the **Common Loon** sound almost like human laughter, as the sound echoes from shore to shore. They and a few pairs of the **Common Merganser** raise their young along secluded shores. The **Belted Kingfisher** can frequently be spotted perching on a snag above a lakeshore, stream, or tidal inlet. As this comical-looking bird, with ragged-looking crest, flies over the water, it breaks the stillness with a harsh rattling call; and it may hover like a helicopter, awaiting the right moment to dive into the water for a small fish.

Few birds are more exciting to see than the spectacular crow-sized **Pileated Woodpecker**. The loud call and powerful hammering of this year-round resident resounds through the forest. Although the largest of North American woodpeckers, measuring up to nearly 20 inches long, is extremely wary, cautiously approaching one may reward you with a view of its black body, black-and-white-striped face and neck, and prominent flaming red crest. Wood chips fly in all directions, as it hammers into a tree trunk in pursuit of carpenter ants or beetle larvae. In springtime, the drumming may also be a declaration

of territorial claims and courtship intentions.

The **Northern Raven** is a common resident of Acadia, its deep croaks carrying for miles, as it glides and swoops in aerial acrobatics or circles aimlessly on thermal updrafts. In summer, ravens raise their young in narrow crevices at such high, precipitous places as Penobscot Mountain's Jordan Cliffs. The **Osprey** and **Bald Eagle** breed and raise their young along the coast of Maine. You may now and then catch a glimpse of one of these impressive birds, as it circles over a cove or pond, plummets suddenly to the water's surface, and flaps away with a fish gripped in its talons.

There are other raptors. The **American Kestrel** typically hovers over meadows and fields in search of mice and other small rodents. The **Red-tailed Hawk** rides thermals, circling higher and higher above the mountains. And there are the summering **Broad-winged Hawk** and resident **Northern Goshawk** that fly swiftly through the forest or skim over the treetops. Rarely, the deep mysterious hooting of a **Barred Owl** carries across a valley after the sun has set.

Other bird sounds of summer include the nasal chattering *"yank-yank-yank"* of the busy little **Red-breasted Nuthatch**; the enthusiastic, musical warblings of the **Purple Finch**; the cheerful *"per-chico-ree"* of the **American Goldfinch**; piercing trills of the tiny

Ruby-crowned Kinglet; and the high-pitched "lisping" notes of the **Cedar Waxwing**.

In July, many of the bird songs begin to lose their exuberance and some stop altogether. By early August, the woodlands of Acadia are suddenly nearly as silent as in winter—an occasional **Black-throated Green Warbler** or a persistent **Red-eyed Vireo** here and there, but little else.

The tiny iridescent green-and-red **Ruby-throated Hummingbird**, which spends its winters mostly in Central America, Mexico, and southernmost Florida, is seldom seen in the park. It is commonly attracted to cultivated flower gardens, such as Thuya Garden that is located above the eastern shore of Northeast Harbor.

Great Black-backed and Herring Gulls congregate in harbors or flock behind lobster boats making their rounds of lobster traps. The gulls' raucous calls are an integral part of the Maine coast. Offshore, the little **Black Guillemot** rapidly flaps its short black-and-white wings, as it flies just above the surface of the ocean. The much larger and ungainly looking **Double-crested Cormorant**, perching on bell buoys and ocean ledges, characteristically holds its long wings outstretched to dry. Flocks of cormorants often skim over the surface of the ocean in long lines and V's.

Among the most graceful seabirds is the **Common Tern**. This fork-tailed swallow-like species breeds in colonies on small outer islands. Even though it is typically seen well off the coast, one or two may occasionally be seen flying over the island's bays and harbors. The larger **Arctic Tern** is less common here. This species is one of the world's champion long-distance fliers. After raising its young on an outer coastal island, this tern migrates in the autumn, heading northeastward near Canada's Newfoundland, then eastward across the North Atlantic and southward along the coasts of Europe and Africa, finally reaching its wintering territory in the summer of the Southern Hemisphere's sea around Antarctica. The Arctic Tern's annual migration covers roughly 25,000 miles.

In late August, September, and October, a new attraction begins at Acadia: the southward migration of countless numbers of shorebirds. Pausing briefly on beaches and rocky shores are various species of **Plovers**, **Sandpipers**, **Yellowlegs**, and **Dowitchers**. Flocks of the little **Sanderling** are especially amusing to watch on a sandy beach, as they repeatedly dash in unison behind each receding wave in search of tiny particles of food and then scurry back just ahead of each returning wave.

With the departure of these transients and the multitude of summering birds that have raised their young here, Acadia once again awaits a new season of snow and ice and wintry gales, when great rafts of eiders return to ride the ocean swells off Ocean Drive, and the buffleheads and loons return to the island's coves and harbors. And so, the fascinating, ever-changing cycle of birdlife continues to unfold its ancient patterns and mysteries.

Mammals

Acadia is home to a surprising variety of mammals. If you walk quietly on the trails and carriage roads, you will likely be rewarded with opportunities to observe some of these secretive island residents.

TERRESTRIAL MAMMALS

White-tailed Deer (*Odocoileus virginianus*) are an abundant mammal on Mount Desert Island, but they are frequently hidden away in cedar swamps, boggy thickets, and secluded mountain ravines. Hikers are sometimes startled as one lets out a loud snort and dashes away through the forest, its white tail raised in alarm. Cedar tree foliage is one of this animal's favorite winter foods, and a visual sign of deer is the "browse line" on cedars around the edges of many lakes and ponds. In the years following the 1947 wildfire, Mount Desert's deer population increased dramatically in response to an abundance of more favorable brushy and young-growth deciduous habitat across a large part of the is-

land's East Side. You are most likely to see one or more deer at dusk or dawn along park roads and lakeshores. Especially in autumn, motorists are urged to be extra cautious when driving at night, since deer all-too-often leap across the road in the confusing glare of headlights.

Beavers (*Castor canadensis*) are usually difficult to spot, but their clever dam-building operations are a common sight along many of Acadia's streams—especially where trees such as aspen offer a source of food and construction material for dams and lodges. These 3- to 4-foot-long rodents are usually busy with tree-felling and other gnawing, dragging, and building activities from dusk to dawn. When alarmed, they use their broad flat tails to hit the water surface with a loud slap—a warning to others to be alert for danger. Beavers spend much of the winter locked beneath the ice, burrowed in their large conical-shaped mud-and-stick lodges. At least one underwater entrance leads into the lodge, the floor of which is above the water level.

Muskrats (*Ondatra zibethicus*) are rodents measuring only 1.5 to 2 feet long. They often live in abandoned beaver ponds and cattail marshes, as well as along the edges of ponds and lakes. They either build a small conical lodge of sticks and mud or dig burrows into embankments.

Raccoons (*Procyon lotor*) are quite common but infrequently seen because they normally forage for food at night. A family of these black-masked animals will occasionally be caught in headlight beams along the road. Streams and lakeshores are their natural feeding habitat, where they wash their prey of crayfish or other aquatic life before eating it.

Porcupines (*Erethizon dorsatum*) are fairly common and mostly nocturnal. They can sometimes be seen in late afternoon or early evening, as they shuffle out of the woods to forage on meadow plants. They also climb trees to eat nutritious buds, twigs, and inner bark. Although porcupines cannot throw their quills, it is wise to keep a respectful distance from them, especially because these animals are believed to have poor eyesight. A porcupine's quills are armed with an extremely sharp barb that makes extraction difficult and painful.

Striped Skunks (*Mephitis mephitis*) are another nocturnal mammal that usually forages between dusk and dawn for such food as berries, insects, grubs, carrion, and small rodents. Late one mid-winter night, one of these black-and-white animals, with plumy tail held high, was seen bounding down the middle of the main street of Seal Harbor. In early summer, there is nothing that quite compares with a parade of tiny young skunks following single-file close behind their mother.

Coyotes (*Canis latrans*) have become fairly common members of the Canidae family that also includes wolves, foxes, and dogs. During the latter few years of the 20th century, coyotes extended their range eastward across New England, and now inhabit Mount Desert Island. From nose to tip of tail, these mammals measure roughly 45 to 50 inches long. They have gray or reddish-gray fur, with rusty brown or yellowish legs and a black tip of their bushy tail. Unlike foxes, coyotes hold their tail down close to their hind legs when running. Although coyotes can sometimes be seen during the day, they are mostly nocturnal. Their distinctive call, which is usually heard at dusk, during the night, or at dawn, consists of a series of barks, wails, howls, and rapid yapping. A single coyote can sound like a chorus of several animals.

Red Foxes (*Vulpes vulpes*) are common, although their numbers seem to fluctuate substantially over the years. From nose to tip of tail, they measure roughly 36 to 40 inches

Raccoon

Striped Skunk

Raccoon tracks   Striped Skunk tracks

long. They have reddish fur, a white-tipped bushy tail, and black feet and lower legs. Their thin high-pitched barking and yapping are occasionally heard at night. Even though foxes usually hunt for rodents and other prey under the cover of darkness, you may occasionally see a fox in broad daylight, as it stalks a mouse in a meadow or along a roadside. (The smaller **Gray Foxes** [*Urocyon cinereoargenteus*] do not range this far northeast along the coast of Maine.)

Snowshoe Hares (*Lepus americanus*) are quite common, although their populations fluctuate greatly over the years. These rabbit-like animals are nocturnal and can occasionally be seen along roadsides in the beam of headlights. In summer, their fur is brown. In winter, the end of each hair turns white, enabling them to blend with the snow.

Mink (*Mustela vison*) are fairly common residents but are difficult to spot, since they are mostly nocturnal and extremely shy. They measure about 2 feet in length. Mink live in dens along streams and lakeshores, and among their favored prey are muskrats, rabbits, chipmunks, frogs, and fish. Weasels are also fairly common.

Northern Flying Squirrels (*Glaucomys sabrinus*) are nocturnal and seldom seen, unless you happen to spot one gorging itself on nuts or seeds at a bird-feeding station. Not infrequently on a woodland walk, you may hear their high-pitched

piercing bird-like call during the daytime. These fascinating little mammals, with silky-soft buff-brown fur above and whitish underparts, do not actually fly. A loose fold of fur-covered skin along each side, between front and hind legs, enables them to glide downward from upper tree branches.

Red Squirrels (*Tamiasciurus hudsonicus*) are abundant and are one of the few kinds of Acadia's land mammals that are really diurnal. Hikers in coniferous forests frequently see them and hear their emphatic loud chattering. As one of these animals perches a safe distance above or dashes frantically from tree to tree, it lets loose with what may seem like a "mad-as-a-wet-hen" scolding. These reddish-brown squirrels are about a foot long from nose to tip of tail. They thrive on seeds, nuts, birds' eggs, and various kinds of mushrooms. Here and there, the observant hiker may see a stump or boulder, upon which a squirrel has eaten or stuffed into his cheeks the nutritious seeds of a pine or spruce cone and left behind a neat pile of discarded bracts.

Eastern Gray Squirrels (*Sciurus carolinensis*) typically inhabit deciduous woodlands and some of the island's residential neighborhoods. They are believed to have been introduced onto Mount Desert Island in the 1920s.

Eastern Chipmunks (*Tamias striatus*) are prolific little mammals that hikers frequently see through-

Long-tailed Weasel

Red Fox

Red Fox tracks

out most of the national park. They measure only 8 to 10 inches in length from tip of nose to end of tail. The side of their bodies is patterned with a whitish stripe bordered by two black stripes; and a black stripe runs down its back. Their call is a harsh little *"chuk-chuk-chuk,"* and their favorite foods include seeds, nuts, and berries.

Masked Shrews (*Sorex cinereus*) are tiny grayish-brown long-tailed mammals that favor moist forested habitat. Even though these abundant animals are diurnal as well as noctur-nal, they are secretive and seldom seen by hikers. They daily eat more than their own body weight in food and have been known to consume up to three times their weight when kept in captivity. Their diet largely consists of insects. **Long-tailed Shrews** (*S. dispar*) and **Northern Short-tailed Shrews** (*Blarina brevicauda*) have also been recorded in the park.

Star-nosed Moles (*Condylura cristata*) and **Hairy-tailed Moles** (*Parascalops breweri*) both reside on Mount Desert Island, but since they live beneath the surface of the ground, they are rarely seen. They daily consume up to three times their body weight, mostly favoring insects and earthworms.

Southern Red-backed Voles (*Clethrionomys gapperi*) and **Meadow Voles** (*Microtus pennsylvanicus*) are both abundant—the former in moist dark spruce forests and the latter in meadows, marshy habitat, and along streams and ponds. Both species are diurnal and nocturnal, but these fat mouse-like little animals are so secretive and blend so well with their surroundings that hikers only rarely see them. Both species have grayish-brown fur—the Red-backed with slightly rusty-red coloring on the back. Their diet includes leafy vegetation, grasses, seeds, nuts, bark, and some insects.

White-footed Mice (*Peromyscus leucopus*) and **Deer Mice** (*P. maniculatus*) are both abundant and are similar in appearance, with a slender

Snowshoe Hare tracks

pointed face and prominent rounded ears. Their fur is brownish above and whitish beneath. **Meadow Jumping Mice** (*Zapus hudsonius*) and **Woodland Jumping Mice** (*Napaeozapus insignis*) have also been seen in the park. Both are primarily nocturnal, and the latter species has golden sides and a white-tipped tail. Mice eat seeds, nuts, fruits, and insects.

Other terrestrial mammals include **River Otters** (*Lutra canadensis*), which are fairly common but not often seen; **Black Bears** (*Urus americanus*) and **Moose** (*Alces alces*), which are uncommon visitors from the mainland; and **Bobcats** (*Lynx rufus*), which are either very rare or may no longer inhabit Mount Desert Island.

Of the bats, the **Little Brown Myotis** (*Myotis lucifugus*) is the species most frequently seen because it typically begins its erratic aerial pursuit of insects around dusk. **Big Brown Bats** (*Eptesicus fuscus*) are also common.

MARINE MAMMALS

Harbor Seals (*Phoca vitulina*) frequent ocean ledges in the coastal waters around Mount Desert Island, and they occasionally swim into the island's harbors and coves. These 5- to 6-foot mammals have gray, tan, brown, reddish-brown, or golden fur that is splotchy patterned with brown or black markings. On sailing excursions, it is entertaining to

watch a group of these seals, some with their whiskered heads bobbing above the water, while others lounge on a nearby, rocky, surf-splashed ledge.

Gray Seals (*Halichoerus grypus*) formerly did not range this far northeast along the coast of Maine, but small numbers of them now inhabit the waters around Mount Desert Island. These animals grow to 8 or 9 feet in length and are uniform gray or blackish in color. The males especially have a prominent "Roman" nose, with widely spaced nostrils.

Atlantic Harbor Porpoises (*Phocoena phocoena*) are a common sight on boat trips in bays and the open ocean around Mount Desert Island. This 4- to 6-foot-long species of marine mammal, with a nearly triangular fin on its back, are dark-gray or black above, grading to light gray along the sides and white beneath. In summer months, small groups of them can be seen surfacing gracefully.

Finback Whales (*Balaenoptera physalus*) are generally the most commonly sighted of several species of whales that inhabit bays and open ocean along the coast of Maine. This slender species, also known as the Common Rorqual, reaches 60 to 70 feet in length and weighs 50 to 60 tons. They have a flattened head, dark-gray back, pale beneath, and long parallel throat grooves. A unique characteristic of this whale is the color of the lower lips—dark-gray on the left side, and light-gray or white on the right side. Finbacks are one of the baleen whales, meaning that they have narrow strips of whalebone extending from the roof of their mouth, with which to strain small marine organisms from the seawater. As these sleek giants surface to breathe, they shoot a slender column of water into the air with a whistling sound.

Less frequently seen are **Minke** (or **Piked**) **Whales** (*Balaenoptera acutorostrata*) that measure 20 to 30 feet long and are dark above and light beneath, with a white band across each flipper; and the large **Humpback Whales** (*Megaptera novaeangliae*) that measure 40 to 50 feet long and are dark above and light beneath, with knobby swellings along the top of the flattened head and along the leading edge of long whitish flippers.

Reptiles

There are few species of cold-blooded reptiles in Acadia, and those that do inhabit the national park are generally shy and secretive. All are non-poisonous. You are most likely to see the little Painted Turtles and Garter Snakes, but then only during the warm months. Since reptilian blood has no fixed temperature (unlike that of mammals) and varies with the surrounding air or water temperature, these animals cannot function in cold weather. They must burrow away safely in the earth, mud, or rock piles.

TURTLES

Snapping Turtles (*Chelydra serpentina*) live in abundance in the park's lakes, ponds, and marshes. They measure from 8 to 12 inches long (occasionally to 1.5 feet), with a rather flat carapace (shell) that is made up of rough scutes (plates). This long-tailed species is a powerful swimmer and darts its large long-necked head quickly to capture such prey as frogs, fish, and small birds and mammals. As the name implies, snapping turtles are quick to defend themselves and can inflict a painful bite with their sharp beaked mouth.

Eastern Painted Turtles (*Chrysemys picta picta*) are only about 5 to 6 inches long and have a smooth, slightly domed carapace that is highlighted with reddish spots around the edge and light-colored borders between the scutes. There are yellow markings on the side of the head. These turtles live in many beaver ponds and in the shallower parts of the larger lakes and ponds. They frequently bask in the warmth of the sun—perhaps even a half dozen of them in a row on a log or rock near the surface of the water.

One of the likely places to see Painted Turtles is on fallen, half-submerged logs at a small pond that is beside the carriage road between Witch Hole Pond and Halfmoon Pond. They feed on aquatic plants, insects, and small mollusks and crustaceans.

Garter Snake

Milk Snake

SNAKES

Note: All species are non-poisonous.
Eastern Garter Snakes (*Thamnophis sirtalis sirtalis*) are fairly commonly seen along trails and carriage roads during the late spring, summer, and early autumn months. They usually measure about 1.5 to 2 feet in length and have a checkered pattern, with three yellowish, greenish, or brown lateral bands running from head to tail.

Eastern Milk Snakes (*Lampropeltis doliata triangulum*) are common residents, but are less frequently encountered than garter snakes. This 2- to 3-foot-long species is strikingly patterned, with several rows of black-edged brown or red-dish-brown splotches on a light-buff or grayish background. This pattern and coloring camouflages them well in a wooded habitat.

Eastern Smooth Green Snakes (*Opheodrys vernalis*) are a common green species, measuring 1 to 1.5 feet in length. They are usually seen in meadows and open mountain slopes.

Red-bellied Snakes (*Storeria occipitomaculata*) and **Northern Ringneck Snakes** (*Diadophis punctatus edwardsi*) are both about a foot long and are not often seen. Red-bellied Snakes favor wooded areas and Northern Ringneck Snakes inhabit rocky terrain.

Amphibians

Amphibians, like reptiles, are cold-blooded animals that must hibernate in the earth or in the muddy bottom of a pond. But unlike reptiles, amphibians, such as frogs and salamanders, pass through two or more major phases of their life cycle. For frogs, there is an aquatic larval phase, the tadpole, in which they breathe oxygen from the water with gills; and an adult phase, in which they have lungs and can live on land. Frogs are usually found in and near shallow ponds and around lakeshores, such as at Aunt Betty Pond and the Breakneck Ponds. In springtime, it is amusing to hear the varied calls of Acadia's frogs—from the deep croaking Bullfrogs and quacking Wood Frogs, to the bell-like chirps of Peepers.

Unless you make a concerted effort to hunt for salamanders, you almost certainly will not see them. These little amphibians live beneath rotting logs and rocks in the damp woods of Acadia.

Spring Peepers (*Hyla crucifer*) are the tiniest of the frogs on Mount Desert Island. This species of tree frog measures a mere inch or so in length. Yet, their choruses of high-pitched piercing calls carry far from wet roadside ditches and boggy forested spots, beginning in April and climaxing in May. Their brown color, with a dark X-shaped pattern on the back, camouflages them well.

Wood Frogs (*Rana sylvatica*) are a 2-inch-long brownish species, with a distinctive dark eye mask. They typically favor damp meadows and clearings near ponds and streams, but these frogs are secretive and not often noticed by hikers. Their call is a hoarse quack, suggestive of a duck.

Pickerel Frogs (*R. palustris*) are a very common beautifully mottled 2- to 3-inch-long species. Their background color often varies from pale yellowish-buff to green, with a pattern of square-shaped dark splotches. Hidden inner surfaces of the hind legs are bright orange or yellow. These frogs inhabit ponds, streams, and adjacent meadows.

Green Frogs (*R. clamitans*

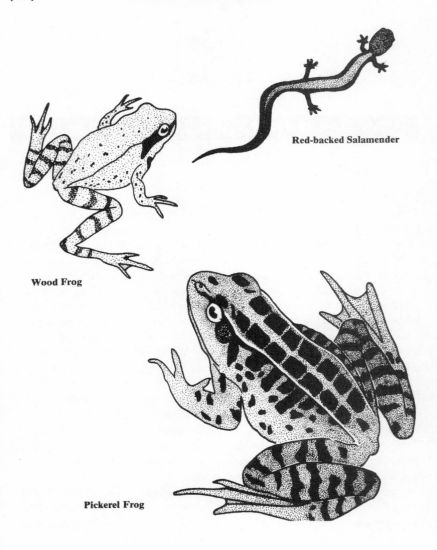

Red-backed Salamender

Wood Frog

Pickerel Frog

melanota) are abundant along shallow lakeshores, streams, and
swampy places. This 2- to 3.5-inch-
long species ranges in color from vibrant green all over, to brown-and-
green. Adult males have a yellow

throat. In the spring and early summer, these frogs often voice their ex-
plosive croaking calls in the evening
and on cloudy or foggy days.

Bullfrogs (*R. catesbeiana*) are
the 4- to 6-inch (occasionally larger)

green or brownish giants whose choruses of deep croaking notes resound across ponds and lakes in the evening.

Several species of salamanders also inhabit the national park—notably the 2- to 4-inch-long **Red-backed Salamanders** (*plethodon cinereus cinereus*). They are common in cool damp woods. The stripe down the back may be reddish, orange, or yellow.

BUTTERFLIES

There are a great many species of butterflies in Acadia, and the following are just a few of the more conspicuous and beautiful ones. Butterflies pass through four stages in their life cycle: egg, caterpillar, chrysalis, and adult butterfly.

Mourning Cloaks (*Nymphalis antiopa*) are apparently the earliest butterflies of the year, first appearing in early April or even late March, after hibernation in the adult butterfly stage. They have approximately a 3-inch wingspread and their wings are rich-velvety dark-brown, with a line of delicate blue dots adjacent to the yellowish outer border. Their flight pattern consists of several quick wing beats, followed by an erratic glide.

Tiger Swallowtails (*Pterourus glaucus*) are the largest and most strikingly beautiful of Acadia's butterflies. They first appear in late May or early June, after wintering in the chrysalis stage. These abundant butterflies of sunny meadows and road-sides have a 4- to 5-inch wingspread and their wings are pale yellow with bold black markings and outer borders. Hind wings have a characteristic "tail" that extends from the outer lower edge.

Monarchs (*Danaus plexippus*) have a 3.5- to 4-inch wingspan, with rounded deep-reddish-orange wings that are strikingly patterned with black veins and white-dotted black borders. Their flight combines slow flapping with glides, in which the wings are held at an upward angle. In late summer, they are often seen feeding on the nectar of goldenrods and thistles. Monarchs are protected from most enemies by their disagreeable scent and taste.

The Monarch is the only butterfly species that annually migrates. These incredible insects leave their northern habitat in the autumn and fly southwestward more than 2,500 miles to their wintering habitat in central Mexico's Sierra Madre Mountains. To protect this vital forested habitat of tall oyamel fir trees from the threat of logging, the

Cecropia Moth

Underwing Moth

Mourning Cloak

Red Admiral

Mexican government in 1986 established the Monarch Butterfly Special Biosphere Reserve, which consists of five sanctuaries, plus a subsequently protected 140,000-acre connecting corridor.

Viceroy Butterflies (*Basilarchia archippus*) are similar in color, shape, and pattern to the Monarch, except for a narrow curving black line that cuts across the black veins of the hind wings; and their wingspan is slightly smaller. The flight pattern consists of very rapid wing beats between glides in which the wings are held horizontally. Because Viceroys so closely resemble the distasteful Monarchs, enemies usually avoid eating them, as well. This is an outstanding example of (unconscious) protective mimicry. Viceroys are generally less common than Monarchs on Mount Desert Island; and unlike the latter, Viceroys do not migrate.

Red Admirals (*Vanessa atalanta*) have approximately a 2-inch wingspread with a dark-brown inner part of the wings, bordered by a nearly circular, broad, bright-orange band that curves midway across the forewings and forms a border along the outer edge of the hind wings. The outer tip of the forewings is black, dotted with white markings. This species favors thistle flowers, and it hibernates either in the chrysalis or adult stage.

Painted Ladies (*Vanessa* spp.) superficially resemble the Red Admiral. The most obvious differences

are the irregular jumble of orange markings, where the Red Admiral has a broad orange band. Painted Ladies favor thistle flowers.

White Admirals (*Basilarchia arthemis*), also called Banded Purples, have boldly marked wings with a broad curving white band across purplish-black wings and a 3-inch wingspan. This species favors deciduous woods of such trees as birch and aspen. Consequently, it is more difficult to spot than species that live in more open habitat. White Admirals hibernate in the caterpillar stage.

Greater Spangled Fritillaries (*Speyeria cybele*) are one of the largest of Acadia's fritillary species, the wingspans of which vary from about 1.5 to 3 inches. Most of them have brownish-orange wings that are intricately patterned with black or dark-brownish dots, crescents, and zigzag bands. Undersurfaces are at least partly speckled with silvery metallic spots. Many species favor meadows and boggy areas, and most hibernate in the caterpillar stage.

Common Sulphur (*Colias philodice*) **and Orange Sulphur Butterflies** (*C. eurytheme*) are abundant around meadows, grassy roadsides, and other open habitat. With a 1- to 2.5-inch wingspan, the Common Sulphur's upper surface of the wings is pale-yellow, the Orange Sulphur's is yellow tinged with orange, and both have black borders along the outer edge of the forewings and hind wings. These are among the earliest

Tiger Swallowtail

Clouded Sulphur

spring butterflies, after usually hibernating in the chrysalis stage. Their flight pattern consists of rapid wing fluttering, as they fly in an erratic zigzag course. They are most active on warm sunny days and frequently gather around the edge of small puddles and pools.

Spring Azures (*Celastrina ladon*) are a common little blue species, with a 1-inch wingspan. The males have pale-blue or bluish-violet upper wing surfaces, and the females have paler purplish or pinkish fore wings and whitish hind wings. Spring Azures are among the earliest native butterflies to emerge from the wintering chrysalis stage—appearing usually in late April and early May.

Cabbage Whites (*Artogeia rapae*) are abundant non-native butterflies from Europe. They have a 1.5- to 2-inch wingspread; and the upper wing surfaces are white, marked with one or two black dots and a black outer tip of the fore wing. They hibernate in the chrysalis stage. Adult Cabbage Whites favor meadows, fields, and grassy roadsides. Many farmers and gardeners consider this now widespread species as a pest.

MOTHS

Moths are mostly nocturnal insects that are typically attracted to lights. As with butterflies, they begin life as an egg, pass through caterpillar and chrysalis stages, and climax as adult moths. Their bodies are usually thicker than those of butterflies, and their antennae are either feather-like or thread-like, the latter without the terminal knobs that are typical of butterflies. Among the more conspicuous species in Acadia are the following:

Cecropia Moths (*Nyalophora cecropia*), the largest species of the giant silk moths, have a 4- to 6-inch wingspread. Both forewings and hind wings are brown, each with a prominent crescent-shaped "eyespot." Whitish and rusty-brown bands run roughly parallel with the outer edges of the wings, and the outer edges are bordered in light tones of buff-brown. Antennae are feather-like.

Polyphemus Moths (*Antheraea polyphemus*), another species of the giant silk moths, have a 3.5- to 5.5-inch wingspan. Their velvety-looking wings are varying shades of yellowish-buff and rusty-brown, with prominent clear oval "eyespots" on all four wings, of which those on the hind wings have a prominent black border. Two segments of a narrow reddish and pink band cut across the base of the forewings. Antennae are feather-like.

Luna Moths (*Actias luna*) are strikingly attractive pale-green giant silk moths, with a 3- to 4-inch wingspread. Both forewings and hind wings have "eyespots," and the hind wings end in a long curved "tail." Antennae are feather-like.

Underwing Moths (*Catocala* spp.), a smaller species of the giant silk moths, typically have brownish forewings that are intricately patterned to blend with tree bark, camouflaging them during the day as they rest. At night, under the beam of a light, the hind wings are colorfully visible: bright red on the Sleepy and Ultrona moths and yellow on the Graceful Underwing. Both are patterned with bold bands of dark-brown that border or are parallel with the curved outer edge of the hind wings. Antennae are thread-like.

A FEW OTHER INSECTS

Dragonflies (Order Odonata, Suborder Anisoptera) are abundant insects typically seen around shallow ponds, swamps, and open marshy habitat. They rapidly and powerfully dart this way and that, and momentarily hover in one place. Dragonflies have huge compound eyes that cover most of the front of the head. Their black body consists of a long slender rigid-looking abdomen; and a thicker thorax. Dragonflies have two pairs of long, narrow wings attached to the thorax that are entirely or nearly transparent and minutely veined, with one pair set behind the other. The forewings and hind wings flap alternately, to reduce air turbulence that would otherwise impair the usefulness of the slightly broader hind wings. As dragonflies zip and swoop through the air or skim low over the surface of a pond, they capture mosquitoes and other smaller insects with their bristle-fringed forelegs and devour them while in flight.

When these dragonflies stop to rest, they continue to extend their wings horizontally.

These prehistoric-looking creatures are among the world's oldest kinds of insects. Roughly 300 million years ago, when warmer, damper conditions of the Pennsylvanian Period were dominated by such early plants as tree ferns and tree-sized clubmosses and horsetails, there were many sizes and varieties of dragonflies. Some, such as *Meganeuropsis permiana,* were giants with a 2- to 2.5-foot wingspread (about the size of a Cooper's hawk). These dragonflies were apparently the world's largest insects ever to inhabit the Earth. They were dominant in the skies more than 100 million years before the evolution of the earliest birds. Today's largest dragonflies have mere 4- to 5-inch wingspan.

Damselflies (Suborder Zygoptera) are smaller, more delicate-looking dragonflies. Some of the narrow-winged varieties have bright blue or red bodies. When damselflies stop to rest, they fold their clear, veined wings together at an angle above their body.

Water Striders (Family Gerridae) are fascinating to watch as they "skate" along on their four slender outstretched legs, supported, as if by magic, on the water's surface film. They are abundant, thrusting themselves from place to place on calm streams and ponds.

Acadia, of course, has a number of stinging insects: **Yellowjackets** and **Hornets** (Family Vespidae) and other **Wasps**; **Bees** (Family Apidae); **Ants** (Family Formicidae); and the non-native **European Fire Ant** (*Myrmica rubra*). No discussion of this subject would be quite complete without including at least a passing mention of two blood-sucking insects that are a nuisance to hikers and campers: the tiny but fierce and venomous **Black Flies** (Family Simuliidae) of late spring and early summer; and the ubiquitous female **Mosquitoes** (Family Culicidae) that jab their sharp proboscis into their victim and inject an itchy fluid that thins the blood.

Intertidal Life

The Intertidal environment of the rugged, rocky seashore is one of the world's most complex and demanding environments. The plants and animals thriving there have developed many ways of coping with the awesome pounding and pulling of the surf. Many of them have the ability to cling tightly to the rocks, as do seaweeds, sea stars, and marine snails. Some are designed to reduce or deflect the full force of the waves, as with flattened, flexible seaweeds and the cone-shaped shells of barnacles and limpets. Still others seek the shelter of crevices in the rocks, as do periwinkles, sea anemones, and the delicate little Corallina.

Many of the intertidal plants and animals have also become adapted to two diametrically opposite environments that are caused by the twice-daily, 8- to 12-foot average rise and fall of the tides along this part of the coast of Maine. A variety of ways have evolved to prevent desiccation and death during periods of exposure to air. Snails and barnacles lock themselves inside their shells. Sea-weeds are covered with a thin, gelatin-like protective layer.

The Intertidal environment is a place of abundant life, in which there is intense competition for space and food between and within the multitude of species. It is a place to observe the ancient processes of predation by one creature against the defenses of another. It is a place to watch the tranquil beauty of a tide pool or the elemental fury of the sea tearing away at the edge of the land.

The following species are among the more common and obvious ones inhabiting the rocky edge of the sea, along this part of the coast of Maine. They are presented within the context of a variety of fairly distinct horizontal bands, in which one form of life or another is dominant. While each of these bands, hereafter referred to as zones, is not restricted entirely to its vertical extent, these zones provide a way to simplify the study and understanding of life along Acadia's shores.

SPRAY ZONE

An irregular black band of *Calothrix*, a primitive blue-green algae, which is classified as a cyano bacteria, forms thin encrusting masses just above the high-tide line, in an area frequently reached by the spray of surf. This band, which is extremely slippery when wet, looks much like a thin deposit of oil or paint washed along the shore rocks. But under a microscope, it appears as a thread-like filament of cells.

PERIWINKLE ZONE

Periwinkles (*Littorina* spp.) are found throughout the intertidal zone environment, but a rough-shelled variety is especially abundant just below the *Calothrix* band. These snails have a spiraled shell that varies from light to dark tones. They are vegetarians that graze on algae, using their file-like radula, with its many rows of roughly 3,500 minute teeth. Because these animals lack the ability to cling to rocks as well as some other animals, periwinkles often congregate in great numbers within sheltered rock crevices.

BARNACLE ZONE

Huge numbers of **Acorn Barnacles** (*Balanus* spp.) mass together to form a whitish band along the rocky shore. These animals are a type of crustacean that is related to the lobster, crab, and shrimp. In spring, a

million-million tiny free-swimming barnacle larvae hatch out per mile of shore waters. In June, they molt and their discarded skeletal casings are suspended in the water in such huge numbers that they actually turn the sea along the shore a milky color. The relatively few larvae that are able to find a suitable place to attach themselves to the rocks now begin their sedentary stage. They secrete a limy conical-shaped shell that is securely cemented to the rocks.

At low tide, these tiny animals close a set of valves at the top of the shell to protect themselves from the desiccating effect of the air. During the brief high tide, the valves open and a delicate feathery little comb-shaped arm reaches out and captures diatoms and other microscopic organisms in the seawater, before quickly withdrawing into the shell. In a race with the outgoing tide, this feeding process is repeated again and again.

ROCKWEED ZONE

The Rockweed Zone is the most prominent of the Intertidal environments and it is out of the water approximately half of the time. It is dominated by a thick mass of branching, stringy, and rubbery brown algae, the rockweeds. There are two main types: *Fucus*, which dominates the upper half of this zone, and *Ascophyllum*, which mainly favors the lower half.

Fucus species have long flattened

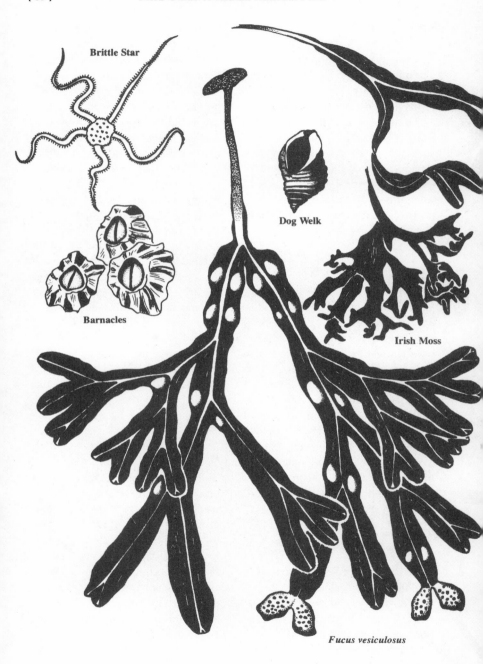

Brittle Star

Dog Welk

Barnacles

Irish Moss

Fucus vesiculosus

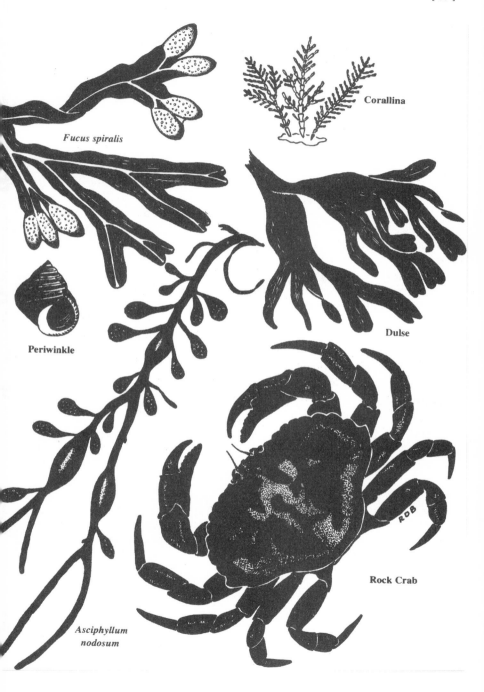

Fucus spiralis

Corallina

Dulse

Periwinkle

Rock Crab

Asciphyllum
nodosum

olive-brown branches that have a distinct midrib, with a flat "wing" along each side. The prolific **Bladder Wrack** (*Fucus vesiculosus*) has Y-shaped branching at the tip of the numerous fronds or branches, and there are small gas bladders that are usually in pairs, one on each side of the midrib. These bladders help to buoy up the plant when it is covered with water, so that its fronds are properly exposed to the sun's rays. During a specific time each year, when reproduction occurs, some of the terminal gas bladders become swollen bumpy receptacles in which reproductive cells develop. These cells mature during the winter and are released into the water during the spring. The receptacles remain attached to the plant throughout the summer.

Fucus spiralis, which grows at the upper edge of the Rockweed Zone, lacks gas bladders. Its fronds spiral in a counterclockwise direction. Another species, *F. endentatus*, which is common in many tide pools, also lacks gas bladders along its branches. Its terminal reproductive receptacles are distinctly long and slender, tapering to a point, and are often branched once or twice.

Knotted Wrack (*Ascophyllum nodosum*) is the other prolific brown algae of this intermediate zone, forming treacherously slippery masses on exposed rocks at low tide. The stems are slender and more rounded than those of *Fucus*, and its branches are irregularly re-branched and

stringy. Numerous tough-skinned gas bladders are located at intervals along the stem, resembling knots along a rope. Reproductive cells are borne in short-stemmed swollen bumpy receptacles that are attached to the branches. Soon after the mature cells have been released into the water in the spring, these receptacles fall off.

In some places near the low-tide line, the stems of Knotted Rockweed are festooned with small bushy and minutely branched tufts of thread-like dark-maroon red algae, **Tubed Weed** (*Polysiphonia lanosa*), that apparently grows only on this species of rockweed. It is an epiphyte that does not harm its host.

Another example of an epiphytic relationship is the very small *Fucus*-favoring brown algae, **Brown Pompom** (*Elachistea fucicola*). This seaweed forms little tufts of dark-brown filaments with a hard knobby base.

Rockweeds typically have, either within their thick mats or directly beneath them, the greatest abundance and variety of life in the Intertidal environment of the rocky shore. During low tide, the moisture and shelter offered by the rockweeds enable many animals to thrive there. Commonly inhabiting these dense "forests" are great numbers of smooth-shelled periwinkles that are usually dark brown with narrow concentric stripes.

The carnivorous **Dog Whelks** (*Thais lapillus*) are also abundant among the rockweeds. Their thick ridged or smooth shells vary in color from white or bright orange, to banded orange-and-white, brown-and-white, and purple-and-white. These marine snails feed on the bivalve **Blue Mussels** (*Mytilus edulis*), which also are prolific here. Whelks attack mussels by boring (dissolving) a cylindrical hole through the mussel shell. They also feed on barnacles, attacking them either by drilling through the shell or by forcing open the valves with their fleshy foot.

IRISH MOSS ZONE

Just above and at the low-tide line, and often somewhat hidden by rockweeds, are a number of interesting and commercially valuable red algae—notably Irish Moss and Dulse.

Irish Moss (*Chondrus crispus*) is a 2- to 4-inch-tall dark maroon-to-blackish bushy little algae that has an iridescent glow when the sun's rays strike it at the right angle. Its somewhat delicate-looking, upward-fanning fronds are short, stubby, and soft to the touch. This seaweed is harvested around the world and is one of this country's major sources of a substance that is used in literally hundreds of products, including medicines, lotions, lipstick, jellies, puddings, and ice cream.

Dulse (*Rhodymenia palmata*) is a 6- to 8-inch-tall rich-red species of algae that is shaped rather like the palm of a hand, with three or more broad flat "fingers." This seaweed favors shady protected places along the rocky shore. Both Dulse and another, more leafy species, *Porphyra umbilicalis*, are dried and eaten with little or no further preparation. Once you get used to its marine flavor, it is really quite pleasant to chew. This species of algae favors the low-tide line, but its red color is often bleached by the sunlight, making it more difficult to recognize.

LAMINARIAN ZONE

This is the zone that is located just at or below the low-tide line, which is out of the water, if at all, only briefly during periods of greater tidal floods and ebbs in the spring and autumn. The Laminarian Zone is named for the various species of brown laminarians—the Kelps, which live from here on down to about 50 feet below the low-tide line. Especially during powerful winter storms, these plants take a tremendous beating from the surf. Of the large brown algae, there are the following five common species:

Winged Kelp (*Alaria esculenta*) has a single long leathery brown blade that grows up to 10 feet long and waves gracefully back and forth with each push and pull of the sea. It has a short stalk that is attached to a well-cemented holdfast. This species of kelp differs from others by having a prominent midrib along its slender 4- to 6-inch-wide ruffle-edged blade. Toward the tip are numerous cuts and tears extending to the midrib, giving the blade a tattered appearance. This species also has two rows of small lateral reproductive blades that grow each year from the upper part of the short stalk.

Sugar Kelp (*Laminaria saccharina*) has a long leathery blade that grows to about 10 feet in length and is 6 to 10 inches wide. There is no central midrib; and especially during the summer, the blade's edges become wavy. *L. longicruris* is similar to *L. saccharina*, but it has a longer stem in proportion to the length of the narrower blade. It also has two rows of reproductive sacs that give a lengthwise pattern to the blade.

Horsetail (or **Oarweed**) **Kelp** (*L. digitata*) has a short stalk that abruptly broadens to a wide-based blade. The blade is cut into a number of long rubbery slender ribbons.

Devil's-apron (or **Sea Colander**) **Kelp** (*Agarum cribrosum*) has a single broad leathery blade that is completely riddled with holes, except along the midrib.

TIDE POOLS

Tide pools are temporarily isolated, tremendously varied, extremely fragile miniature marine environments. They provide refuge for a host of plants and animals that cannot tolerate exposure to the air during low tide. Some pools have almost no life, while others are exquisitely beautiful and colorful little "gardens."

Of the larger brown algae of tide pools, *Fucus edentatus* is typically common. Horsetail and Devil's-apron kelps are occasionally found in some of the lower, deeper pools. Rock surfaces of tide pools are commonly encrusted with other algae. Typical brown species are the dark-brown or blackish patches of *Ralfsia verrucosa* and rust-colored expanses of *Hildenbrandia prototypes*.

Of the red algae, **Irish Moss** is abundant in many pools, sometimes forming carpets across the bottom. **Dulse** is less common. An especially intriguing red algae is **Corallina** (*Corallina officinalis*). It is a distinctive delicate little plant that forms 1- to 2-inch-tall clumps, sometimes growing sideways from the sheer side of a pool. Clusters of main stems are attached to a crust-like holdfast. Each stem has upward-reaching branches, most of which are, in turn, re-branched once or twice. The rigid-looking stems and branches consist of flexible-jointed wedge-shaped bead-like segments. They are coated with shiny appearing deposits of whitish calcite—a crystalline substance that this plant precipitates from the calcium and magnesium carbonates in seawater.

One of the encrusting red algae, *Lithothamnium lenormandi*, also has the ability to extract these minerals from the water. It forms deep-pink patches that are beautifully patterned with concentric rings of darker and lighter shades of pink. *Lithophyllum incrustans* is another species of encrusting red algae that forms pink knobby patches on rocks and on the shells of mussels and whelks.

There are a number of green algae in tide pools. *Cladophora gracilis* grows in small tufts of stringy branching dull bluish-green threads. *Spongomorpha areta* produces a coarser and more tangled growth of hooked branches that form small spongy green clumps. **Sea Lettuce** (*Ulva lactuca*) has delicate, very thin and wavy green leaves that grow in clumps or may float free in the water. This species is an indicator of high organic content, such as sewage in coastal coves. **Maidenhair Algae** (*Enteromorpha intestinalis*) has long slender and nonbranched bright-green tubular stems that grow to a foot or more in length and from 0.25 to 0.5 of an inch wide. The tubular stems are often partially inflated with gas that buoys up the plant.

Marine algae in tide pools can tolerate a fair degree of change in environmental conditions, such as temperature, salinity, and oxygen content. Animal life, by contrast, is extremely vulnerable to substantial variations. Depending on the depth and size of a pool, water temperature can increase more or less rapidly. As the temperature increases, the oxygen content decreases—posing an increasing danger that animals will die from insufficient oxygen. Increasing water temperature also elevates the rate of evaporation, which in turn increases the proportion of salts in the pool. If salinity becomes

too great, it causes an imbalance in osmotic pressure, which then causes an outward movement of an animal's body fluids. Such loss can ultimately lead to dehydration and death. If too much fresh water, as from heavy rainfall, dilutes a tide pool's seawater, the imbalance in osmotic pressure causes an animal to swell up with too much water, which can ultimately lead to death.

There are a few hardy animals that have adapted remarkably well to tide pool environments. The more common species include the following:

Crumb-of-Bread Sponges (*Halichondria panacea*) are primitive animals that form a rough bumpy yellowish, pale-green, or orange layer that is dotted with raised tubular openings. In favorable locations below the low-tide line, these tubes sometimes reach 1 to 1.5 feet tall. A current of seawater filters through tiny pores located on the surface of the crust. Microscopic food particles are extracted from the water by colonies of nearly self-sufficient sponge cells. Water circulates out of the sponge through cone-shaped openings. No species has ever evolved from these primitive animals; they are a dead-end branch in evolution.

Starfish (*Asterias vulgaris*) and **Brittle Stars** (*Ophiopholis aculeate*) are both occasionally found in tide pools, as well as more commonly below the low-tide line. Both types of sea stars have five arms (rays)—the starfish's are thick, tapering to slender tips. The 6- to 11-inch-wide spiny starfishes vary from purplish or pink to pale orange. They use a hydraulic system to move their 800 or more tiny tubular sucker-tipped feet. Mussels and other bivalve mollusks are among the carnivorous starfish's prey. In a contest of strength and endurance, a starfish wraps its arms around the tightly closed shells and literally pulls them open. The predator's stomach is then everted (turned outward) through its mouth to envelope its food. The 6- to 8-inch-wide brittle stars move by a graceful writhing motion of their flexible slender arms. Both kinds of sea stars have the ability to regenerate a lost arm.

Green Sea Urchins (*Strongylocentrotus droebachiensis*) have thickly packed, short, pale-green spines. They slowly move about on some of these spines, as they graze on areas of algae. The mouth is located in the middle of the undersurface.

Sand Dollars (*Mellita testudinata*) are a close relative of sea urchins and are also occasionally washed up on beaches. They burrow into sandy shores at or just below the low-tide line. When alive, they are thickly covered with furry looking spines. After death, the spines are shed, exposing their whitish disc-shaped shell the upper surface of which is marked with a five-rayed, flower-like pattern.

Sea Cucumbers (*Cucumaria frondosa*) have soft leathery elongated bodies, usually measuring 9 or 10 inches in length. The tapered front end contains the mouth, which is surrounded by a ring of branched tentacles that can be retracted. Several rows of small tubular feet along the body enable these unlikely looking relatives of the starfish to move around slowly. While these weird reddish-brown creatures are occasionally seen in lower tide pools or stranded on rocks at low tide, they are more commonly found below the low-tide line. When disturbed, sea cucumbers are likely to disgorge their stomach contents.

Sea Anemones (*Metridium* spp.) grow in clusters within a few sheltered tide pools and sea caves. These sedentary animals actually resemble erect 1- to 4-inch-wide flowers. Their rings of narrow fleshy whitish or pink petal-like tentacles that surround its mouth are located at the top of a short stocky brownish stem-like body, the base of which is attached to the rocks. Sometimes it is possible to observe sea anemones creeping along with a slow gliding movement of the stem's "foot." Stinging cells on the tentacles paralyze small fish, crustaceans, and other organisms, after which a number of its tentacles wrap around the prey and hand it to the mouth. When all the tentacles are retracted, as when the animal has been disturbed, only the knobby stump of the stem is visible. These animals are prolific in some places at a depth of roughly 10 to 30 feet below the low-tide line. Vandalism and collecting have unfortunately depleted or wiped out some of Acadia's former colonies of sea anemones.

Other animals of tide pools include two single-shelled mollusks: the variously patterned 1- to 1.5-inch conical-shaped **Atlantic Plate Limpets** (*Acmaea testudinalis*); and the primitive **Chitons** (*Chaetopleura apiculata*) with their slightly rounded 0.5- to 2-inch oval shell that is divided into eight transverse plates. There are also **Periwinkles**, **Dog Whelks**, and dense colonies of **Blue Mussels**.

Crabs of various sizes and colors can often be seen in tide pools, as they crawl around or hide among seaweed. These include **Rock Crabs** (*Cancer irroratus*); the slightly larger but less common **Jonah Crabs** (*C. borealis*), which have rougher shells and shorter legs than rock crabs; the 2- to 3-inch **Green Crabs** (*Carcinides maenas*), which typically hide beneath rocks or bury themselves in sandy beaches; and the pinkish 1- to 3-inch **Hermit Crabs** (*Pagurus longicarpus*). The latter, with their eyes at the end of stem-like appendages, live in empty shells of the periwinkle and moon snail—moving quickly from one to another when they outgrow their prior adopted home.

MUDFLATS

The mudflats, in the upper reaches of many harbors and bays, are another intertidal habitat around the shores of Mount Desert Island.

Soft-shelled (or **Long-necked**) **Clams** (*Mya arenaria*), which are typically 2 to 3 inches long, but may grow to 4 or 5 inches, bury themselves in mudflats that are exposed at low tide. Much less common are the 5-inch-long **Quahogs** (also known as **Littleneck Clams** or **Cherrystones**) (*Venus mercenaria*), which are found near the surface of muddy-sandy beaches. The fairly common **Atlantic Razor Clams** (*Ensis directus*) have slender 5- to 7-inch-long shells that help them burrow quickly into the mud.

Northern Moon Snails (*Lunatia heros*) have a single smoothly rounded, whitish or gray 2- to 4-inch shell. As these snails search for soft-shelled clams and other mollusks, they use a huge "foot" to dig as far as 12 inches beneath the surface of a mudflat. Like dog whelks versus mussels, these carnivorous snails drill a hole through the clam's shell and devour their prey.

SALT MARSHES

Salt marshes and tidal estuaries are ecologically rich environments that support an abundance of life. Many species of finfish and shellfish, especially in their juvenile stages, depend upon the nutrient-rich tidal waters that constantly flow back and forth in this sheltered habitat. At the lowest level of these expanses of saltgrass meadow, beginning slightly below the mean-tide level, is the stout reed-like broad-leaved **Smooth Cordgrass** (*Spartina alterniflora*). This species grows from about 2 to 8 feet tall and has a 1- to 4-inch-long spike-like terminal inflorescence (a flower cluster on a common axis).

At a level reached only at high tide is the more delicate narrow-leaved **Saltmeadow Cordgrass** (*S. patens*). It grows from about 1 to 3 feet tall and has a number of 1- to 2-inch-long flower spikes that branch alternately on short stems from the stalk. Mixed in with the latter species and reaching to a slightly higher tide level is **Blackgrass** (*Juncus gerardi*), which is identified by its dark-green color and tiny blackish flowers.

Other plants in the upper reaches of salt marshes include **Seaside Plantain** (*Plantago juncoides*), **Seaside Goldenrod** (*Solidago sempervirens*), **Sea Lavender** (*Limonium nashii*) (see the Wildflowers section); and the erect branching clumps of **Glasswort** (*Salicornia* spp.). The latter species is a distinctive little plant that grows about a foot tall, with jointed fleshy cylindrical stems. Leaves are reduced to mere scales along the stem. This plant is bright green in summer and typically turns a blazing red in autumn.

Bass Harbor Marsh is one of Acadia's most extensive salt marshes. It sprawls along the meandering course of Marshall Brook and its tributaries, above the head of Bass Harbor, with Western Mountain providing a scenic backdrop to the north. In summer, the salt grasses are bright green; and in autumn, they turn a rich golden-russet color that contrasts with the bordering dark-green spruce forest.

Offshore Marine Life

The ocean waters surrounding Mount Desert Island are inhabited by many species of marine animals. (See the Mammals section for whales, seals, and porpoises.) Among them are the following:

Northern Lobsters (*Homarus americanus*) usually grow to about 18 or 20 inches long. In summer, these animals move in closer to shore, dwelling in crevices and other sheltered places below the low-tide line, where they spawn. In early autumn, they shed their old shells and begin growing new ones. In winter, they migrate into deeper offshore waters.

Scallops (*Pecten* spp.) are bivalve mollusks, with beautifully fluted fan-shaped 4- to 6-inch-wide shells. They live in the mud and sand at or below the low-tide line and inhabit the ocean floor. These animals move around, both in mud and water, by rapidly clapping their shells together and ejecting a jet of water that propels them along.

Floating in the cold waters of the Gulf of Maine in summer are two va-rieties of jellyfish: **Moon Jellies** (*Aurelia* spp.) and the less common **Red Arctic Jellyfishes** (*Cyanea* spp.). The latter, which are commonly from 1 to 3 feet wide (especially large ones reach 6 or 8 feet across), have long tentacles that inflict a painful sting. As the name implies, jellyfish are boneless animals.

A number of commercially important finfish live in the ocean waters around Mount Desert Island. Among them are the following:

Atlantic Cod (*Gadus morhua*) usually measure from 2 to 4 feet long and weigh from 6 to 12 pounds (exceptional individuals weigh between 50 and 100 pounds). These fish live mostly near the ocean bottom in deeper offshore waters, where they consume a wide variety of marine animals, including mollusks, crustaceans, starfish, and smaller fish, such as herring and mackerel. Cod have three dorsal fins (above) and two anal fins (below), a barbel (a thread-like growth) on the chin, and are thickly speckled with dark-brown or grayish spots, with a narrow pale lateral line from head to unforked tail.

Pollock (*Pollachius virens*) are another member of the Cod Family. They grow from 1 to 2.5 feet long and usually weigh from 5 to 15 pounds (some weigh as much as 35 pounds). These fish are olive-green with a whitish lateral line along the body, and they have a long lower jaw that projects beyond the upper jaw. Adults live in deeper waters offshore, but they tend to stay near the surface as they feed on small fish.

Haddock (*Melanogrammus aeglefinus*), a smaller member of the Cod Family, usually measure 1 to 2 feet long and weigh 2 to 5 pounds (some weigh from 12 to 15 pounds). They are distinguished from cod and pollock by having a dark line along the side; and from cod by lacking a speckled pattern. Haddock feed on mollusks, crustaceans, and other invertebrate animals of the deep-sea bottom.

Winter Flounder (*Pseudopleuronectes americanus*) are among the most common species of flatfish inhabiting the waters around Mount Desert Island. They are distinctly flattened fish that are adapted to lying on, lying partially embedded in, or skimming over the muddy-sandy bottom of sheltered harbors, bays, and other coastal waters. The upper surface of their body varies from reddish-brown or brown to dark gray, and the undersurface is usually light-colored. A narrow lateral line extends from head to tail. They usu-

ally measure 12 to 15 inches long and weigh 0.5 to 2 pounds (a few weigh up to about 5 pounds). Both eyes are on the right-hand or upper surface. Single dorsal and anal fins form continuous fringe-like borders. These small-mouthed fish feed on crustaceans, mollusks, small fish, and other sea-bottom organisms. They spawn in the winter and early spring.

Summer Flounder (or **Fluke**) (*Paralichthys dentatus*) are one of the "left-handed" species of flounder—so named because their eyes and the darker upper surface are on the fish's left side. The color and pattern of the upper surface can vary greatly, to blend with the ocean bottom where the fish is resting. In an amazing example of protective camouflage, the fish's background color can range from brown or olive-green to gray, with tints of color that range from pink to dark brownish-black. A scattering of spots or round splotches also varies from light to dark shades, depending upon the ocean bottom's colors and textures.

Summer flounder have teeth and a larger mouth than winter flounder, and they usually grow 1 to 2 feet long and weigh 2 to 5 pounds (sometimes up to about 15 pounds). This species is usually found in shallow waters of bays and harbors in summer, moving to deeper waters in winter.

Atlantic Halibut (*Hippoglossus hippoglossus*) are large dark-colored large-mouthed "right-handed" flatfish of the Flounder Family. They average 2 to 5 feet in length and weigh from 20 to 200 pounds. Except for their much larger size and more pointed fins, these fish look much like other species of flounder. They, too, change color and pattern to blend with the ocean floor. Halibut feed mostly on a wide variety of other fish. They spend the summer in shallower coastal waters, moving to the deep-sea bottom farther offshore during the winter.

Atlantic Mackerel (*Scomber scombrus*) are a sleek-looking fish that usually measure about 1 to 1.5 feet long and weigh 1 to 2 pounds (sometimes up to 5 or 6 pounds). Mackerel have two widely-spaced dorsal fins and one anal fin, and between them and the deeply forked tail are rows of tiny fins. The nearly scale-less iridescent skin is boldly patterned above with blackish wavy lines, contrasting with the unmarked, silvery underside. These fish usually swim in large schools and tend to spend the summer close to shore. In winter, they are absent from Maine's coastal waters.

Atlantic Herring (*Clupea harengus*) are silvery scaled fish that mature to about 10 or 15 inches in length and weigh 1 to 1.5 pounds. They have single dorsal and anal fins, a metallic-bluish or greenish-blue back, deeply forked tail, and projecting lower jaw. Herring congregate in enormous schools. In spring and summer, when the juveniles are 3 to 4 inches long, huge quantities of them are caught and canned as sardines.

ANADROMOUS FISHES

Alewives (*Alosa pseudoharengus*) are a member of the Herring Family. These silvery-gray 10- to 12-inch-long fish have single dorsal and anal fins and a deeply forked tail. They are anadromous—a living link between the sea and freshwater lakes and ponds. In May, large numbers of them migrate upstream from coastal waters to their ancestral freshwater spawning habitat. They are driven relentlessly, swimming against a stream's currents, battering themselves against rocks and each other,

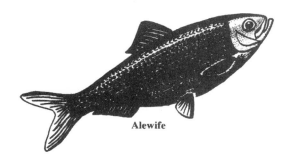

Alewife

and finally reaching the tranquil waters where they once again assure the survival of their species. Soon after spawning, the adults return to the sea. The juveniles spend the summer growing to 3 or 4 inches in length, before dashing down to the sea in early autumn. Seal Cove Pond is one of Acadia's major spawning areas for these fascinating fish.

American Smelts (*Osmerus mordax*) are another species of anadromous fish inhabiting the Maine coast waters. They live in coastal waters and spawn in streams during the spring. Smelts have slender 6- to 9-inch-long greenish-and-silver bodies, with single dorsal and anal fins. They also have a small adipose fin that is located between the dorsal fin and tail, indicating that smelts are related to salmon and trout.

Atlantic Salmon (*Salmo salar*) have silvery scaled bodies, with a scattering of blackish spots above, a dark back, single dorsal and anal fins, and a small adipose fin between the dorsal fin and forked tail. These fish are usually about 1 to 3 feet long and weigh 10 to 12 pounds (sometimes to 50 pounds or more). They feed on small fish and crustaceans. Atlantic salmon are anadromous, migrating from the ocean up rivers and streams, where they spawn in late October and early November. The following spring, their reddish or yellowish eggs hatch juveniles, which usually remain in the freshwater environments for 2 or 3 years, before swimming down to the sea.

FRESHWATER FISHES

Landlocked Salmon (*Salmo salar*) are a freshwater race of the same species as Atlantic salmon, but are generally smaller, with slight differences in appearance. These salmon, which are common in Jordan Pond, Eagle Lake, Echo Lake, and Long (Great) Pond, usually measure about 16 to 20 inches long and weigh from 2 to 2.5 or 3 pounds.

Eastern Brook Trout (*Salvelinus fontinalis*) are a beautiful species of freshwater fish, measuring 8 to 10 inches in length and weighing about half a pound. Their sides are dark-brownish, patterned with yellow spots and a scattering of red spots, each of which is surrounded by bluish aureoles. Lower along the sides is a broad pinkish-orange streak. The dorsal fin and the tail are patterned with dark lines on a yellowish-orange background, and the pectoral and ventral fins are pinkish-orange, with a white leading edge. Typical of trout and salmon, there is also a small adipose fin between the dorsal fin and tail. These fish inhabit Jordan Pond, Eagle Lake, and Echo Lake.

Lake Trout (or **Togue**) (*S. namaycush*) are white-speckled brownish, greenish, or grayish fish that live in the deeper parts of Jordan Pond and Eagle Lake. They average 16 to 18 inches in length and weigh about 3 pounds (a few weigh as much as 8 or 9 pounds). Two other species of trout are found on Mount

Desert Island: **Brown Trout** (*Salmo trutta*), which are a non-native species from Europe, inhabit Lower Hadlock Pond and Seal Cove Pond; and **Rainbow Trout** (*S. gairdneri*), which were originally native to the Rocky Mountains.

Smallmouth Bass (*Micropterus dolomieui*) inhabit Long (Great) Pond and Seal Cove Pond, where they measure 12 to 15 inches long and weigh 1 to 1.5 pounds. As with other members of the Sunfish Family, the lower jaw projects beyond the upper, and a spiny dorsal fin and a larger dorsal fin are joined as a single continuous fin. Broad brownish-bronze sides are faintly patterned with a series of dark bars.

Trees

One of the aspects of nature that makes Acadia National Park such a beautiful and fascinating area is the great variety of trees. Most obvious is the blend of needle-bearing conifers—the pines, spruces, balsam fir, and cedar—and the broad-leaved deciduous trees, such as maples, oaks, birches, aspens, and ashes.

CONIFERS

Eastern White Pine (*Pinus strobes*) is the stateliest of Acadia's evergreen trees. Its soft thin bluish-green 3- to 5-inch needles grow in bundles of 5. They produce a gentle whispering sound when a summer breeze blows through a grove of these trees. In good years, the upper branches "drip" with dozens of their 5- to 8-inch-long pendent cones. The White Pine often rises majestically above the other forest trees—to as much as 75 or 100 feet tall.

This species is unfortunately vulnerable to harm by a weevil that kills the leader, which sometimes results in the development of two or more main stems. Groves of the White Pine are typically mixed with the Red Pine, as they are on a beautiful point at the northwest corner of Eagle Lake. You can also find a few of these pines around the carriage road bridge near the Bubble Pond parking area.

Red Pine (*P. resinosa*) grows tall and straight and has reddish plated bark. The rich-green 4- to 6-inch needles grow in bundles of 2 and are thicker and more rigid than those of the White Pine. Scattered Red Pines can be seen around the northern end of Eagle Lake, along the trail that leads up Acadia Mountain from the west, and along the south ridge trail up Norumbega (Brown) Mountain.

Jack Pine (*P. banksiana*) is typically a tall and slender tree in parts of the upper Midwest and Canada and northward to the limit of trees. But in Acadia, it is usually rather small, scrubby, and asymmetrical. Its stiff 1- to 1.5-inch needles grow in bundles of 2. The 1- to 2.5-inch-long asymmetrical cones are usually bent

White Pine

Red Pine

Hemlock

White Spruce

Pitch Pine

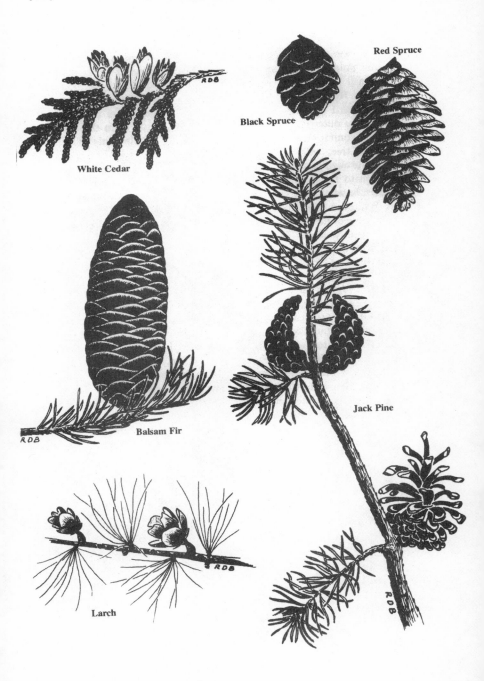

White Cedar

Black Spruce

Red Spruce

Balsam Fir

Jack Pine

Larch

over to one side, frequently growing in pairs and opening their scales unevenly. The scaly bark is gray or reddish-brown.

This species is found at only a few locations in Acadia, including a small grove along State Highway 3, just south of Huguenot Head; an extensive stretch along Cadillac Mountain's South Ridge Trail, about a mile up from Eagles Crag; a few scattered near the summit of Norumbega (Brown) Mountain; and more abundantly in the park's Schoodic Peninsula unit.

Pitch Pine (*P. rigida*) is a picturesque tree, especially where it grows on some of the exposed mountain ledges and ridges and along stretches of rocky seashore. In such locations, this species often branches in angular asymmetrical patterns that resemble carefully trimmed pines in a Japanese garden. Its rigid rich-green 3- to 6-inch needles grow in bundles of 3. The squat 1.5- to 3.5-inch-long cones typically grow in clusters of from 2 to 5 that are closely attached to branches or even the trunk, where they remain for years. The scales of the cones are armed with sharp, recurved prickles. The bark of this species has broad purplish-tinged reddish-brown ridges.

Groves of these trees grow along the Ocean Drive section of the Park Loop Road; on Great Head and The Beehive; on Champlain, Gorham, Dorr, Norumbega (Brown), and Acadia mountains; along parts of the north and south ridges of Cadillac Mountain; and along part of the Wonderland Trail, near Ship Harbor.

Tamarack (or **Eastern Larch**) (*Larix laricina*) is the only needle-bearing conifer in Acadia that sheds its foliage in winter. This gracefully symmetrical tree is transformed to a bluish-green color, as its roughly 1-inch-long needles emerge in clusters. In late October, after the maples, aspens, birches, and other broad-leaved trees have reached their height of color, the Tamarack is transformed to a softly glowing dull-gold color. The delicate reddish-brown cones are slightly less than an inch long. This species typically grows with the Black Spruce in boggy areas, around sphagnum heaths, and along swampy lakeshores, such as the northern shore of Upper Hadlock Pond. The Tamarack ranges from the northeastern United States and eastern Canada to Alaska.

White Spruce (*P. glauca*) is a beautiful conifer that ranges to the limit of trees from Newfoundland to Alaska. It has nearly 1-inch sharp-pointed bluish-green needles and 2- to 2.5-inch-long cylindrical cones. This species is best seen along rocky seashores and on points jutting into the sea. You can find the White Spruce along the shore from Seawall Picnic Area southward to Ship Harbor, and on the outer cliffs of Otter Point. It is commonly a strikingly symmetrical tree, with its boughs sweeping gracefully outward—its lowest branches often extending to the ground. If you are uncertain whether a particular tree is a White Spruce or Red Spruce, try crushing some of its needles. If they smell pungently skunk-like, it is White Spruce.

Black Spruce (*P. mariana*) is another conifer that ranges far to the north, to the edge of the Arctic tundra, from Newfoundland to Alaska. Its short, sharply pointed needles are only about 0.3 to 0.6 of an inch in length and its grayish-brown or purplish-black cones measure about 1 inch long. The tree itself has a very slender, gradually tapering profile. In Acadia, the Black Spruce typically grows around the edges of sphagnum bogs, such as between Seawall Campground and Ship Harbor.

Red Spruce (*Picea rubens*) is probably Acadia's most abundant tree species. Its yellowish-green needles are 0.5 to just under 1 inch long and the cones measure about 1.3 to 2 inches in length. In some years, the tops of the Red Spruce are covered with masses of cones, attracting such birds as crossbills, grosbeaks, and nuthatches. The Red Spruce forms dense dark old-growth stands in many areas of Acadia, such as along part of the west shore of Jordan Pond; at the end of Otter Point; on some of the lower slopes of Pemetic Mountain; along Valley Cove Road, between Flying Mountain and St. Sauveur Mountain; and

on much of heavily forested Western Mountain.

Eastern Hemlock (*Tsuga canadensis*) grows almost exclusively in shaded damp cool stream valleys, where it becomes a large rugged tree, with wide-spreading branches. It has flat 0.3- to 0.7-inch-long needles that lie mostly along a single plane of a twig (unlike spruce needles). The little cones, which grow at the end of twigs, measure only about 0.5 to 1 inch in length. Some beautiful old hemlocks can be found along the carriage road between Bubble Pond and the junction with the Eagle Lake carriage road loop; at the upper carriage road bridge in the Amphitheater; at one of two adjacent carriage road bridges in Upper Hadlock valley, on the Around Mountain carriage road loop; and bordering many valley streams flowing down from the mountains.

Balsam Fir (*Abies balsamea*) is perhaps best known for the extremely sweet fragrance of its needles when crushed or used in small balsam pillows. Like Eastern Hemlock, its flat needles grow along a single plane of a twig, giving the bough a flattened appearance. The fir's needles measure about 0.5 to 1.5 inches in length. They are shiny and dark-green above, and silvery beneath. Cylindrical 2- to 4-inch-long cones are dark purple; and, characteristic of all true fir species, they grow upright from branches, rather than hanging down, as do spruce cones. Also, unlike spruce cones, which fall to the ground whole, the scales of fir cones fall individually, leaving only the central stem attached to the branch.

This species is common throughout the moist forests of Acadia, most often in the company of spruces. The Balsam Fir can develop into a beautifully symmetrical tree, but all too frequently its symmetry is spoiled by a budworm that attacks the leader and may even succeed in killing the tree.

Northern White Cedar (or **Eastern Arborvitae**) (*Thuja occidentalis*) grows in cool swampy habitat along lakeshores and streams and on some damp mountain slopes. The leaves and twigs of this prolific conifer are made up of small overlapping yellowish-green scales that completely cover the sprays of flattened branches. The foliage has a pleasant pungent aroma when crushed. Its cones, which measure about 0.3 to 0.5 of an inch long, grow in erect clusters near the ends of twigs. The bark is pale brown, stringy, and fibrously ridged. Mature cedars often become densely cone-shaped, and when deer browse the lower branches, the tree appears manicured. Such pruned cedars can be seen along the western shore of the southern end of Long (Great) Pond, along the edge of Upper Hadlock Pond, and across much of the west face of Cadillac Mountain above Bubble Pond.

BROAD-LEAVED TREES

American Beech (*Fagus grandifolia*) is a large, abundant tree with characteristically smooth pale gray bark that is sometimes marred by dark knobby blotches. In moist sheltered valleys between the mountains, such as along the carriage road south of Bubble Pond, between Cadillac and Pemetic mountains, this species forms nearly pure stands. Pale brown leaf buds are long and slender. The 2.5- to 6-inch-long leaves taper from a rounded base to the tip, and they have sharp slightly incurved marginal "teeth." Beech foliage is bright green when it initially unfurls in late May. In summer, it takes on a darker and more papery quality. In October, a grove of these trees is transformed to a colorful blend of green, yellow, and rust. Beech leaves often remain attached to their twigs long into winter, rustling like dry paper in the wind. In the autumn, ripened fruits consist of a small prickly bur that splits open, releasing 2 or 3 nuts. This species reproduces both with its seeds and by putting out underground sucker shoots. Consequently, a large, old Beech may be surrounded by a cluster of young trees, growing in the shade of the parent.

Northern Red Oak (*Quercus rubra*) is perhaps the stateliest of Acadia's broad-leaved trees, with its thick trunk, broadly rounded crown, and outward-sweeping branches. It is a common species throughout much of Acadia. The 5- to 8-inch-long leaves are deeply cut into from 7 to 11 angular pointed bristle-tipped lobes. As the foliage unfurls in late May, the young leaves are initially a soft pink, becoming a yellowish color before turning green. In October, following the peak of brilliant foliage of maples, birches, and aspens, the Red Oak turns briefly a rich coppery red. The fat shiny 1- to 1.5-inch-long acorns are mounted in shallow scaled cups. An extensive stand of this species borders the carriage road along the west side of Eagle Lake.

Bear (or **Scrub**) **Oak** (*Q. ilicifolia*) is one of the rarest and least conspicuous trees of Acadia, where it is at the northeastern end of its range. This species grows only on dry ledges of Acadia Mountain's western slope and summit, and in several places on St. Sauveur Mountain. It is little more than a shrub, growing among open stands of Pitch Pine and Red Pine. Bear Oak has thick 2- to 5-inch-long leaves that are smaller, less deeply cut, and have fewer angular pointed lobes than those of the Red Oak. Their undersurface is covered with whitish fuzzy hairs. Acorns are about 0.5 of an inch in length.

Eastern Hophornbeam (or **Eastern Ironwood**) (*Ostrya virginiana*) is an uncommon slender little tree of cool shady woods. Its brownish-gray bark is patterned with vertical shredded strips and grooves. In spring, pendent red-tinged male catkins grow to about 2 inches in length. Its 3- to 5-inch-long oval leaves taper from a rounded base to the tip, and are thin but rather firm-textured, with double-toothed margins. Hophornbeam nuts are enclosed within small inflated green or reddish bladder-like pods that overlap one another in a pendent cone-like cluster. The wood of this species is extremely dense and hard.

Yellow Birch (*Betula lutea*) is one of Acadia's larger broad-leaved trees. Its bark is a lustrous silvery bronze that peels into irregular papery thin curls. The 2- to 3-foot trunk of mature trees is typically short, abruptly dividing into many ascending branches. In spring, the pendent male catkins grow to more than 3 inches in length, and the female catkins to less than an inch. The 3- to 5-inch-long leaves are long-tapering from a rounded base to the tip, with double-toothed margins. Three-winged seeds are borne in short-stemmed cone-like, 1- to 1.5-inch-long seed pods. In autumn, Yellow Birch foliage turns bright yellow. This species favors moist woods of stream valleys and shady mountain ravines.

Paper (or **Canoe**) **Birch** (*B. papyrifera*) is arguably Acadia's most beautiful broad-leaved tree. Its trunk and larger ascending branches are covered with paper-like bark that has a whitish outer layer and creamy white, orange, or brownish inner layers. These smooth layers are charac-

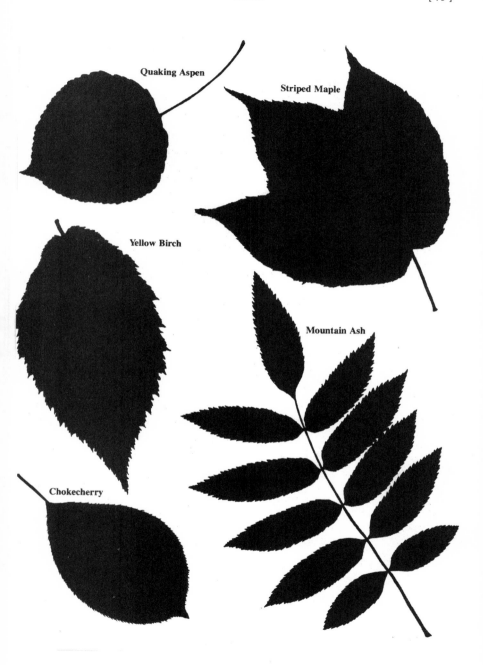

Quaking Aspen

Striped Maple

Yellow Birch

Mountain Ash

Chokecherry

Beech

Bigtooth Aspen

Witch-Hazel

Mountain Maple

teristically patterned with narrow, horizontal lenticels and blotched here and there with dark branch scars. In spring, pendent male catkins grow to 3 or 4 inches in length, and the more erect female catkins to about 2 inches. By autumn, the latter develop into pendent cone-like fruits filled with seeds. Paper Birch leaves measure about 2 to 4 inches long and taper from a rounded base to the tip, with a double-toothed margin. In autumn, the leaves turn brilliant yellow. It was the bark of this species that some early Native Americans used in constructing canoes.

Gray Birch (*B. populifolia*) is the smallest of Acadia's birches. It is a delicately slender short-lived tree that typically grows in small clumps, reaching only about 15 or 20 feet in height. The bark is chalk-white or grayish-white and does not readily peel off. The shiny 2- to 3-inch-long leaves are roughly triangular, tapering from a nearly flat base to the tip, with double-toothed margins. In autumn, its foliage turns yellow. The Gray Birch is often among the first tree species to grow in an abandoned field or to reseed after fire.

Balsam Poplar (*Populus balsamifera*) is not common in Acadia. Only a few small groves of young, straight-trunked trees are widely scattered here and there, one of which is adjacent to the junction of State Highways 198 and 233. This is a species of the far northern extremity of North American trees, thriving along lakes and streams from Labrador to Alaska. Finely serrated 3- to 8-inch-long leaves are more tapered toward the tip than those of aspens. Long-tapering buds are covered with a sticky pungent-smelling resin (balsam).

Quaking Aspen (*P. tremuloides*) is an abundant slender rather delicate-looking tree. Although elsewhere, as in the mountains of the West, it typically grows in pure groves, here in Acadia, it typically grows with maples, birches, and other species. This tree usually reaches 20 to 40 feet in height, with a trunk diameter up to a foot or so. One of the earliest signs of spring in Acadia is the Quaking Aspen's 1.5- to 2.5-inch-long pendent flowering-bearing catkins that appear on bare branches in April. The rounded heart-shaped leaves have tiny marginal "teeth." The leaf stems are flattened at right angles to the blade, causing the leaves to flutter and quiver delicately back and forth even in the slightest breeze. In autumn, the foliage turns bright pale-yellow. The Quaking Aspen is a favorite tree of the beaver, both for food and dam- and lodge-building material. It is also among the first species to grow back after a fire. Although this is a modest tree, it has a huge range that extends from Labrador to Alaska and south to the mountains of northern Mexico.

Bigtooth Aspen (*P. grandidentata*) looks much like the Quaking Aspen, but it is typically a somewhat

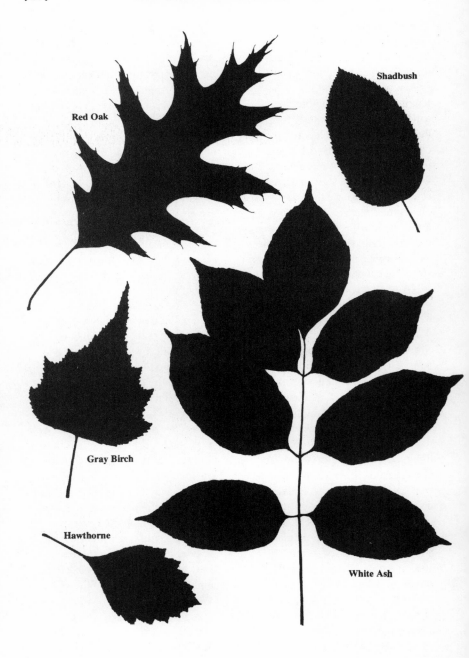

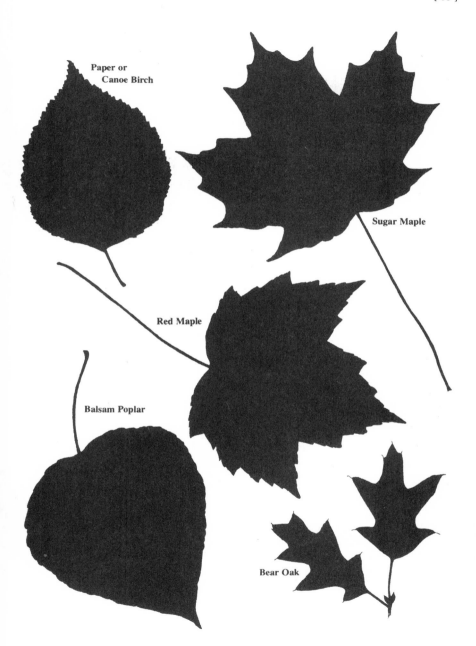

Paper or
Canoe Birch

Sugar Maple

Red Maple

Balsam Poplar

Bear Oak

larger tree. It reaches 30 to 50 feet in height, with a trunk diameter of from 1 to 2 feet. Although Bigtooth Aspen leaves are only slightly larger than those of Quaking Aspen, they have more prominent and more rounded marginal "teeth." This species, which is less common than the smaller species, grows in scattered small clumps. The bark of young trees is smooth and yellowish-greenish-gray; but with age, the bark becomes deeply furrowed. In the early spring, the Bigtooth Aspen puts out long catkins, followed by leaves that are initially a silvery color and thickly covered with fuzzy down. As with the Quaking Aspen, the leaf stems are flattened, causing the leaves to flutter in a breeze. In autumn, the leaves turn bright golden-yellow.

Black Willow (*Salix nigra*) is an uncommon tree in Acadia. A few grow around Beaverdam Pond, just beyond Bear Brook Picnic Area, along the Park Loop Road. An old wind-battered clump is also located at Seal Harbor beach, opposite the park-entrance road at Stanley Brook. This species develops a thick trunk and branches, with deeply furrowed bark. Because the wood is relatively weak and branches often break off in storms, the Black Willow often has an asymmetrical appearance. The 2- to 6-inch-long round-based leaves are slender, with finely toothed margins.

Common Chokecherry (*Prunus virginiana*) is a small tree or shrub of the Rose Family that grows to about 15 or 20 feet tall. Its rounded leaves are 2 to 4 inches long, tapering to a sharp point, with sharp and often double-toothed margins. Small white flowers of early summer are clustered in 3- to 6-inch-long spikes that are either erect or drooping. Very bitter cherries are initially bright red, ripening to a dark crimson-maroon color. Chokecherry bark is grayish-brown, breaking into a scaly surface on larger trees, with light-colored lenticels. This species favors thickets and young woods, often coming in after fire.

Black Cherry (*P. serotina*) is similar to Chokecherry, except that its leaves are longer (to about 5 or 6 inches) and narrower, with blunt-toothed margins. Small whitish flowers are borne in 3- to 6-inch-long slender spikes that are either erect or drooping. Bitter cherries are dark red, ripening to purplish-black. Mature trees grow to 50 feet or more in height, and the fragrant bark of the trunk and branches of young trees is smooth, dark reddish-brown, and patterned with dark lenticels. The bark of mature trees becomes dark and rough, with irregular scales of outer bark and reddish inner bark. This species favors thickets and wooded habitat.

Pin Cherry (*P. pensylvanica*) is a small tree or shrub that grows about 10 to 20 feet tall, with smooth reddish-brown bark that is patterned with lenticels. Its 3- to 5-inch-long leaves are even more narrowly tapering than those of Black Cherry, and have sharply serrated margins. Unlike Black Cherry and Chokecherry, it has creamy white flowers and sour, pale-red cherries that are borne in long-stemmed loose clusters. This species favors thickets and young woods.

American Mountain-Ash (*Sorbus americana*) is a 10- to 30-foot-tall tree or shrub, with light-gray bark. It is fairly common on Acadia's mountain ridges and in rocky woodlands. Spreading branches are covered with 6- to 8-inch-long compound leaves that are divided into 11 to 17 tapering 2- to 4-inch-long leaflets that have sharply serrated margins. Dense flat-topped clusters of small creamy white flowers bloom in early June. In autumn, this otherwise modest tree is festooned with rounded bunches of bright-red or orange-red quarter-inch berry-like fruits that remain after the leaves have turned red or pale yellow.

Shadbush (or **Downy Serviceberry**) (*Amelanchier laevis* or *A. arborea*) is a rather modest tree or shrub of the Rose Family that grows about 15 to 30 feet tall. It is commonly found around lakeshores, on open mountain slopes, and in thickets on exposed mountain summits. It is one of Acadia's earliest flowering species. In early or mid-May, it suddenly bursts forth with showy drooping white clusters of narrow-petalled flowers. As the petals blow away, the 3- to 4-inch-long finely serrated oval leaves unfurl. In early summer,

round dark-purplish fruits dangle briefly in long-stemmed clusters.

Hawthorns (*Crataegus* spp.) are small broad-crowned trees, with long, slender thorns at intervals along twigs and branches. The alternate rounded 1- to 2-inch leaves have serrated sharply pointed shallow lobes. Small white-petalled flowers grow in twig-end clusters, followed by long-stemmed bright-red berry-like fruits. In autumn, after the leaves have fallen, abundant clusters of these fruits are conspicuous. Hawthorns favor roadside thickets and meadow edges, but are not common in Acadia.

Mountain Maple (*Acer spicatum*) is a small understory tree or shrub that usually grows 10 or 15 feet tall, but occasionally to 20 or 30 feet. Its 4- to 5-inch-long leaves have 3 (occasionally 5) coarsely serrated, tapered, and pointed lobes. Their undersurface may be slightly fuzzy, as are twigs and buds. Quarter-inch-long pale-yellow flowers of late spring are borne on long erect racemes, with male flowers above the female flowers. Seeds are borne in two-winged pairs that hang down in clusters. The wings turn a combination of red and yellow in late summer. In autumn, the foliage is a blend of orange and red. Mountain Maple favors rocky shady ravines and other cool wooded habitat.

Striped Maple (or **Moosewood**) (*A. pensylvanicum*) is typically a small understory tree or shrub that favors moist woods. Occasionally, it reaches 30 or 40 feet in height. Its 5- to 6-inch-long rounded leaves have three slender-pointed lobes and sharply double-toothed margins. As the leaves have nearly unfurled, bright-yellow quarter-inch flowers are borne on 4- to 6-inch-long pendent racemes. The most distinctive characteristic of this species is the light-green bark of its trunk and branches that are patterned with long vertical whitish or pale-green stripes. Seeds are borne in two-winged pairs that hang down in long-stemmed clusters. In autumn, the foliage turns bright pale-yellow, seeming to flood areas of the dark forest with pale-golden light.

Red Maple (*A. rubrum*) is an abundant forest tree in Acadia, favoring moist, even swampy habitat, around lakeshores, along streams, and in mountain valleys. Small clustered flowers, blooming in mid- to late-April, briefly produce a soft reddish flush of color that spreads across many of Acadia's valleys and mountainsides. Later in spring, the leaves unfurl, measuring about 3 to 6 inches long, with 3 or 5 pointed lobes that are irregularly serrated. Seeds are borne in two-winged pairs that hang down in short-stemmed clusters. The wings are often red or reddish-brown. In late September and early October, the Red Maple's foliage typically turns blazing crimson.

Sugar Maple (*A. saccharum*) is the largest of the four native maples in Acadia. It is a common forest species in rich moist valleys and along lower mountain slopes. An open-grown Sugar Maple develops a rounded symmetrical shape; but within a forest, it is typically more slender and taller, often reaching 50 to 75 feet or more in height, with a 2- to 4-foot trunk diameter. The rough grayish-brown bark of a mature Sugar Maple is deeply furrowed. The 4- to 8-inch-long leaves usually have five angular pointed lobes, with only a few large teeth, and smooth or slightly wavy margins. Small yellowish flowers are borne in narrow clusters at about the same time as the leaves unfurl. Seeds are borne in two-winged pairs. In autumn, the foliage turns stunning shades of yellow, orange, and red. As the name implies, this is the tree from which maple syrup is derived in March, just as the sap begins to flow.

White Ash (*Fraxinus americana*), of the Olive Family, is the most common species of ash in Acadia's forests, typically growing with maples and other broad-leaved species. It has 8- to 12-inch-long compound leaves. These are usually divided into 7 (occasionally 5 or 9) oval short-stemmed 3- to 5-inch leaflets, with serrated margins. Seeds hang in clusters, each attached to a single 1- to 2-inch-long wing that is pointed at both ends. In autumn, the White Ash's foliage turns bright yellow that appears to glow in the forest. Its yellow is often softly tinged with a purplish-bronze color. The gray bark of the trunk is patterned with diamond-shaped fissures and flat-topped ridges, caused by the expanding outer bark as the trunk grows in size.

Black Ash (*F. nigra*) has 12- to 16-inch-long compound leaves. These are divided into 7 or 11 (or occasionally even 13) stemless leaflets that measure 4 to 5 inches long. Clustered single-winged seeds are blunt-tipped. This uncommon species in Acadia favors low swampy ground.

American Elm (*Ulmus americana*) and **American Basswood** (or **Linden**) (*Tilia americana*) both grow on Mount Desert Island, but are believed to have been introduced here for ornamental purposes. They are found in villages, around old farmhouses, and along highways.

Shrubs

Acadia has an abundant, varied, and interesting array of native shrubs. Among them are the low-growing Juniper that adds so much beauty to mountain and seashore ledges and cliffs; fragrant patches of low-growing Crowberry that thrive on some rocky shores and mountain ridges; the spectacularly blooming Rhodora and Sheep Laurel; Sweetfern, Sweetgale, and Bayberry, the leaves of which are pungently aromatic when crushed; Cranberries, Blueberries, Raspberries, and Blackberries; and numerous others.

Common Juniper (*Juniperus communis*) is an abundant low-growing shrub that typically forms attractive bushy mats on open mountain ledges and coastal cliffs. Sharp 3-sided whitish-green scale-like needles grow in whorls of 3. Fruits are typical juniper berries that are dark-blue covered with a whitish powdery substance. This species is found along the Shore Path on Otter Point, at various places along the Ship Harbor Trail, on Penobscot Mountain's

Jordan Ridge, and other similar places.

Trailing (or **Creeping**) **Juniper** (*J. horizontalis*), also called Bar Harbor Juniper, forms beautiful prostrate mats, with long creeping branches. Twigs are covered with tight scale-like leaves. This species, which is much less abundant than the Common Juniper, is limited mostly to a few places along the brink of ocean cliffs between Bar Harbor and Northeast Harbor.

Black Crowberry (*Empetrum nigrum*) is a densely branching 2- to 4-inch-tall ground-covering evergreen shrub. It has quarter-inch-long 4-ranked needle-like leaves. In early June, tiny pinkish-purple flowers bloom in long clusters, followed by juicy little black fruits, called drupes, which ripen in July and August and hold 6 to 9 seeds. This species is typically found on the brink of ocean cliffs. It also grows in sphagnum bogs and occasionally around small pools on exposed mountain ridges, as on Penobscot Mountain and the

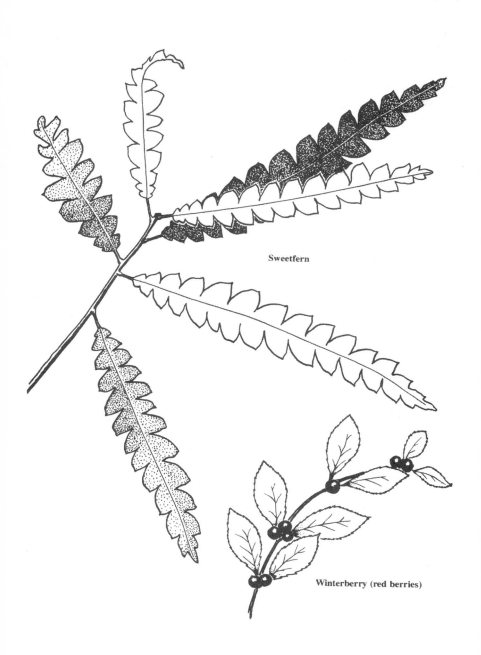

Sweetfern

Winterberry (red berries)

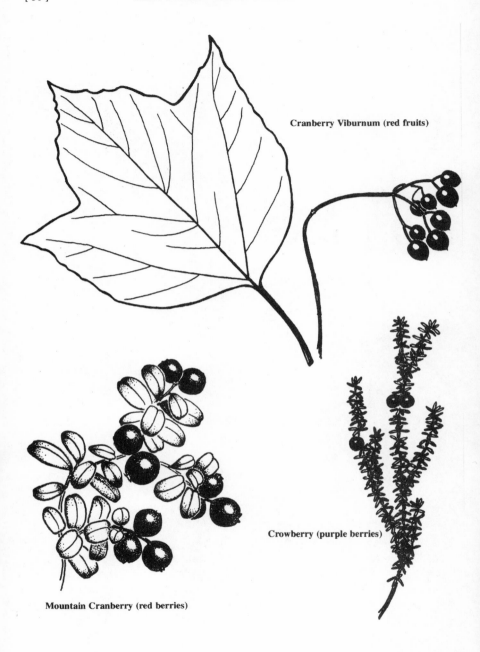

Cranberry Viburnum (red fruits)

Crowberry (purple berries)

Mountain Cranberry (red berries)

South Ridge of Cadillac Mountain. Patches of Crowberry have a subtle sweet aroma that is especially delightful when blended with the fragrant sea air, such as along the shore around Otter Point and between Seawall and Bass Harbor Head. This heather-like species also grows far to the north—from Labrador and Newfoundland, westward across northern Canada and throughout nearly all of Alaska.

Mountain (or **Rock**) **Cranberry** (*Vaccinium vitis-idaea*), of the Heath Family, is an abundant 2- to 8-inch-tall creeping evergreen plant of exposed mountain ridges, rocky shores, and semi-shaded conifer woods. It has thick 0.25- to 0.75-inch-long oval leaves, with rolled margins and minute blackish bristles on the paler undersurface. Bell-shaped pink flowers grow in terminal clusters, followed by 0.25- to 0.5-inch red berries that ripen in mid-summer. This shrub also grows in the Arctic.

Small Cranberry (*V. oxycoccus*) is fairly common in sphagnum bogs. Its creeping branches have slender pointed leaves, with a whitish undersurface and slightly rolled margins. Long delicate flower stems grow from the end of branches, and each pinkish flower has recurved petals, making it appear like a tiny nodding shooting star. This species also grows in the Arctic.

Large Cranberry (*V. macrocarpon*) is a common bog species. It has narrowly oval leaves and half-inch-long pinkish flowers that bloom in July. Flower stems do not grow from the end of branches. Red berries, measuring 0.5 to 0.75 of an inch, ripen in August.

Bearberry (*Arctostaphylos uvarusi*) is an attractive little ground-covering evergreen of the Heath Family that favors exposed dry rocky or sandy habitats on just a few of Acadia's mountain summits and ridges. Its dark-green 0.5- to 1-inch-long paddle-shaped leaves grow from stems with reddish bark. In early June, white-and-pink-edged bell-shaped flowers, measuring less than a quarter-inch in length, are borne in terminal clusters, followed by red berries.

Rhodora (*Rhododendron canadense*), of the Heath Family, is an abundant 2- to 4-foot-tall shrub of bogs and marshy habitat, as well as damp depressions and crevices on the mountains. This species becomes one of Acadia's most impressive wildflower displays, when it suddenly bursts into terminal clusters of purplish-pink azalea-like blossoms in late May and early June. Boggy places, such as Great Meadow, near Sieur de Monts Spring, become "flooded" with expanses of its vibrant color. Individual flowers have two 1-inch-long slender lobes, a lobed upper lip, and 10 long stamens. Bright-green 1- to 2-inch-long oval leaves unfurl after the earliest flowers.

Labrador Tea (*Ledum groenlandicum*) is an attractive and abundant member of the Heath Family.

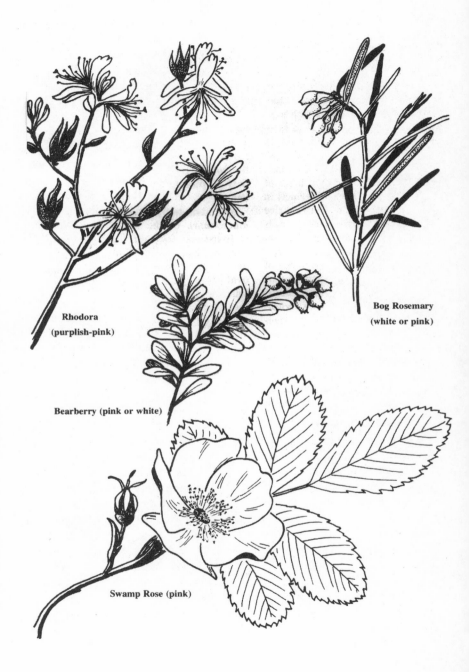

Rhodora
(purplish-pink)

Bog Rosemary
(white or pink)

Bearberry (pink or white)

Swamp Rose (pink)

Leatherleaf (white)

Sheep Laurel (pink)

Large Cranberry (pinkish-white)

Labrador Tea (white)

Hobblebush (white)

This 2- to 3-foot-tall evergreen shrub favors sphagnum bogs, as well as damp depressions and crevices on Acadia's mountain ridges and summits. It has 1- to 2-inch-long leathery and narrowly oblong leaves that have conspicuously rolled margins. The whitish or rusty brown undersurface is covered with woolly hairs. Small whitish flowers bloom in June, and their stamens give the erect, terminal clusters an almost fuzzy appearance. This species grows on such exposed places as Penobscot Mountain's Jordan Ridge. It also grows far to the north, from Labrador and Greenland, westward across northern Canada, and throughout much of Alaska.

Sheep Laurel (*Kalmia angustifolia*), of the Heath Family, is a common 2- to 3-foot-tall shrub of bogs, sunny ledges, and depressions and crevices on Acadia's exposed mountain ridges and summits. It has 1- to 2-inch-long narrowly oblong evergreen leaves. The older olive-green leaves droop downward; and the new bright-green terminal leaves stand erect. Between the old and new foliage, there is a whorl of half-inch bright crimson-pink flowers that are shaped like little 5-sided bowls. They bloom from mid-June to mid-July. Sheep laurel can be found on Penobscot Mountain's Jordan Ridge and other similar places.

Pale (or **Bog**) **Laurel** (*K. polifolia*) is less common than Sheep Laurel and is mostly restricted to sphagnum bogs. This evergreen shrub has 0.5- to 1.5-inch-long stemless oblong or linear leaves that are dark-green above and whitish beneath, with rolled margins. Terminal rose-purple flowers are shaped like little 5-sided bowls. This species ranges far to the north, from Newfoundland, westward across northern Canada, to Southeast Alaska.

Bog Rosemary (*Andromeda glaucophylla*), of the Heath Family, is a small evergreen bog plant that grows 1- to 2-feet tall. It has 1- to 2-inch-long slender leathery leaves, with rolled edges and a whitish minutely hairy undersurface. Flowers grow in nodding terminal clusters of small white or pale-pink bells that bloom in May and June.

Leatherleaf (*Chamaedaphne calyculata*) is a fairly common 1- to 4-foot-tall evergreen bog shrub of the Heath Family. It has 1- to 2-inch-long narrowly oblong leaves that are covered on both surfaces with minute round scales. Older leaves are brownish and new ones are bright green. Little white bell-shaped flowers, which bloom in May and June, are uniquely clustered in racemes— with leaves along one side and flowers along the other. This species can be seen growing densely in such places as the boggy borders of Witch Hole Pond.

Black Huckleberry (*Gaylussacia baccata*), of the Heath Family, is an abundant 1- to 3-foot-tall shrub that grows on exposed mountain ridges and summits, as well as along sea cliffs. Its 1- to 3-inch-long narrowly oval bristle-tipped leaves are speckled on both surfaces with yellowish resin dots. Small clusters of whitish flowers bloom in late May and early June. Round blackish berries ripen by mid-summer. Unlike the many small-seeded fruits of the Blueberry, this species generally has 10 nutlets in each fruit. In October, Black Huckleberry leaves turn a vivid shade of scarlet. The berries are edible when stewed and sweetened.

Lowbush Blueberry (*Vaccinium angustifolium* and *V. vacillans*) is a prolific shrub of the Heath Family in Acadia. It generally grows to a foot or two in height. The 0.5- to 2-inch-long narrowly oval leaves sometimes have finely serrated margins and are dull green above and whitish-green beneath. Unlike the Black Huckleberry, the twigs of Lowbush Blueberry are thickly covered with tiny wart-like speckles. Small creamy white bell-like flowers bloom in late May and early June. The mouth-watering berries, which ripen in July and August, are dark blue and covered with a thin layer of whitish powder. Blueberries thrive in dry sunny openings along trails and carriage roads, as well as on exposed mountain ridges and summits, and along some stretches of rocky seashore. In autumn, the bright-red foliage provides beautiful expanses of glowing color. **Highbush Blueberry** (*V. corymbosum*) grows in swamps and damp thickets.

Common Winterberry (or

Black Alder) (*Ilex verticillata*), of the Holly Family, is usually an inconspicuous 4- to 8-foot-tall shrub that favors swampy habitat and wet lakeshore thickets. It is especially abundant beside the carriage road that runs along the west shore of Bubble Pond, where it grows in the company of Royal Fern; and at a number of wet places around the north end of Eagle Lake. Its oval 2- to 4-inch-long deciduous leaves vary from narrow to broad, with finely toothed margins. Tiny whitish pistillate (female) and staminate (male) flowers bloom in early summer. In autumn, Winterberry becomes conspicuously adorned with shiny, round, and intensely red berries that grow on short stems—singly or in two's or three's—at regular intervals along the branches. After the leaves have fallen off in October, these berry-laden shrubs are especially beautiful against the bright blue background of a lake, before the berries disappear by around mid-November.

Mountain-holly (*Nemopanthus mucronata*), of the Holly Family, is a 4- to 6-foot-tall shrub, with light-gray bark. It has 0.5- to 2-inch-long slightly bristle-tipped oval leaves. In June, long-stemmed 4 or 5 slender-petalled yellow flowers bloom singly or in small clusters; followed in late July and August by round, 0.4-inch long-stemmed dull-red berries. This species grows in a variety of habitats, from damp thickets and boggy areas to exposed mountain ridges and summits. On the latter, it is typically a small nearly prostrate little shrub.

Sweetfern (*Comptonia peregrina*), of the Wax Myrtle Family, is a 2- to 4-foot-tall shrub that is prolific in dry sunny meadows, clearings, and roadsides. Its slender 2- to 6-inch-long pungent leaves have round-lobed margins that give them a fern-like appearance. A small nut is enclosed within a round spiny looking green bur or catkin. This plant can be seen along many stretches of the carriage roads.

Black Chokeberry (*Pyrus melanocarpa*), of the Rose Family, is a shrub of just a few inches to 2 feet in height. It has dark-green finely serrated narrowly oblong 0.5- to 2-inch-long leaves. Pale-pink or whitish half-inch 5-petalled flowers of June grow in terminal clusters. Its clusters of long-stemmed 0.4-inch berry-like black fruits ripen in August. This species is very common as low-growing thickets in depressions and crevices of most exposed mountain ridges and summits. A good place to find Black Chokeberry is along the trail up Huguenot Head.

Common Ninebark (*Physocarpus opulifolius*) is a member of the Rose Family that grows to 10 or 12 feet tall. Its 1- to 3-inch-long leaves are 3-lobed, with slightly rounded marginal teeth—suggestive of a miniature Mountain Maple leaf. In July, this species briefly puts out small, dense, rounded clusters of tiny 5-petalled white flowers. Clusters of berries ripen to a dull reddish color. The bark tends to peel in papery strips. Common Ninebark favors fairly open, brushy areas along the eastern part of Mount Desert Island, such as near Thunder Hole, The Tarn, and Sieur de Monts Spring.

Hobblebush (*Viburnum alnifolium*), of the Honeysuckle Family, is a 5- to 8-foot-tall shrub, with straggling, irregular branches. It has 4- to 8-inch-long oval or heart-shaped leaves, with finely serrated margins. Twigs of the reclining branches are covered with rust-colored hairs. Its small white flowers bloom in flat-topped clusters from early May to early June. In these clusters, the outer flowers are sterile and have conspicuously larger petals than the much smaller inner flowers. Clusters of pinkish-red berry-like fruits ripen by mid-August. In autumn, the leaves turn yellow and red. Hobblebush favors moist cool woods, such as along Stanley Brook near Seal Harbor and some of the brooks above Upper Hadlock Pond.

Highbush Cranberry (or **Cranberry Viburnum**) (*V. trilobum*) grows to 10 or 12 feet tall. Its 2- to 4-inch-long leaves superficially resemble those of the Striped Maple, with 3 slender-pointed lobes. Flat-topped flower clusters are similar to Hobblebush: a few large 5-petalled white sterile flowers surrounding many tiny greenish fertile flowers. Drooping clusters of bright shiny red berries ripen in autumn and are especially conspicuous after the leaves have fallen. These fruits are quite tart, but can be substituted for true cranberries. They are a popular food for Ruffed Grouse. Highbush Cranberry inhabits fairly open brushy places.

Witherod (or **Northern Wild-raisin**) (*V. cassinoides*) is a very common shrub or small tree that grows 3 to 10 feet tall. Its 2- to 5-inch-long narrowly oval or elliptical leaves are thick, smooth, and dull on the upper surface. Leaf stalks have narrow "wings." Small creamy white flowers bloom from mid-June to July, in slightly rounded flat-topped stalked clusters that measure 2 to 5 inches across. The clustered berry-like fruits are initially yellowish-white, ripening in September to bluish-black, with a thin covering of whitish powder. After most other autumn foliage color has disappeared, the leaves of Witherod add touches of red and yellow to the landscape. This species favors thickets in depressions and crevices on exposed mountain ridges, as well as damp thickets and cool woods at lower elevations.

Mapleleaf Viburnum (*V. aceri-folium*) has serrated 3-lobed, 2- to 5-inch leaves that are velvety on their undersurface. This species grows infrequently in Acadia's woodlands and thickets.

Red Elderberry (*Sambucus pubens*), of the Honeysuckle Family, is a common modest shrub that grows 3 to 12 feet tall. It has 4- to 10-inch-long compound leaves of 5 to 7 narrowly oval leaflets, with coarsely serrated margins. Small yellowish-white round-topped flower clusters bloom in May or early June. Red berry-like fruits are borne in conspicuous cone-shaped clusters that ripen in July and August. This species grows along stretches of Ocean Drive.

Common Elderberry (*S. canadensis*) has dense flat-topped clusters of whitish flowers and dark-purplish berries. This species grows infrequently in Acadia.

Alternate-leaved Dogwood (*Cornus alternifolia*) is a common shrub or small tree in Acadia's forests. Its 2- to 5-inch-long oval leaves taper from a broad base to the tip, with parallel veins that follow the curve of the leaf margins. As the name implies, this is the only dogwood species that has alternate leaves. Small white early summer flowers are borne in loose fairly flat-topped clusters. Dark-blue berry-like fruits grow in clusters.

Pussy Willow (*Salix discolor*) is a shrub or small tree that is well known for its grayish softly fuzzy staminate flower catkins that appear in late March and early April. The 2- to 5-inch-long leaves taper sharply toward each end and have serrated margins except near the base. This species grows in damp places along streams, lakeshores, and roadsides.

Speckled Alder (*Alnus rugosa*) is an abundant shrub or small tree that typically forms dense clumps

Mapleleaf Viburnum (red fruits)

and thickets in low swampy habitat. The 2- to 5-inch-long leaves are broadly oval, with a sharp-pointed apex and single- and double-toothed margins. Seeds are produced in hanging clusters of 0.5- to 0.8-inch-long miniature-pine-cone-like woody catkins. This species is named for the whitish transverse lenticels that pattern its dark bark.

Mountain (or **Green**) **Alder** (*A. viridis*) is a common shrub, similar to but usually smaller than Speckled Alder. The undersurface of its leaves is either velvety or shiny without hairs. Seeds are borne in small clusters of what resemble miniature 0.4- to 0.6-inch-long pine cones. Its bark is smooth and lacks a pattern of lenticels. It typically grows in drier habitat than Speckled Alder, as in low-growing (sometimes prostrate) thickets on exposed mountain ridges. Mountain Alder is abundant on Penobscot Mountain's Jordan Ridge, on the North Bubble, and in many other similar places.

Witch Hazel (*Hammamelis virginiana*) is an inconspicuous but common shrub or small understory tree of shaded woods. Its 4- to 6-inch-long oval leaves have wavy round-toothed margins; and the rounded leaf base is distinctly unsymmetrical. This species is the last to bloom, waiting until its leaves are falling in mid-October to November. Along outer branches, it then unfurls slightly fragrant tiny flowers with 4 slender 0.4- to 0.6-inch wavy yellow petals. Seeds are produced the following year in 2-beaked woody capsules.

Northern Bush Honeysuckle (*Diervilla lonicera*) is a fairly common 2- to 4-foot-tall shrub. Its 2- to 4-inch-long finely serrated slender-tipped leaves are slightly folded along the mid-vein. Yellow to reddish short-stemmed half-inch-long tubular flowers have 5 widely spreading petals and long stamens. They grow 2 or 3 to a cluster and bloom in late June and July. Twigs have narrow ridges that connect the leaf scars. This species favors semi-open rocky hillsides, clearings, and thickets.

Meadowsweet (*Spirea latifolia*), of the Rose Family, is an abundant 2- to 5-foot-tall shrub. Its quarter-inch-wide fuzzy-looking creamy-white or pinkish flowers grow in a terminal cluster. The 1.5- to 3-inch-long ovate to lanceolate leaves are sharply serrated. This species, which blooms from late June to September, favors sunny moist meadows, thickets, and roadsides.

Steeplebush (*S. tomentosa*), of the Rose Family, is a fairly common 2- to 4-foot-tall shrub. Similar to Meadowsweet, its tiny pink flowers grow in a more narrowly tapering spike-like cluster, the shape of which is suggestive of a church steeple. This species, which blooms from July to September, favors meadows, thickets, and sunny stream banks, lakeshores, and roadsides.

Beaked Hazelnut (*Corylus rostrata* or *cornuta*) is a rather uncommon shrub or small tree of thickets and edges of woods. Its 3- to 5-inch-long oval leaves have sharply double-toothed margins. Nuts are enclosed in a green husk that has a pronounced long-tapering bristle-tipped beak.

Staghorn Sumac (*Rhus typhina*) is a common distinctive-looking shrub of sunny thickets. Its 1- to 2-foot-long compound leaves have from 11 to 31 narrow serrated leaflets. This irregularly branched shrub has velvet-hairy twigs. Erect tight clusters of hairy red fruits are borne at the end of angular branches. Staghorn Sumac is abundant along the Park Loop Road, near the base of Champlain Mountain.

Poison Ivy (*R. radicans*), a member of the Sumac Family, is uncommon in Acadia, but is scattered here and there, such as along a few stretches of seashore cliffs and banks of the south shore of Mount Desert Island's East Side. It has long-stemmed 5- to 12-inch-long leaves that are divided into 3 pointed narrowly oval leaflets, with margins that are smooth or slightly serrated and/or wavy. The middle leaflet has a short stem, while the others are usually sessile. Small whitish-yellow flowers, growing in branched clusters from the leaf axis, bloom in early summer, followed by clusters of round whitish fruits. All parts of this species contain a toxic oily substance that is poisonous to humans.

Wildflowers

A tremendous variety of wildflowers in Acadia provides a seemingly endless parade of floral color, from the earliest pink and white Arbutus to the latest purple Aster. The following species are presented roughly within habitat types, such as Forest, Meadow, and Bog. Within these groupings, they are arranged approximately in their flowering sequence—from spring to autumn.

In most instances, no specific indication of where individual species can be found has been given—simply because ecological conditions can too easily change over time; and because too many visitors (even extremely careful visitors) drawn to a particular site can easily and inadvertently destroy what they came to see. With a general guide to the wildflower characteristics and habitats, it should be a pleasurable adventure to discover your own patches of Arbutus, Orchids, Violets, Pyrola, or whatever.

FOREST FLOWERS

Trailing Arbutus (*Epigaea repens*), of the Heath Family, is one of Acadia's very earliest wildflowers. In early May, or even as early as mid- to late-April, dense little clusters of pink-and-white 5-petalled flowers come into bloom, half-hidden among the leathery oval evergreen leaves. This plant forms ground-covering mats in semi-shaded coniferous or mixed woods, as well as along roadsides and trails through the forest. The faint sweet fragrance of arbutus flowers offers one of the lasting memories of Acadia's long-reluctant springtime and is a fitting prelude to summer.

Goldthread (*Coptis groenlandica*), of the Buttercup Family, is a fairly common little 3- to 5-inch-tall dark evergreen plant of shaded mossy areas of damp conifer woods. Its attractive shiny leaves are divided into 3 leaflets that have scalloped and minutely serrated margins. The leaves are borne at the end of long delicate stems that are attached to the base of the plant. In

May, a solitary tiny white flower, with 5 to 7 petal-like sepals, blooms at the end of a 3- to 5-inch-tall stalk. Goldthread takes its name from its bright yellow thread-like roots.

Early Saxifrage (*Saxifraga virginiensis*), of the Saxifrage Family, favors Acadia's sunny cliff ledges, where it is frequently rooted in mounds of moss. A delicately hairy stalk rises 3 to 12 inches tall from a rosette of 1- to 3-inch-long spatula-shaped basal leaves with toothed margins. Branched terminal clusters of tiny flowers, with 5-pointed white petals and 10 bright yellow stamens, come into bloom from early May to early June.

Starflower (*Trientalis borealis*), of the Primrose Family, is an erect plant that grows 4 to 6 inches tall, with a terminal whorl of 5 to 9 narrowly tapering 2- to 4-inch-long leaves. In late May and June, one or two delicate 0.5- to 0.75-inch white flowers, with 6 to 8 pointed petals, come into bloom. Each blossom is borne at the end of a short stem that grows from a leaf axil (the upper angle created where a leaf is attached to its stem). This common species favors cool coniferous woods.

A number of species of the Violet Family inhabit Acadia, blooming from early May to June in woods, meadows, and along stream banks. **Northern White Violet** (*Viola pallens*) and **Sweet White Violet** (*V. blanda*) are similar in appearance, except that the leaves and flowers of the latter have reddish stems. The former species favors damper habitat than the latter, which favors cool, shaded ground, as in cedar and spruce woods. **Canada Violet** (*V. canadensis*) is a fragrant white-flowered species, with a hint of yellow at the base of the petals. Its heart-shaped leaves have finely toothed margins. This species favors dry sunny pine woods. **Marsh Blue** (or **Bog-bice**) **Violet** (*V. cucullata*) is one of several species of blue violets. Its purplish-blue 0.75-inch flowers bloom in late May and early June. Long-stemmed heart-shaped leaves are 1 to 4 inches in length. As the name implies, this species favors wet habitat. **Northern Blue Violet** (*V. septentrionalis*) has downy stems, heart-shaped leaves, and bearded lower 3 petals. It favors open conifer woods.

Creeping Snowberry (*Gaultheria hispidula*), a ground-creeping evergreen of the Heath Family, has 0.25- to 0.5-inch-long oval pointed leaves along its vine-like branches. In late May, this species puts out 4-lobed quarter-inch bell-like white flowers that bloom from the axil of an occasional leaf. Later in the season, shiny white berry-like fruits ripen. Their flavor resembles wintergreen. This uncommon delicate little plant grows in cool shady damp conifer woods, sphagnum bogs, and occasionally in groves of Pitch Pine.

Wood Betony (*Pedicularis canadensis*), of the Figwort Family, is a 5- to 15-inch-tall stout little plant of open woods and clearings. It has a

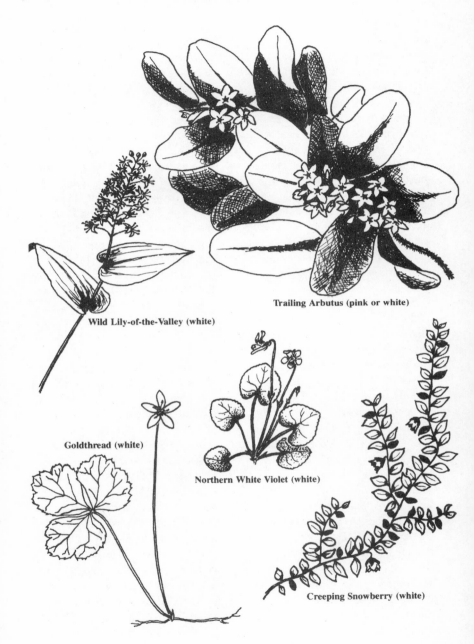

Trailing Arbutus (pink or white)

Wild Lily-of-the-Valley (white)

Goldthread (white)

Northern White Violet (white)

Creeping Snowberry (white)

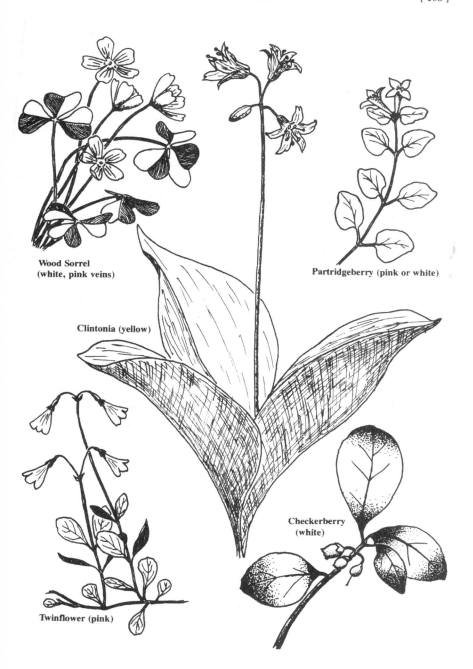

Wood Sorrel
(white, pink veins)

Partridgeberry (pink or white)

Clintonia (yellow)

Twinflower (pink)

Checkerberry
(white)

short and rather round terminal
spike of 0.75-inch-long purple-and-
greenish-yellow flowers that have a
hood-shaped upper lip and a 3-lobed
lower lip. Leaves are deeply lobed
and resembling miniature fern
fronds. They become progressively
smaller, the higher up the stalk they
are. This species blooms from late
May to June.

Canada Mayflower (or **Wild
Lily-of-the-Valley**) (*Maianthemum
canadense*), of the Lily Family, grows
abundantly in cool damp woods and
semi-shaded clearings. In late May
and June, its tiny, cream-colored 4-
petalled star-shaped flowers are
borne in a terminal spike on a delicate 2- to 6-inch stalk. The flower's 4
outreaching stamens give the flower
spike a fuzzy appearance. This plant
has from 1 to 3 leaves, which measure 1 to 3 inches long. They taper
from a heart-shaped deeply cleft
base that appears to wrap partway
around the stalk. Quarter-inch
berries are initially green and then
turn whitish or reddish with minute
spots.

Twisted Stalks (*Streptopus
roseus* and *S. amplexifolius*) are fairly
common species of the Lily Family
that favor cool damp woods. They
both have half-inch-wide bell-shaped
flowers (the former are dull pinkish-
purple and the latter are greenish),
which bloom in late May and June.
Each flower has a thread-like stem
that is attached to a stemless leaf
axil. Tapering leaves clasp the
slightly twisting stalk and branches.

Yellow Clintonia (or **Bluebead
Lily**) (*Clintonia borealis*) is another
member of the Lily Family and is often found in the company of Canada
Mayflower. It has 2 to 4 large shiny
tapered basal leaves. In June, 2 to 6
yellowish-green inch-wide lily-
shaped flowers nod on short stems
from the top of a 5- to 15-inch stalk.
By mid-summer, round berries ripen
to a rich shade of deep blue.

Smooth Solomon's Seal (*Polyg-
onatum biflorum*) and **False
Solomon's Seal** (*Smilacina race-
mosa*) are two more woodland members of the Lily Family. They have a
similar appearance, with oval 2- to 6-
inch-long leaves that grow along a
gracefully arching 1- to 3-foot stem.
The yellowish 0.5- to 0.6-inch bell-
like flowers of Solomon's Seal, in 5
to 10 or more pairs, hang from the
underside of the stem, each pair attached at a leaf axil. The tiny
creamy-white flowers of False
Solomon's Seal are borne in a
branched terminal raceme. Both
species bloom in June. A much
smaller species, the **Three-leaved
False Solomon's Seal** (*S. trifolia*)
blooms in late May and June, with a
spike of small white flowers. It favors
damp thickets and meadows.

Painted Trillium (*Trillium un-
dulatum*) is a rare 10- to 20-inch-tall
member of the Lily Family that
grows in damp woods and shaded
stream valleys. Its single terminal
flower, which blooms in late May
and early June, has 3 graceful wavy-
edged petals that are red-streaked at

Eagle Lake, Sargent Mountain from Cadillac Mountain

Eagle Lake and Pemetic Mountain

Hadlock Brook waterfall

Carriage Road bridge across Duck Brook

Canoeing on Bubble Pond

Cliffs at Hunters Beach

Cross-country skiers above Jordan Pond

*Icicles on cliffs
at the base of the
Triad*

*Trail sign on
Penobscot
Mountain-
Sargent
Mountain
Saddle*

Surf, Schoodic Point; Cadillac Mountain beyond

Cinnamon Ferns

Red Fox pups

*Great (Long)
Pond from
Beech
Mountain*

*Waterfall,
Hadlock Brook*

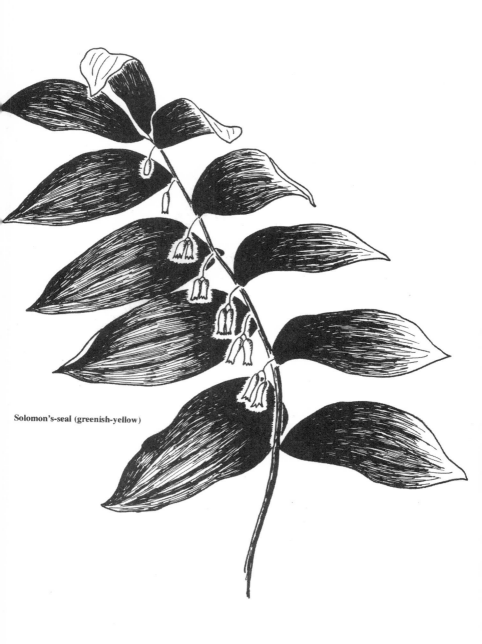

Solomon's-seal (greenish-yellow)

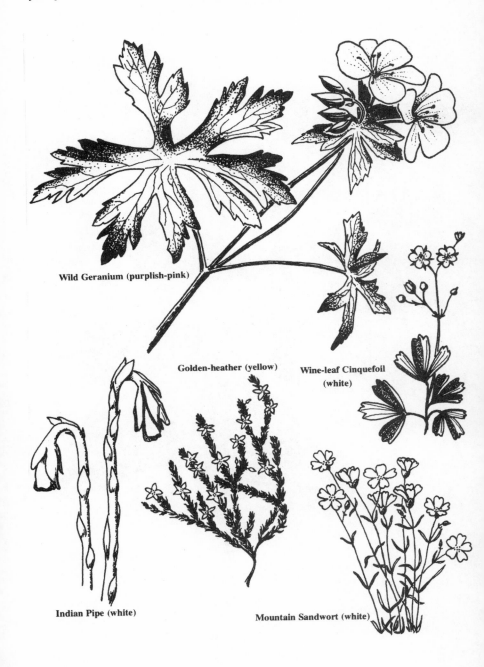

Wild Geranium (purplish-pink)

Golden-heather (yellow)

Wine-leaf Cinquefoil
(white)

Indian Pipe (white)

Mountain Sandwort (white)

the base. Three broadly oval 3- to 8-inch-long pointed leaves grow in a whorl just below the flower.

Bunchberry (*Cornus canadensis*) is an abundant member of the Dogwood Family. It often forms extensive ground-covering patches in cool sun-dappled woods, as well as in more open habitat. This species is about 6 to 8 inches tall, with a terminal whorl of oval 1- to 4-inch-long leaves. Typical of dogwoods, the leaf veins are parallel, following the curve of the margins. What appear to be 4 rounded white petals are actually bracts that surround a central cluster of small greenish flowers. Bunchberry blooms in June, followed by tightly clustered and shiny bright-red fruits.

Pink Lady's-slipper (or **Moccasin Flower**) (*Cypripedium acaule*), of the Orchid Family, produces its conspicuous 1.5- to 2-inch-long inflated pink pouch that nods from the top of a 6- to 15-inch-tall stalk in late May and June. Each plant has a pair of oval deeply parallel-veined 6- to 8-inch-long basal leaves that are finely hairy. This orchid especially favors dry acidic, needle-covered ground beneath pine trees. The Pink Lady's-slipper grows here and there in scattered groups. As with all orchids, collecting and picking unfortunately pose a threat to their welfare. **Showy Lady's-slipper** (*C. reginae*) blooms with large pink-and-white flowers in July. It is rarely found in Acadia, favoring wet and swampy woods.

Wild Geranium (or **Cranesbill**) (*Geranium maculatum*), of the Geranium Family, grows 1 to 2 feet tall and is a common species of open woods, thickets, and shaded roadsides. Delicate 1- to 1.5-inch-wide magenta-pink or pale-purple flowers, which bloom in late spring and early summer, have 5 rounded petals and grow in loosely branched terminal clusters of 2 to 5 blossoms each. Hairy leaves have 3 or 5 deeply cut wedge-toothed lobes. Fruits have a long tapered beak-like protuberance. Another species of geranium, **Herb Robert** (or **Musk-Geranium**) (*G. robertianum*) is found less commonly in Acadia. It grows 5 to 18 inches tall and favors rocky thickets and coastal shores. Half-inch-wide reddish-purple flowers bloom in terminal pairs. Fruits have a long slender beak-like protuberance.

White Baneberry (*Actaea pachypoda*) is a fairly rare member of the Buttercup Family in Acadia. It has a rounded terminal raceme of whitish flowers that bloom in June. Individual flowers have from 4 to 10 very slender blunt-tipped petals and long stamens. The twice- or thrice-compound leaves have tapered sharply toothed leaflets. Mid-summer fruits, which are borne on short thick reddish stems, ripen to striking white berries, each of which has a conspicuous black spot that gives rise to its nickname, "Doll's-eyes." This 1- to 2-foot-tall plant favors shady wooded habitat—sometimes growing along stream banks.

Teaberry (or **Wintergreen**)
(*Gaultheria procumbens*), of the
Heath Family, is an abundant small
creeping evergreen of cool woods. It
has thick shiny oval and slightly serrated 1- to 1.5-inch-long leaves that
grow on 2- to 5-inch-tall erect
branches. In late June and early July,
0.25- to 0.4-inch urn-shaped white
pendent flowers come into bloom—
half-hidden beneath the leaves. Both
the leaves and the bright-red berries
of late summer have a pleasant aromatic flavor. Teaberry should not be
confused with a species that has not
been recorded in Acadia: the Spotted
(or Striped) Wintergreen
(*Chimaphila maculate*) of the Wintergreen Family.

Partridgeberry (*Mitchella
repens*), of the Bedstraw Family, is a
common, little ground-creeping evergreen. Its 0.25- to 0.5-inch-long
rounded dark-green leaves grow in
pairs and have a creamy-white mid-
vein. In June, fragrant, 0.5- to 0.75-
inch funnel-shaped flowers come
into bloom. They have 4 flaring
creamy-white lobes that are fringed
on the inner surface, and are borne
in pairs at the ends of long creeping
stems. In an example of *dimorphous*
reproduction, the ovary of the one
flower is joined with that of its twin,
while one blossom contains the functional pistil and the other contains
the functional stamens. Later in the
season, the twin flowers ripen into a
single bright-red berry. This species
favors both damp and dry woods.

Common Pipsissewa
(*Chimaphila umbellate*), of the Wintergreen Family, is an uncommon
small evergreen plant. Its narrow
dark-green and slightly serrated 1- to
2-inch-long shiny leaves grow in
whorls from the stem. Erect
branches are 4 to 10 inches tall,
growing from creeping underground
stems. A terminal cluster of quarter-
inch nodding pink-and-white flowers
blooms in July and early August.
This species favors shady dry
woods.

Common Wood Sorrel (*Oxalis
montana*), of the Wood Sorrel Family, is an abundant 3- to 4-inch-tall
plant that grows in cool damp
woods. Its 5-petalled 0.75-inch-wide
flowers bloom in July. They have
notched pink-veined white or pale-
pink petals. The clover-like leaf is divided into 3 delicate heart-shaped
leaflets. This species favors damp
woods.

Twinflower (*Linnaea borealis*), a
member of the Honeysuckle Family,
is an inconspicuous little evergreen.
Its creeping stems are covered with
small rounded opposite leaves. A
pair of very fragrant half-inch-long
bell-shaped pink-and-white flowers
nods from the forked top of each delicate 4- to 6-inch-tall branch. Flowers
boom from June to August, and even
into September. This species favors
cool moist woods, but also has been
found growing in groves of Pitch
Pine.

Dewdrop (or **False Violet**) (*Dal-

ibarda repens), of the Rose Family, is a delicate inconspicuous 2- to 5-inch-tall plant. Its violet-like heart-shaped 1- to 2-inch-wide dark-green leaves have slightly wavy-toothed margins and long stems that are attached near the base of the plant. Leaves and stems are softly hairy. Usually a single half-inch-wide 5-petalled flower is borne at the end of a long reddish flower stalk. The self-pollinating flowers bloom in late July and August. This species is occasionally found in Acadia's cedar swamps and other cool mossy damp woods.

Shinleaf (*Pyrola elliptica*), of the Wintergreen Family, is occasionally found in Acadia's woods. It has elliptical long-stemmed basal evergreen leaves (the stem is not as long as the blade of the leaf). In July and August, fragrant loosely clustered greenish-white nodding terminal flowers bloom in a spiral along the upper part of the 5- to 10-inch stalk. This species favors damp woods.

Round-leaved Pyrola (*P. rotundifolia*) is the tallest species of Pyrola. Its flower stalk grows 0.5 to 1.5 feet from a basal cluster of 1- to 2-inch rounded or slightly oval shiny evergreen leaves. The leaf stem is about as long as the leaf blade. The loosely clustered nodding waxy white flowers spiral down the upper part of the stalk. The half-inch-wide 5-petalled flowers bloom in mid-summer. This species is fairly common, sometimes forming large colonies in dry wooded habitat.

One-sided Pyrola (*P. secunda*), an infrequent species in Acadia, is the smallest Pyrola, growing only 3 to 8 inches tall. Its terminal white or greenish flowers, which bloom in early July, all nod in a row along one side of the often slightly bent-over stalk. The oval pointed evergreen leaves are clustered around the base.

Downy Rattlesnake Plantain (*Goodyera pubescens*), of the Orchid Family, is uncommon in Acadia. In late July and early August, it blooms briefly with a 6- to 18-inch-long cylindrical raceme of 0.25- to 0.5-inch white flowers. Dark evergreen 1- to 3-inch-long oval basal leaves grow in flat rosettes and are delicately patterned with a network of pale-green or whitish veins. This species typically grows in colonies, within dry shady deciduous and coniferous woods.

Wild Sarsaparilla (*Aralia nudicaulis*), of the Ginseng Family, is an abundant 1- to 1.5-foot-tall plant. Its single long-stemmed leaf is divided into 3 compound leaflets, each of which has 3 or 5 oval sub-leaflets with finely serrated margins. In July and August, inconspicuous little greenish-white flowers grow in 3 to 7 rounded long-stemmed umbrella-like clusters that are partially hidden below the leaf. Clustered quarter-inch berries ripen to purplish-black. This species favors moist woods, in both shady and semi-open habitat.

Bristly Sarsaparilla (*A. hispida*),

Blue-eyed Grass (bluish-purple)

Bluet (blue and yellow)

Jewelweed (orange-yellow)

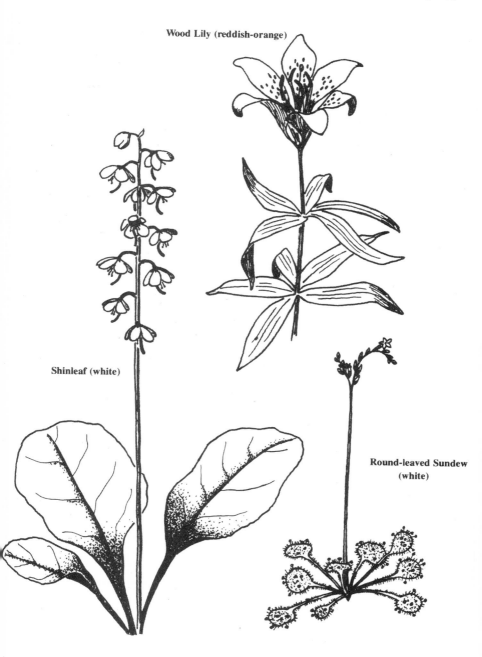

Wood Lily (reddish-orange)

Shinleaf (white)

Round-leaved Sundew
(white)

which grows 1 to 3 feet tall, is named for its bristly-stemmed base. In late July, small whitish flowers come into bloom. Its purplish-black fruits are borne in tall terminal umbels. This species usually favors clearings, brushy habitat, and roadsides.

SAPROPHYTIC AND PARASITIC FOREST FLOWERS

Indian Pipe (*Monotropa uniflora*), of the Wintergreen Family, hardly looks like a flower. Its fleshy 4- to 10-inch-tall stalk is white, with small leaf-like alternate bracts. The single white or occasionally pink nodding terminal flower has 2 to 4 scales and 4 to 5 petals. This saprophytic and parasitic plant derives its sustenance from decaying organic matter and from the roots of living plants. Thus, the Indian Pipe does not need the green chlorophyll of most other higher plants. After flowering, the seed pod is held erect and becomes a pinkish-buff color. This species, which appears from late July to mid-August, grows in darkly shaded damp woods. Its scattered clumps are especially abundant during rainy summers.

Pinesap (or **False Beech Drops**) (*M. hypopithys*) is much less common in Acadia than Indian Pipe. This 4- to 14-inch-tall species varies in color from whitish and lemon-yellow to pale-reddish. Many small alternate bracts cover the stalk. A number of little nodding, vase-shaped yellowish-tinged pale-red flowers are clustered along the slightly drooping top of the stalk. Seed pods are held erect. The saprophytic and parasitic habits and damp woodland habitat of Pinesap are similar to Indian Pipe.

Beechdrop (*Epifagus virginiana*), of the Broomrape Family, is an inconspicuous purplish-brown or yellowish 0.5- to 2-foot-tall parasitic plant that grows in scattered clumps within Beech woodlands, where it feeds on the roots of the Beech tree. Its slender branches are covered with small scales. A terminal spike of little tubular flowers blooms in August and September. The upper flowers are open and sterile, and the lower ones are closed and self-fertilizing.

Coralroots, of the Orchid Family, are found rather commonly, in some years, in shaded, moist woods. **Northern Coralroot** (*Corallhorhiza trifida*) blooms in early summer, with a terminal spike of whitish tubular flowers. **Spotted Coralroot** (*C. maculata*) has a mid-summer spike of purplish-brown flowers, with a pale red-spotted lower lip. Both species lack chlorophyll and leaves, and grow in decaying organic matter.

MOUNTAIN FLOWERS

Wine-leaved (or **Three-toothed**) **Cinquefoil** (*Potentilla tridentata*), of the Rose Family, is a prolific low-growing little plant of dry exposed mountain ridges and summits, as well as coastal cliffs. Its quarter-inch-wide white flowers have 5 rounded petals. Leaves, which turn deep maroon-red in autumn, have 3 narrow 1.5- to 2-inch-long leaflets, with rounded 3-toothed tips. This 2- to 12-inch-tall plant blooms in June and July.

Golden-heather (*Hudsonia ericoides*), of the Rockrose Family, is a 4- to 8-inch-tall little shrub. Its clustered branches are densely covered with narrow, needle-like upward-spreading leaves that are only about an eighth-of-an-inch long. In mid-June through early July, this neat little plant comes into bloom with bright golden-yellow quarter-inch 5-petaled star-shaped flowers. It grows at just a few dry exposed mountain-top locations in Acadia.

Mountain Sandwort (*Arenaria groenlandica*), of the Pink Family, is a true Arctic species that grows in dry sandy depressions and crevices on exposed mountain ridges and summits. It forms inconspicuous 2- to 5-inch-tall tufts and clumps. The stems bear minute opposite slender leaves. Terminal quarter-inch-long flowers have 5 white petals that are notched at the tip. This species blooms during most of the warmer months, generally from late May to October or even into November.

Wood Lily (*Lilium philadelphicum*) is a strikingly beautiful bright-orange or reddish-orange flower. Unlike other species of this genus, its terminal flower opens upward and stands erect. Usually there is only a single blossom on each plant. Al-though the Wood Lily typically grows about 3 feet tall, Acadia's plants often reach not much more than about a foot in height. The flower, which briefly blooms in mid- to late-July, has 6 petals that are speckled with purplish spots. Slender tapered leaves grow in whorls around the stalk. This plant grows singly or in loose clumps on only a very few exposed mountain and coastal locations.

Harebell (*Campanula rotundifolia*), of the Bluebell Family, is a 5- to 15-inch-tall plant. It has small round basal leaves, as well as slender 1- to 3-inch-long grass-like leaves that grow upward from the stems. This species comes into bloom from mid-July to September, with its delicate 0.5- to 1-inch-long purplish-blue 5-petalled bell-like flowers that nod from the end of branches. Harebell favors exposed ledges on mountain ridges and summits, as well as coastal cliffs.

BOG FLOWERS

Baked-apple Berry (or **Cloudberry**) (*Rubus chamaemorus*), a member of the Rose Family, is an Arctic plant of sphagnum bogs. It has creeping stems with erect 3- to 18-inch-tall branches. Each plant has only two or three leaves that are 2.5 to 3 inches wide, with 5 or 6 rounded and serrated lobes. In June, it blooms with solitary, long-stemmed 4 or 5 round-petalled flowers. Its orange raspberry-like fruits

Evening Primrose (yellow)

Tawny Hawkweed (orange)

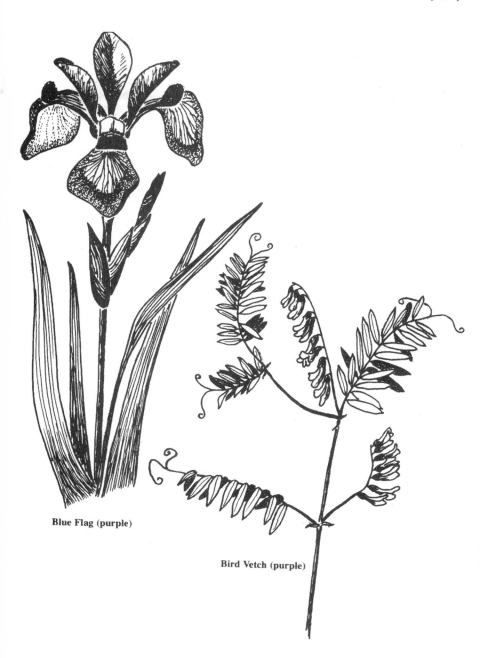

Blue Flag (purple)

Bird Vetch (purple)

suggest the flavor of baked apple. This species is rare in Acadia's bogs.

Dragon's Mouth (or **Swamp Pink**) (*Arethusa bulbosa*), of the Orchid Family, is a delicate 5- to 12-inch-tall plant, which blooms in June. There is usually only a single 1- to 2-inch-long flower at the top of each stalk. Flowers consist of 3 upraised magenta-pink sepals that reach above the petals, which in turn arch over a conspicuous pink-and-yellow downward-curving and spreading lip. The latter is marked with deep-magenta splotches and several rows of minute whitish or yellow hairs. This species is fairly common in Acadia's sphagnum bogs.

Grass Pink (*Calopogon pulchellus*), of the Orchid Family, is a delicate 6- to 18-inch-tall plant that blooms in July and August. It has a 12-inch-long slender basal leaf. On each stalk, there are usually from 3 to 6 fragrant flowers in a loose terminal raceme. Its 1- to 1.5-inch-wide purplish-pink flowers have outward-fanning pink sepals and petals, and an upraised and flared lip that is crested with minute whitish-yellow hairs. This species grows in Acadia's sphagnum bogs and wet meadows.

Rose Pogonia (*Pogonia ophioglossoides*), of the Orchid Family, is a delicate, 6- to 20-inch-tall plant that blooms in July and August. A single broad tapered 4- to 5-inch-long leaf is located about midway up the stalk. Usually only a single 1.5- to 2-inch-wide flower is borne at the top

of the stalk. The flower's rose-pink sepals and petals overhang a deeper pink, fringed and yellow-bristled protruding lip. This species grows in Acadia's sphagnum bogs and along shallow lakeshores.

Bog Goldenrod (*Solidago uliginosa*), of the Sunflower Family, is a 2- to 5-foot-tall plant. Tiny yellow flowers are borne in pyramidal short-branched clusters. The lower leaves, which are prominently larger than upper ones, measure up to a foot long, with serrated margins and long-tapering stems. This species, which blooms in August and September, favors swampy meadows and sphagnum bogs.

INSECTIVOROUS BOG PLANTS

Northern Pitcher Plant (*Sarracenia purpurea*), of the Pitcher Plant Family, is a distinctive species of sphagnum bogs. This species takes its name from the 4- to 10-inch-tall, hooded, ascending pitcher-shaped fleshy green basal leaf that is patterned with reddish veins. Insects, which are attracted by a sugar-like secretion, are trapped inside the leaf that is usually partially filled with liquid. It is believed that the drowned insects are absorbed into the plant, contributing to its sustenance. The solitary 1.5- to 3-inch reddish-purple and green flower, nodding from the top of an erect 1- to 1.5-foot-tall stalk, has 5 reddish petals that arch under and partly cover the greenish-yellow umbrella-shaped style. Five purplish sepals spread outward from the top of the flower, which blooms in June and July.

Round-leaved Sundew (*Drosera rotundifolia*), of the Sundew Family, is an inconspicuous but abundant little plant of sphagnum bogs and other marshy habitat. Its slender hairy-stemmed 0.4- to 0.75-inch rounded basal leaves form a rosette at or near the ground. The upper surface of the leaves is covered with reddish glandular hairs that secrete sticky sparkling sugar-like "dewdrops" that attract and capture insects. Once an insect is ensnared, the leaf folds inward and absorbs its prey. In July and August, tiny quarter-inch 5-petalled white terminal flowers come into bloom, clustered along one side of the 4- to 9-inch-tall stalk. The upper end of the stalk is usually bent over slightly. The similar **Spatulate-leaved Sundew** (*D. leucantha*) is much less common in Acadia's bogs. Its longer smooth-stemmed oval leaves assume a more ascending position than those of the Round-leaved Sundew. The flower stalk is typically only about 2 to 8 inches tall.

MARSH AND SWAMP FLOWERS

Blue Flag (*Iris versicolor*), of the Iris Family, is the beautiful and common *fleur-de-lis* of marshy habitat, wet roadside ditches, and tidal inlets where streams meet the sea. Its purple flowers have 3 erect petals and 3 larger outward-spreading sepals that are patterned with deep-purple veins and yellow-and-white markings. This species blooms in June and July.

Yellow Loosestrife (or **Swamp Candles**) (*Lysimachia terrestris*), of the Primrose Family, is an attractive 10- to 30-inch-tall plant. It has a spike-like terminal cluster of half-inch-wide 5-petalled yellow star-shaped flowers. At the base of each petal is a pair of reddish spots, giving the appearance of a circle around the base of the stamens. Below the flower cluster are slender 2- to 4-inch-long opposite leaves that are sharply pointed at both ends. This species, which blooms from late June to August, favors Acadia's swampy and damp grassy habitat. (See the Whorled Loosestrife, under Meadow and Roadside Flowers.)

Purple-fringed Orchis (*Habenaria fimbriata*), of the Orchid Family, is an uncommon but very striking 1- to 3-foot-tall species favoring swampy thickets, such as around the edges of old beaver ponds. In July, the terminal spike of flowers is more than 2 inches wide and up to 10 or 12 inches long. The individual flower has a prominent 3-part outward-fanning and fringed lip. Another swamp or bog orchid of Acadia is the 1- to 2.5-foot-tall **Leafy White Orchid** (or **White Rein-Orchid**) (**H. dilatata**). Its greenish-white late-June and July flowers have a narrow tapered protruding smooth-edged lip. Leaves are long and narrowly tapering. This species is found only occasionally.

A number of other orchids have been recorded as rare or infrequent. Among them are the 7- to 16-inch-tall yellowish-green-flowered **Hooker's Orchis** (*H. hookeri*) of swampy woods; the larger 1- to 2-foot-tall whitish-flowered **Round-leaved Orchid** (*H. orbiculata*), both species with large nearly round or oval basal leaves; and the inconspicuous 5- to 10-inch-tall **Northern Bog Orchid** (or **One-leaved Rein-Orchis**) (*H. obtusata*), whose spike of greenish-white flowers blooms in late July and early August, and favoring shallow shaded lakeshores and damp woods and bogs. The single smooth basal leaf broadens from its axil.

Nodding Ladies' Tresses (*Spiranthes cernua*), of the Orchid Family, is a fairly common 6- to 18-inch-tall plant. Its half-inch-long creamy-white outward-projecting flowers are borne in a slender spike and form a double spiral that extends a third to halfway down the stalk. The individual flower has a downward-arching wavy-edged lip. Narrow basal leaves are 8 or 10 inches long. This species, which blooms in August and early September, favors marshy habitat, and damp meadows and thickets. **Slender Ladies' Tresses** (*S. gracilis*) has a delicate single spiral of white flowers. This species blooms in late summer and favors damp grassy habitat.

Cardinal Flower (*Lobelia cardinalis*), of the Bluebell Family, is a conspicuous, but uncommon species of Lobelia. It grows from 2 to 4 feet tall and bears a spike of dazzling scarlet flowers, which bloom from July to September. This species grows infrequently in swampy habitat and along or in shallow streams.

Jewelweed (or **Spotted Touch-me-not**) (*Impatiens capensis*), of the Touch-me-not Family, is a loosely branching, 2- to 5-foot-tall shrubby plant, with pendent, speckled inch-long, tubular orange flowers, which bloom in August and early September. Ripe seed pods explode at the slightest touch, shooting seeds in all directions. Alternate oval leaves are serrated and stalked. This species favors semi-shaded wet habitat, such as around Sieur de Monts Spring.

Skunk Cabbage (*Symplocarpus foetidus*), of the Arum Family, is a rare Acadia swamp species, found mostly in the vicinity of Seawall and Wonderland (also on the Cranberry Islands). Its peculiar mid- to late-April flower consists of a compact round spadix (a club-like spike); surrounded by a hooded shell-like spathe that is streaked with reddish-purple and yellowish-green patterns. By late spring, the 1- to 2-foot-long oval bright-green "cabbage" leaves unfurl.

Jack-in-the-Pulpit (*Arisaema triphyllum*) is an uncommon member

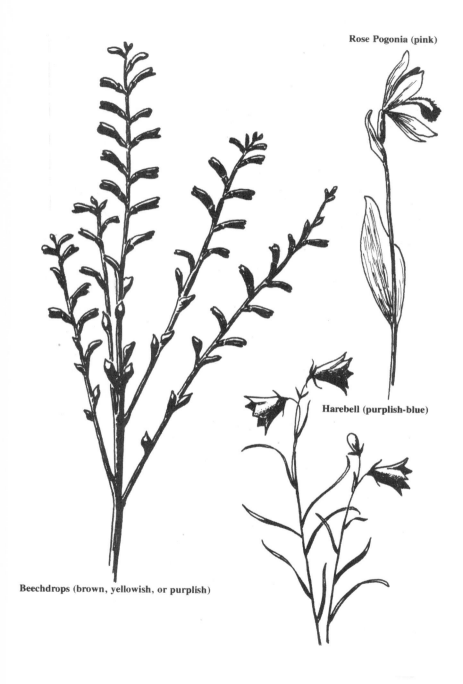

Rose Pogonia (pink)

Harebell (purplish-blue)

Beechdrops (brown, yellowish, or purplish)

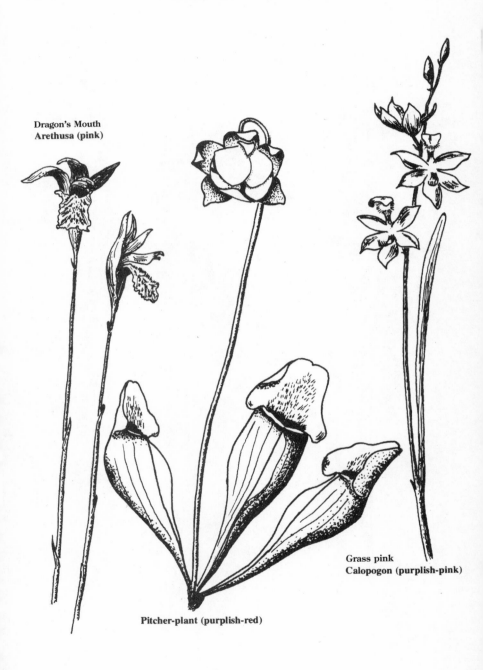

Dragon's Mouth
Arethusa (pink)

Grass pink
Calopogon (purplish-pink)

Pitcher-plant (purplish-red)

of the Arum Family in Acadia. It grows infrequently in certain swampy and damp wooded places. The inconspicuous flowers of late May and early June are tightly crowded on a spadix, which is enclosed by a green-and-white-striped spathe that stands erect on its stalk. The 1- to 3-foot-tall plant usually has 2 large long-stemmed leaves, each of which is divided into 3 broadly tapered leaflets.

Common Cattail (*Typha latifolia*), of the Cattail Family, has 4- to 8-foot-tall slender bladelike leaves and a brown sausage-shaped terminal pistillate flower spike. This species grows commonly in dense stands around shallow ponds and other marshy areas.

POND FLOWERS

Fragrant Water Lily (*Nymphaea odorata*), of the Water Lily Family, is a very common aquatic plant. The rounded 3- to 10-inch leaves, which float on the surface of the water, are shiny and green above and purplish beneath. Its strikingly beautiful and fragrant 3- to 5-inch-wide white or pink-tinged flowers, which bloom from late spring through most of the summer, have many tapered upraised petals. Another Water Lily has smaller leaves and flowers. It covers part of Sargent Mountain Pond, which lies in the saddle between the summits of Sargent and Penobscot mountains.

Yellow Pond Lily (*Nuphar varie-*

gatum), of the Water Lily Family, is an abundant aquatic plant, the leaves and flowers of which float on the surface of shallow ponds. Its oblong leaves are 4 to 15 inches long. Yellow cup-shaped flowers, which bloom from late spring through most of the summer, have 5 or 6 curved petal-like sepals. This species can be seen on the surface of The Tarn and other shallow ponds.

Arrowhead (*Sagittaria latifolia*), of the Water Plantain Family, is an aquatic plant that has emphatically arrow-shaped erect 3- to 15-inch-long leaves that vary from slender to broad. Its 0.6-inch-wide flowers, which bloom through much of the summer, have 3 rounded white petals. This species grows in shallow ponds.

Pickerelweed (*Pontederia cordata*), of the Pickerelweed Family, is a prolific aquatic plant that has erect 3- to 10-inch-long arrowhead-shaped leaves. Spikes of densely clustered bluish-purple flowers bloom during much of the summer. Each 0.25- to 0.4-inch-long tubular flower has 3-lobed upper and lower lips. Two yellow spots highlight the middle of the upper lobe. This species can be seen in the shallows of the Breakneck Ponds.

Greater Bladderwort (*Utricularia vulgaris*), of the Bladderwort Family, is a common small aquatic plant, with 6- to 12-inch stems. It grows either from the mud of shallow ponds or is kept afloat by numerous little bladders that are located

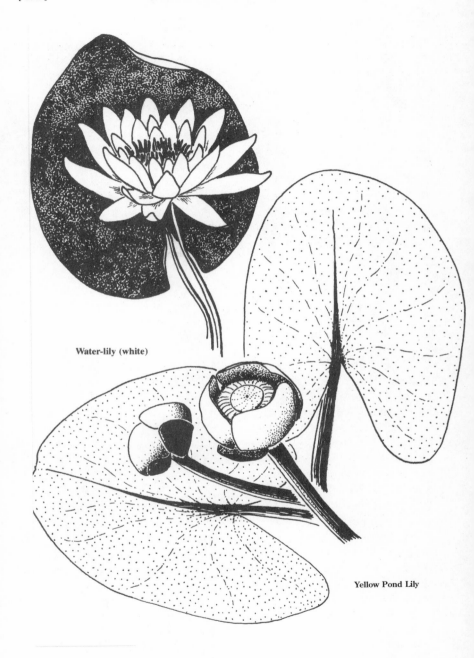

Water-lily (white)

Yellow Pond Lily

Pickerelweed (purplish-blue)

Lupine (purplish-blue, pink or white)

within the root system. Clustered terminal flowers resemble tiny hoods or bonnets, with a curved spur beneath. This species, which blooms during July and August, can be seen around the edge of The Tarn and other shallow ponds and sluggish streams.

Water Lobelia (*Lobelia dortmanna*), of the Bluebell Family, is an inconspicuous 6- to 18-inch-tall aquatic plant, with small thick slender basal leaves that are submerged. A loosely clustered terminal spike bears pale-purple or white tubular flowers, which are about a half-inch long and have 2 erect lobes and 3 lower lobes. This species, which blooms from late July to early September, favors shallow borders of ponds.

MEADOW AND ROADSIDE FLOWERS

Bluets (*Houstonia caerulea*), of the Bedstraw Family, are tiny delicate flowers of grassy meadows and roadsides. They typically bloom in thick patches during May and June. The individual half-inch-wide flower, which is borne singly and erect atop a 3- to 6-inch-tall stem, has 4 pale-blue or whitish petals and a yellow center.

Blue-eyed Grass (*Sisyrinchium angustifolium*), of the Iris Family, grows commonly in sunny, grassy meadows. Grass-like 4- to 10-inch-long leaves curve gracefully upward from the winged stalk. Its delicate

half-inch-wide 6-petalled flowers, which bloom from May to July, are violet-blue with a yellow center.

Wild Strawberry (*Frageria virginiana*), of the Rose Family, is an abundant 3- to 6-inch-tall plant of meadows and grassy roadsides. Its small 5 round-petalled white flowers bloom from early May to early June. Its leaves are divided into 3 sharply serrated leaflets and have long hairy stems. The berries are smaller than domestic strawberries.

Fringed Polygala (or **Gaywings**) (*Polygala paucifolia*), of the Milkwort Family, is an uncommon 3- to 6-inch-tall plant. Its broadly oval inch-long evergreen leaves are clustered near the top of the stalk. In June, delicate 0.75-inch-long purplish-pink orchid-like flowers come into bloom. They have tubular petals, the lower one ending in a protruding fringe; and 2 wide-spreading wing-like sepals of the same color. One, two, or three flowers are borne at the end of each stalk. This species, which favors damp meadows and open woods, has been recorded from only a few places in Acadia.

Large-leaved Lupine (*Lupinus polyphyllus*), of the Pea Family, is a beautiful 1- to 2-foot-tall non-native species that was introduced from the Pacific Northwest. Extensive patches of this plant typically grow along grassy roadsides. The purplish-blue or occasionally pink or white flowers, which bloom in June and early July, are borne on an 8- to

12-inch terminal spike. Palmate leaves are divided into 7 to 15 slender radiating leaflets. Fruits ripen within hairy bean-like pods.

Canadian Dwarf Cinquefoil (*Potentilla Canadensis*), of the Rose Family, is an abundant erect or sprawling meadow plant. Its long-stemmed half-inch-wide flowers, which bloom in June and early July, have 5 slightly notched yellow petals. Compound leaves usually have 5 wedge-shaped 1.5-inch-long leaflets, the outer ends of which are toothed. A similar abundant species is the **Common Cinquefoil** (*P. simplex*), which favors meadows and grassy lakeshores. Its larger compound leaves are about 2.5 inches long.

Common Buttercup (*Ranunculus acris*), of the Buttercup Family, is a non-native species that was introduced into North America from Europe. It grows from 1 to 3 feet tall, with slender branches. Basal leaves are deeply cut into 5 or 7 long-toothed segments. The bright-yellow flowers usually have 5 shiny overlapping petals. This abundant roadside plant blooms mostly in June and July.

Orange Hawkweed (*Hieracium aurantiacum*), of the Sunflower Family, is a common non-native species of grassy roadsides and meadows, which was introduced into North America from Europe. Each plant has a number of 0.5- to 0.75-inch-wide ray-petalled flowers, which bloom from June to September. They are borne at the top of its 1- to 2-foot-tall hairy stalk, at the base of which is a whorl of 2- to 5-inch-long slender and hairy leaves.

Yellow Hawkweed (*H. pretense*) is a non-native species from Europe. It grows abundantly in grassy habitat, where masses of their bright-yellow ray-petalled flowers bloom from June to August. Another yellow-flowered species that looks similar is the **Fall Dandelion** (*Leontodon autumnalis*). But unlike the hawkweeds, its flower stalk is sometimes branched, is not hairy, and the smooth, narrow basal leaves are deeply cut into slender lobes.

Oxeye Daisy (*Chrysanthemum leucanthemum*), of the Sunflower Family, is a 1- to 3-foot-tall non-native species that was introduced into North America from Europe. Its 1.5- to 2-inch-wide flowers, which bloom from June through August, have 25 to 35 white ray-petals and a slightly depressed golden center. Its narrow leaves are irregularly lobed. The Oxeye Daisy is abundant in meadows and along grassy roadsides.

Rabbit's-foot Clover (*Trifolium arvense*), of the Pea Family, is a 4- to 15-inch-tall non-native plant from Europe. It has fuzzy pinkish-gray flower spikes. The leaves are divided into 3 narrow leaflets. This species is common in meadows and along grassy roadsides.

Red Clover (*T. pretense*) is a 6- to 20-inch-tall non-native plant from Europe. It has clusters of bright-purplish-red half-inch-long pea-like

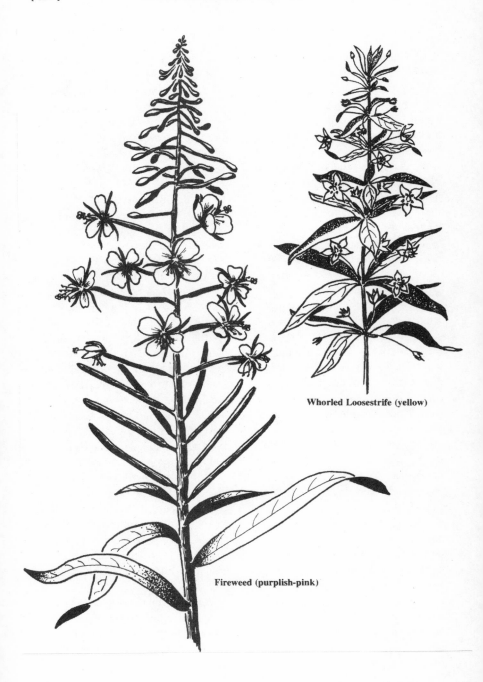

Whorled Loosestrife (yellow)

Fireweed (purplish-pink)

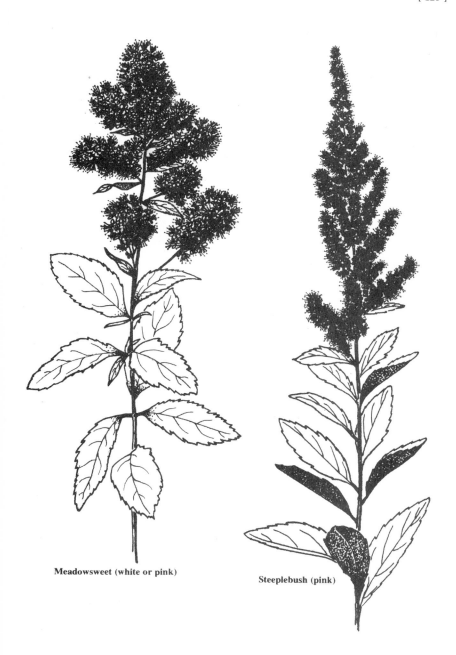

Meadowsweet (white or pink)

Steeplebush (pink)

flowers that are borne in rounded 1-inch heads. The leaves are divided into 3 (sometimes 4 or 5) rounded leaflets, each of which is marked with a triangular whitish pattern. This species is common in meadows and along grassy roadsides.

White Clover (*T. repens*) is a prolific 4- to 10-inch-tall non-native plant from Europe. It has clusters of 0.25- to 0.5-inch-long white or pinkish pea-like flowers that are borne in 0.75-inch-wide rounded heads. The leaves are divided into 3 leaflets, each of which is marked with a pale-whitish, triangular pattern. This species is abundant in meadows and along grassy roadsides. **Alsike Clover** (*T. hybridum*) is similar to the White Clover, but its flower stems grow from branching stalks and its leaflets lack the triangular whitish pattern.

Hop Clover (*T. agrarium*) is a common 6- to 18-inch-tall non-native plant from Europe. It has clusters of quarter-inch-long pea-like flowers that are borne in 0.5- to 1-inch-wide oblong heads.

Blue (or **Cow**) **Vetch** (*Vicia cracca*), of the Pea Family, is a vine-like non-native plant from Europe. In summer, bluish-purple half-inch-long pea-like flowers come into bloom in long one-sided clusters. Inch-long pod-like fruits ripen in late summer. Its grayish-green compound leaves typically have from 8 to 12 narrow bristle-tipped leaflets. Two tendrils, used in climbing, are located at the end of each leaf-stalk. This species favors open, grassy habitat.

Spreading Dogbane (*Apocynum androsaemifolium*), of the Dogbane Family, is a shrubby 1- to 2-foot-tall plant. It has opposite ovate 2- to 3-inch-long smooth-edged leaves. Its flowers, which bloom in late June and early July, are light pink 5-lobed 0.25- to 0.4-inch-wide pendent bell-like flowers, which bloom in late June and early July, and have deep-pink stripes inside. The clustered flowers are attached to the axils of the outermost leaves. The stems are often partly reddish in color. This species favors sunny thickets, meadows, and roadsides.

Yellow Rattlebox (*Rhinanthus crista-galli*), of the Snapdragon Family, is a common 6- to 30-inch-tall plant. From mid-June to July, it has half-inch-long stemless yellow flowers that are borne in a one-sided spike. Each blossom protrudes from a green cup-like calyx. Later in the summer, the seeds rattle in their ripened pods. The narrow opposite 1- to 2.5-inch-long leaves have serrated margins. This species, which is parasitic, favors open grassy habitat and thickets.

Whorled Loosestrife (*Lysimachia quadrifolia*), of the Primrose Family, is a 1- to 2-foot-tall plant. It has several whorls of 4 to 6 tapered 3- to 5-inch-long leaves that extend to the top of the stalk. Small long-stemmed 5-inch-wide yellow flowers grow from the leaf axils. A circle of tiny reddish dots gives the appearance of a circle around middle of the flower's 5-lobed corolla. This species, which blooms from late June to early July, favors sunny openings and roadsides. (See the Yellow Loosestrife, under Marsh and Swamp Flowers.)

Yarrow (*Achillea millefolium*), of the Sunflower Family, is a common 1- to 2-foot-tall non-native species from Europe. It consists of a flat-topped terminal cluster of tiny whitish (occasionally pale-pink) flowers, each of which has usually five, eighth-inch-long ray petals. Intricately dissected, feathery, carrot-like leaves are pungently aromatic when crushed. This species, which blooms from late June to autumn, favors meadows and grassy roadsides.

Fireweed (*Epilobium angustifolium*), of the Evening Primrose Family, is a 3- to 5-foot-tall plant that grows in dense clumps that sway gracefully in a breeze. Bright purplish-pink 1-inch-wide flowers are borne on a terminal spike-like raceme. They have 2 rounded upper petals; and 2 slightly larger and rounded lower petals. Buds droop downward, flowering begins from the bottom of the cluster, and seed pods reach upward. Alternate, 3- to 8-inch long leaves are slender, resembling those of willows. This showy species, which is at the peak of blooming in July and early August, favors clearings, spruce-forest blow-downs, and areas swept by fire. Fireweed also grows far to the north, across northern Canada and throughout much of Alaska.

Evening Primrose (*Oenothera biennis*), of the Evening Primrose Family, is a very common 2- to 5-foot-tall plant. Its terminal 1- to 2-inch-wide long-stemmed flowers have 4 large yellow petals and 4 backward-spreading sepals. Flower stems are attached at the leaf axils. Alternate 3- to 7-inch-long slender leaves are slightly serrated. True to its name, the flowers of the Evening Primrose open in the evening and fade by the middle of the following day. They have a mildly lemon-like scent. This species, which blooms from July to September, favors meadows and sunny roadsides.

Common St. Johnswort (*Hypericum perforatum*), of the St. Johnswort Family, is a common 1- to 2.5-foot-tall non-native shrubby plant from Europe. It has 1-inch-wide 5-petalled golden-yellow flowers that are clustered on short terminal branches. The petals have minute black dots along their margins. The branches are covered with slender 1- to 2-inch-long opposite leaves. This species, which blooms from late June to August, favors meadows and sunny roadsides.

Common Mullein (*Verbascum thapsus*), of the Snapdragon Family, is a fairly common 2- to 5-foot-tall non-native species from Europe. The rosette of basal leaves and those growing upward from the stalk are thickly covered with velvety hairs that give the plant a whitish woolly appearance. The dense cylindrical terminal spike is also woolly; and only a few of the 5-petalled 0.25- to

Nodding Ladies' Tresses (white)   )

Yarrow (white)

Gray Goldenrod (yellow)

Common St. Johnswort (yellow)

0.5-inch-wide yellow flowers are in bloom at any one time, from July to September. This species favors sunny roadsides.

Tall Meadow Rue (*Thalictrum polygamum*), of the Buttercup Family, is a fairly abundant 3- to 6-foot-tall plant. Its white 0.4-inch-wide flowers, which lack petals, are borne in plume-like erect and loose terminal clusters. Petal-like sepals soon drop off, and the numerous thread-like stamens give the flower heads an especially fuzzy or misty appearance. Compound leaves are divided into rounded 3-lobed 1-inch-long leaflets. This species, which blooms in July and August, favors damp meadows and roadsides, and swampy thickets.

Black-eyed Susan (*Rudbeckia hirta*), of the Sunflower Family, is a conspicuous and cheerful 1- to 2-foot-tall plant. Its flowers have 8 to 15 rich-yellow 1- to 2-inch-long ray-petals and a dark-brown raised center. Long slender alternate leaves and branching stems are hairy. This species, which blooms from late June to September, favors sunny roadsides and meadows.

Common Tansy (*Tanacetum vulgare*), of the Sunflower Family, is a 2- to 4-foot-tall non-native species from Europe. Its half-inch-wide flowers, which are usually devoid of ray-petals, are borne in flat-topped yellow terminal clusters. Alternate 3- to 6-inch-long leaves are deeply cut, fern-like, into serrated leaflets. Clumps of this species, which blooms from late July to September,

are found only occasionally on Mount Desert Island—notably along the Park Loop Road, between Sand Beach and Thunder Hole.

Heal-all (or **Selfheal**) (*Prunella vulgaris*), of the Mint Family, is a very common 3- to 12-inch-tall non-native species from Europe. Its short terminal spike has purplish half-inch-long tubular-shaped flowers, with a hood and fringed lip. Narrow to oval leaves are opposite, 1 to 4 inches long and tapered. This species, which blooms from July to September, favors grassy roadsides, as well as a variety of sunny and semi-shaded habitats.

Joe-Pye Weed (*Eupatorium purpureum*), of the Sunflower Family, is a fairly common 2- to 5-foot-tall plant. Its dull purplish-pink flowers are borne in branching round-topped terminal clusters. Long stamens give the 0.4-inch-wide flower head a fuzzy appearance. Whorls of 4 tapered 3- to 8-inch-long serrated leaves grow from the stalk. This species, which blooms in late-summer and early autumn, favors open, wet meadows and thickets.

Boneset (*E. perfoliatum*), of the Sunflower Family, is a 2- to 4-foot-tall plant. It has rounded branching terminal clusters of dull-white flowers. Tapered 4- to 7-inch-long hairy leaves grow in pairs, with their bases joined completely around the hairy stalk. This species, which blooms in late summer and early autumn, favors wet meadows and thickets.

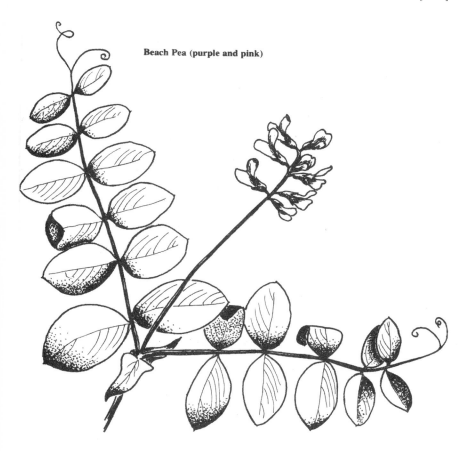

Beach Pea (purple and pink)

Pearly Everlasting (*Anaphalis margaritacea*), of the Sunflower Family, is a common 1- to 2.5-foot-tall plant. It has branching flat-topped terminal clusters of white flowers. The individual round quarter-inch-wide flower consists of papery petal-like white bracts that surround a yellow center. Alternate upward-sweeping 3- to 5-inch-long leaves are grayish-green above; and whitish and densely wooly beneath.

This species, which blooms from July to September, grows in clumps and patches within dry forest clearings and meadows, and along roadsides.

Common Thistle (*Cirsium arvense*), of the Sunflower Family, is a common 1- to 5-foot-tall plant. It has numerous 0.5- to 0.75-inch-wide pale-violet flowers, which are within 1- to 3-inch-wide terminal heads at the end of branching stems. Leaves are

Canada Goldenrod (yellow)

Lance-leaved Goldenrod (yellow)

1 to 3 inches long, deeply lobed, and sharply bristle-tipped. This species, which bloom in late-summer and early-autumn, favor sunny roadsides and meadows.

Goldenrods, of the Sunflower Family, are abundant late-summer and early-autumn wildflowers that grow in a wide variety of open, sunny habitat—mostly in meadows, fields, and grassy roadsides. Among the many species are the following:

Early Goldenrod (*Solidago juncea*) has tiny yellow flower heads that are borne in a gracefully branching pyramidal terminal cluster. The 2- to 4-foot-tall stalk has long tapered alternate leaves that have a pair of very small leaflets at their axils. Long-stemmed basal leaves are much larger and wider, and are serrated along the outer end. This is Acadia's earliest goldenrod species to bloom, beginning in July.

Canada Goldenrod (*S. Canadensis*) is similar to the Early Goldenrod, except that its slender leaves are all sharply serrated, there are no leaflets at leaf axils, and basal leaves are not as wide. This very common 2- to 5-foot-tall species blooms in August and September.

Rough-stemmed Goldenrod (*S. rugosa*) is a 1- to 7-foot-tall very hairy species, with wide, tapered, and sharply serrated leaves. Lower leaves are larger, with gradually tapering stems. Clusters of small yellow flower heads are usually borne on long, leafy, and upward-spreading branches. Each upward-tapering flower cluster has short branches. This species, which blooms in August and September, favors grassy meadows and roadsides.

Lance-leaved Goldenrod (*S. graminifolia*) is a common slender-leaved plant that has a branched flat-topped cluster of flower heads. This species, which blooms in August and September, favors damp meadows, stream banks, and roadsides.

Gray Goldenrod (*S. nemoralis*) is a delicate 1.5- to 2-foot-tall plant that grows in scattered clumps. Its delicately hairy stalk has a slender one-sided, slightly curving terminal cluster of tiny yellow flower heads. Long-tapering leaves become progressively smaller up the stalk, and a pair of tiny leaflets grows from the axil of each leaf. This species, which blooms most commonly in September and early October, favors dry meadows, forest openings, and open mountain ridges and summits. Several varieties of goldenrod bear their flowers in slender symmetrical terminal spikes, notably the 1- to 3-foot-tall **Downy Goldenrod** (*S. puberula*), with yellow flowers that bloom from August to October; and the **Silverrod** (*S. bicolor*), which is the only member of this genus to bear white or pale creamy-yellow flowers, which bloom in August and September. (See the **Bog Goldenrod** (*S. uliginosa*) in the Bog Flowers section and **Seaside Goldenrod** (*S. sempervirens*) in the Seaside Flowers section.)

Asters of many species are abundant members of the Sunflower Family, and their blooming is a sure sign that summer is drawing to a close and frosty autumn days are fast approaching. Just a few of Acadia's species are the following:

Flat-topped Aster (*Aster umbellatus*) is a prolific 2- to 7-foot-tall plant. Its 0.5- to 1-inch-wide flowers have 10 to 15 white rays and yellow centers. They are borne in a branched flat-topped terminal cluster. The leaves are narrow and tapered, without serrated margins. This species, which is one of the earliest blooming of this genus—from early August through September, favors a wide variety of habitats, from dry, exposed mountain ledges to meadows, grassy roadsides, and areas of brushy second-growth.

Big-leaved Aster (*A. macrophyllus*) is an abundant 2- to 3-foot-tall plant. Its 1-inch-wide flowers have 10 to 16 light-purple rays and yellow centers. They are borne in a loosely branching terminal cluster. Alternate, tapered leaves have serrated margins; and the 4- to 8-inch-wide lower leaves are roughly heart-shaped and deeply serrated. This species, which blooms from mid-August through September, favors clearings, open woods, and roadsides.

New England Aster (*A. novae-angliae*), which is Acadia's showiest aster, grows from 3- to 6-feet-tall. Its 1- to 2-inch-wide flowers have 35 to 45 rich-purple rays and bright-yellow centers. They are borne in terminal clusters. Numerous alternate 1.5- to 5-inch-long slender leaves clasp the rigid stem. This species, which blooms from August to October, typically grows in extensive clumps and favors damp thickets, meadows, and roadsides.

Calico Aster (*A. lateriflorus*) is a 1- to 5-foot-tall plant. Its very small flowers—barely a half-inch wide—have pale-purple to white rays and deeper purple centers. The narrow tapered 2- to 6-inch-long leaves have a few marginal teeth. This species, which blooms in late summer and early autumn, favors forest openings, meadows, and roadsides.

Whorled Wood Aster (*A. acumiatus*) is a common 1- to 3-foot-tall plant. Its white-rayed flowers are borne on small branching terminal clusters. Sharply toothed long-tapered pointed leaves grow from the stalk in an imperfect whorl. This rather inconspicuous species, which blooms in late summer and early autumn, favors semi-open clearings.

SEASIDE FLOWERS

Beach Pea (*Lathyrus japonicus*), of the Pea Family, is an abundant 1- to 2-foot-tall vine. The 0.75-inch-long pea-like flowers vary from pink to lavender, or a combination of the two. They are borne in long-stemmed clusters. The 1- to 2-inch-long compound leaves are divided into 6 or 12 bristle-tipped oval leaflets. Two arrowhead-shaped stipules grow at the base of each leaf.

New England Aster (deep violet and yellow)

Two-inch-long pods contain 2 tiny peas. Terminal tendrils are used for climbing. This species, which blooms from late May to August, favors the upper shoreline of sandy and rocky beaches of Mount Desert Island and the outer islands.

Silverweed (*Potentilla anserine*), of the Rose Family, is a common 1- to 3-foot-long prostrate plant. A single 0.5- to 1-inch-wide 5-petalled bright-yellow flower is borne at the end of each delicate leafless stalk. The compound basal leaves are up

Whorled Wood Aster (white)

to 1 foot in length. They are borne on stalks without flowers and are divided into a number of narrow-toothed leaflets, which are green above and have silvery hairs beneath. This species, which blooms from June to August, favors the upper shoreline of sandy and rocky beaches and salt marshes.

Hedge Bindweed (*Convolvulus sepium*), of the Morning Glory Family, is an abundant vine. Its 2- to 3-inch-wide funnel-shaped white flowers are often tinged with pink. Grayish-green 2- to 5-inch-long alternate leaves are arrowhead-shaped with blunt basal lobes. This species, which blooms from July to September, favor many shoreline areas.

Seaside Goldenrod (*Solidago sempervirens*), of the Sunflower Family, is a 1- to 5-foot-tall stout-looking plant. Its thick 1- to 6-inch-long narrowly tapering alternate leaves diminish in size up the stalk. The smallest leaves grow among the terminal one-sided cluster of small yellow flower heads. This species, which blooms in August and September, favors the upper shoreline of

rocky and sandy beaches, and tidal inlets including salt marsh habitat of Mount Desert Island and the outer islands. (See other goldenrods under Meadow and Roadside Flowers.)

Seaside Plantain (*Plantago juncoides*), of the Plantain Family, is a common 2- to 8-inch-tall plant. It has long slender upward-sweeping fleshy basal leaves. Tiny grayish flowers, with 4 whitish sepals but no petals, grow in slender compact terminal spikes. This species, which blooms in mid- to late-summer, often grows in the same places as Seaside Goldenrod.

Sea Lavender (*Limonium carolinianum*), of the Leadwort Family, is a common 1- to 2-foot-tall plant. Its many minute pale-purple flowers have 5 spatula-shaped lobes and a funnel-shaped corolla. They line the upper surface of the delicate branches that grow in sprays. Basal 3- to 6-inch-long leaves are broadly tapering, with long-tapered stems. This species, which blooms from late July through September, favors salt marshes and tidal flats.

Ferns

Some of the most gracefully beautiful plants in Acadia are the non-flowering Ferns that reproduce by microscopic spores. These low-growing plants of the northeastern part of North America are small relics of tree ferns that were the dominant plants, along with the Clubmosses and Horsetails, during a warmer, more humid period of Earth's history, roughly 240 to 300 million years ago—long before the appearance of today's dominant coniferous and deciduous, seed-bearing trees. The most common species in Acadia are grouped below according to very general habitats.

MOUNTAIN LEDGES AND ROCKY RAVINES

Common Polypody (*Polypodium vulgare*) is an abundant little evergreen species that grows in colonies on shaded rocky ledges and in boulder-filled woods. Its smooth leathery dark-green fronds may grow to a foot or more in length, but are frequently shorter. The margins of the 10 to 20 pairs of leaflets, which are not divided into subleaflets, are smooth, slightly wavy, or minutely toothed. Toward the upper end of the frond, round reddish-brown spore cases typically form two rows on the undersurface of leaflets.

Rusty Woodsia (*Woodsia ilvensis*) is a coarse little species that grows in stiff erect tufts. The underside of the roughly 6-inch-long pinnately divided frond is covered with silvery fuzz that turns to rusty-brown in dry periods or in autumn. This species favors mountain ledges and crevices.

Christmas Fern (*Polystichum arostichoides*) is a beautifully spreading evergreen fern. Its leathery dark-green fronds are roughly 3 feet long, tapering rapidly from around the middle to the tip. The frond's 20 to 40 pairs of sharp-pointed leaflets, which are not cut into subleaflets, have minutely bristle-toothed margins and a prominent, pointed "ear" or lobe near the base. Spore-bearing fertile fronds grow more rigidly erect and taller than sterile fronds;

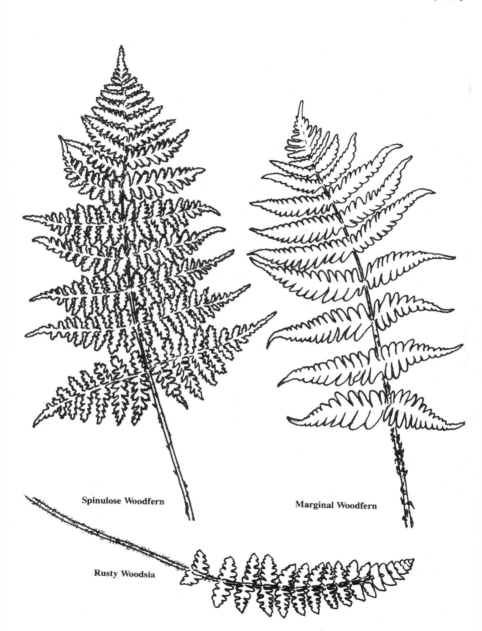

Spinulose Woodfern

Marginal Woodfern

Rusty Woodsia

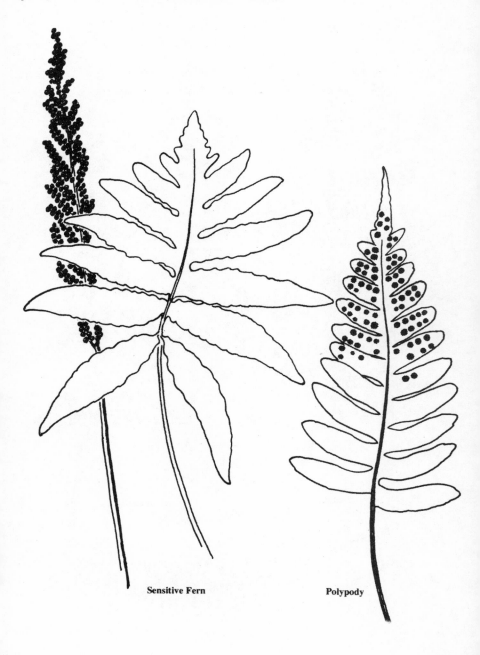

Sensitive Fern   Polypody

and their upper, fertile leaflets are noticeably smaller with a dense covering of spore cases. This species favors rocky shaded woods and ravines.

Marginal Wood (or **Marginal Shield**) **Fern** (*Dryopteris marginalis*) is an attractive hardy evergreen species that grows in gracefully spreading individual clumps. Pinnately divided fronds are typically 1 to 2 feet long. Spore cases are prominent along the undersurface margins of the subleaflets. The stalk is covered with golden-brown scales. This species is common within wooded mountain slopes and rocky ravines.

Long (**Narrow**) **Beech Fern** (*Phegopteris connectilis*) is a common non-evergreen species that has a roughly 1-foot-long triangular-shaped frond. The lowest pair of leaflets typically sweeps downward and somewhat forward, suggestive of scissor blades. From the middle to the tip of the frond, the slender pointed leaflets rapidly diminish in length. Leaflet margins are cut (not quite to the mid-vein) into lobes. The stalk is hairy and scaly. This species favors rich moist rocky ravines. It often provides attractive borders drooping over shaded brooks and rocky streambanks.

Oak Fern (*Gymnocarpium dryopteris*) is a delicate little species that resembles a miniature Bracken. Its 5-inch-long fronds are broadly triangular, dividing into 3 horizontally spreading leaflets. Blunt-pointed subleaflets are divided into blunt lobes. The slightly scaly brittle stem is typically dark at the base. This species favors shady damp rocky habitat, especially along streambanks.

MOIST WOODS

Spinulose Wood Fern (*Dryopteris spinulosa*) is a fairly common delicate lacy-looking species that is usually evergreen, with pinnately divided fronds that generally grow 2 to 3 feet long. This species has a number of confusing variations. On some, for example, the pairs of leaflets are attached to the stem opposite each other; on others, they are noticeably alternate. Both forms are found in Acadia. The spore cases are glandular-shaped and the stem is covered with brown scales. This species favors rich moist woods.

Lady Fern (*Athyrium Filix-femina*) is a common very lacy and showy non-evergreen species, with pinnately divided fronds that are about 2.5 feet long and about 10 inches wide. There are roughly 24 pairs of leaflets, which grow slightly offset from each other along the stalk; and each leaflet has about a dozen subleaflets. Dark-brown spore cases are curved or horseshoe-shaped. This species favors moist semi-shaded woods, but also grows in clearings, meadows, and ravines, and along streams and roadsides.

WET OR SWAMPY WOODS

Crested Fern (*Dryopteris cristata*)
is a tall slender evergreen species.
Its leaflets are widely spaced and often twisted into a horizontal plane,
giving the 1- to 2.5-foot-long frond a
ladder-like appearance. Sub-leaflets
have blunt points and slightly
toothed margins. Kidney-shaped
spore cases, on the undersurface of
the upper leaflets, are midway between the midvein and the edge.
This species favors wet or even
swampy woods.

    Cinnamon Fern (*Osmunda cin-
namomea*) is a common gracefully
arching and coarse non-evergreen
species that grows in circular
clumps. In late spring, several slender fertile fronds appear from the
center of the crown. Their many,
spore-bearing pairs of leaflets are
club-shaped and upward-reaching,
close to the stalk. They are initially

Interrupted Fern

New York Fern

green and mature to cinnamon-brown. After these spore-bearing stalks have dispersed their spores, they quickly wither away. Surrounding the fertile fronds are the outspreading sterile fronds that are about 2 to 5 feet tall. The margins of the roughly 20 leaflets are deeply cut into oblong lobes that are more pointed than are those of the Interrupted Fern. This species favors wet or swampy woods, as well as streambanks and lakeshores.

SWAMPS AND BOGS

Sensitive Fern (*Onoclea sensibilis*) is a very common non-evergreen 1- to 2-foot-tall species that has a wide triangular sterile frond, which has roughly 12 pairs of leaflets. The leaflet margins are either smooth or slightly wavy lobed. The separate fertile spore-bearing frond is about 1 foot tall, with short compact upright branches containing hard bead-like spore cases that mature to dark brown. This species is one of the earliest to die back after the first autumn frost, leaving only the rigid fertile stalk standing. The Sensitive Fern favors boggy areas, streambanks, and other damp habitat.

Royal Fern (*Osmunda regalis*) is a very graceful 2- to 5-foot-tall species that typically forms dense stands. Its large bright-green fronds have leaflets that are actually branches, on which are 6 to 12 oblong and widely spaced subleaflets.

Bright-brown spore-bearing leaflets grow at the upper end of the fertile fronds. This species is common in boggy habitat.

SUNNY OR SEMI-SHADED MEADOWS, DRIER WOODS, THICKETS, AND ROADSIDES

Interrupted Fern (*Osmunda claytoniana*) is an abundant large graceful non-evergreen species. It is easily identified by the distinctive fertile fronds, which usually have 4 or more pairs of small dense spore-bearing leaflets midway up the frond. The spore cases are initially green, maturing to brown, and then soon withering away—leaving a gap in the middle of the frond. The rest of the fertile fronds (below and above the spore-bearing leaflets) and the sterile fronds have numerous pairs of regular leaflets that taper to slightly rounded ends (more rounded than those of Cinnamon Fern). The brown, woolly fiddleheads of the Interrupted Fern are among the earliest to appear in the spring. This species favors a wide variety of relatively dry habitats, including drier woods, forest openings, meadows, and roadsides.

New York Fern (*Thelypteris noveboracensis*) is a common delicate yellowish-green species that typically grows in dense colonies. Its 1- to 2-foot-tall fronds taper distinctly toward *both* ends. Their undersurface is finely hairy; and their slender leaflets, which are cut nearly to the mid-vein by narrowly rounded lobes, are arranged alternately on the stalk. This species favors sunny forest openings.

Hay-scented Fern (*Dennstaedtia punctilobula*) is another common delicate yellowish-green species that typically grows in extensive dense colonies. Its 1.5- to 3-foot-tall fronds are hairy on the lower surface. Leaflets are cut into subleaflets, on the indented margins of which are little cup-like spore coverings that surround tiny fruit dots. The stem is hairy, and brown at the base. The Hay-scented Fern is pleasantly fragrant in late summer; and with the first frost, it quickly turns very pale yellow and russet. This species favors dry sunny openings, meadows, forest edges, and roadsides.

Bracken (*Pteridium aquilinium*) is an abundant coarse species that grows in colonies. Its knee-high horizontally spreading fronds are roughly 3 feet wide and divided into 3 parts. Lower leaflets are cut into subleaflets. Spore-bearing fruit dots are arranged in narrow lines near the leaflet margins, the edges of which are rolled under and covering or partially covering the spores. In early summer, the fronds are initially bright green, but gradually turn darker. In early autumn, they may turn golden-yellow, or with an early frost, will turn brown. This species favors meadows, forest clearings, and roadsides.

Clubmosses are low-growing non-flowering plants that reproduce by microscopic spores. They, and the ferns and horsetails, were tree-sized plants, during a warmer and more humid period of Earth's history roughly 240 to 300 million years ago—long before the appearance of today's dominant coniferous and deciduous seed-bearing trees. The evergreen Clubmosses are not especially abundant in Acadia, but patches of one species or another grow here and there. One group of them has erect, unbranched or simply branched stems:

Shining Clubmoss (*Lycopodium lucidulum*) has erect 6-inch-tall stems that are single or once-branched, with minute slender pointed 6-ranked leaves. Unlike the next species (below), these tiny leaves spread in various directions from the stem, with sections of alternately longer and shorter ones along the stem. Unlike most other clubmosses, this species lacks cylindrical spore-bearing cones. Instead, it has yellowish-orange spore cases that

are attached to the axils of the upper leaves. Erect stems branch from short horizontal stems. This species is fairly common in some of Acadia's shady moist woods and along stream banks.

Stiff (or **Bristly**) **Clubmoss** (*L. annotinum*) typically has erect, unbranched stems that are 6 inches or more in length. Rigid sharp-pointed slender 5-ranked (or more) leaves spread uniformly outward or slightly downward, and are interrupted periodically by annual growth constrictions along the stem. Stalkless cylindrical 1- to 2-inch-long cones are borne at the end of some stems. Unlike the previous species, the upright stems branch from long horizontal runners that are only sparsely covered with leaves. Stiff Clubmoss is relatively common in some areas of Acadia's moist woods.

Staghorn Clubmoss (*L. clavatum*) has erect simply branched 10-inch-tall stems that are thickly covered with narrow, upward-reaching, hair-tipped 10-ranked leaves. Three or more of its slender 2- to 3-inch-

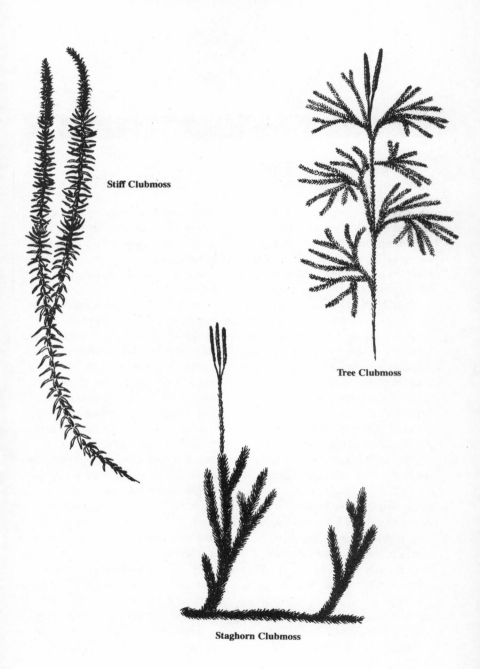

Stiff Clubmoss

Tree Clubmoss

Staghorn Clubmoss

long cones are borne at the end of a stem. The upright stems branch from long creeping above-ground runners that are densely covered with tiny leaves. This species is fairly common in some of Acadia's dry open woods and thickets.

A second group of Clubmosses has miniature-tree-like stems, with branches that are intricately and delicately forked and often twice-forked: **Tree Clubmoss** (or **Ground Pine**) (*L. obscurum* var. *dendroideum*) has erect stems that grow to about 1 foot tall and resemble miniature pine trees. They are forked and re-forked, with a fan-like outer edge of each upward-reaching branch. Densely growing sharply pointed narrow 6- or 8-ranked leaves are either outward-spreading or slightly incurved along the stem. Cylindrical stalkless 1.5-inch-long cones are borne at the top of each stem in erect clusters. The upright stems branch from long underground runners. This species is very common in some areas of Acadia's woods.

Ground Cedar (*L. tristachyum*) has erect bluish-green miniature-tree-like stems that grow to about 1 foot in height. It often forms dense "shag-rug" patches. The lower branches are flattened horizontally and are neatly fan-shaped. Upper forked branches are erect, rather cup-shaped, and flat-topped, with numerous small branches. Minute scale-like 4-ranked leaves resemble those of the Northern White Cedar tree. They grow close together for about half their length, then narrow to a tapered sharp point. The 1- to 2-inch-long cylindrical cones are borne at the end of 3- to 4-inch-long stalks, with 3 or 4 cones on each stalk— looking like a miniature candelabra. The upright stems branch from long runners that are as much as 5 or 6 inches underground. This species grows in some areas of Acadia's open dry woods and clearings.

Running Pine (*L. complanatum*) is quite similar to the previous species, but is less erect, with more open-spreading and shorter upper branches. Minute scale-like 4-ranked leaves grow together for more than half their length and then taper to a slender point. From 2 to 4 cylindrical 1- to 2-inch-long cones are borne at the top of a 3-inch-tall stalk. The upright stems branch from an intricate maze of horizontal runners, which, unlike Ground Cedar, are either on or just beneath the surface of the ground. This species grows occasionally in semi-open woods.

Horsetails

Horsetails, like the ferns and club-mosses, are miniature remnants of what were the world's dominant forms of plants roughly 240 to 300 million years ago. These leafless plants have distinctly different-looking fertile and sterile stalks. Stems and branches consist of hollow, cylindrical, and segmented tubes that are divided at the sheath-covered nodes. Like the Ferns and Clubmosses, these plants reproduce by microscopic spores. Both stems and branches of most Horsetails (also known as Scouring Rushes) carry out the process of photosynthesis, which the leaves of most other plants perform.

Wood Horsetail (*Equisetum sylvaticum*) has fertile stalks that appear first in the spring. They grow to about 8 inches tall and each has a terminal spore-bearing cone. Later, after the spores have been released and the cone has dropped off, these stalks put out intricately branching plumy whorls of flattened green branches that are similar to those of the sterile stalks. The symmetrical delicately forked branches of the sterile stalks are about 6 inches wide and are slightly drooping. This is the most abundant species of Horsetail in Acadia's damp woods and swampy habitat.

Field Horsetail (*E. arvense*) has sterile stalks that are bushier than those of the Wood Horsetail. Their whorled upreaching straight branches are typically not forked. The stout cone-tipped fertile stalk, which soon withers away, is either unbranched or has short whorled branches. There are confusing variations exhibited by the Field Horsetail. This species generally favors open or semi-open habitat.

Mosses

Among the smallest of Acadia's plants are the prolific mosses that often cover the ground and decaying logs. This is a miniature world where a magnifying lens can help you explore their seemingly endless variety. Perhaps the most intriguing and beautiful of Acadia's array of mosses are the **Sphagnums**, known also as peat mosses, which form thick spongy mats in heaths, along banks of sluggish brooks, and in other boggy places. Their color varies among the many species from bright green, as in *Sphagnum palustre*, and yellowish-green, as in *S. pulchrum*; to brownish-yellow, as in *S. papillosum*, and deep red, as in *S. rubellum*. When these mosses are dry, their colors are pale.

The most interesting characteristic of Sphagnums is their ability to absorb many times their weight in water. Large hollow cells, which are filled with air when the plant is dry, absorb moisture through small pores in the cell walls. This moisture moves by capillary action from cell to cell, until the whole plant is saturated like a sponge. The leafy branches make Sphagnums easy to distinguish from all other groups of mosses. The branches at the top of each plant form a characteristically compact rosette. When the ground is thickly covered with one of the reddish species, its rosettes create an especially beautiful pattern.

Hair-cap Moss (*Polytrichum commune*) is quite possibly Acadia's most abundant conspicuous species of moss. It forms soft dark-green carpets in a variety of habitats—most luxuriantly in forest clearings and meadows, as well as along many stretches of Acadia's trails and carriage roads where sunlight reaches the ground. The Hair-cap Moss is named for the long silky "hairs" that grow from the golden calyptra—the veil or hood enclosing the erect spore-capsule (cornuous), which is borne at the end of the 2- to 4-inch-tall stalk (pedicel). In late summer and autumn, when the veil has fallen off, the 4-angled capsule tips to a horizontal or drooping position. Narrow 0.75-inch-long pointed leaves, with minutely serrated edges, grow around the plant's stem. When the plant is wet, these tiny leaves are held at right angles to the stem; but when dry, they are tightly folded against the stem to reduce the loss of moisture. This species grows to as much as 6 inches tall (occasionally to a foot or more). Other species of hair-caps are smaller, such as the common 1- to 4-inch-tall *P. juniperium*. Unlike *P. commune*, the smooth-edged leaves of this species are bright bluish-green, and they are tipped with a short reddish toothed awn.

Pincushion (or **White**) **Moss** (*Leucobryum glaucum*) forms smoothly rounded pale whitish-green "pincushions" in shaded conifer woods. Like the Sphagnums, large hollow cells absorb moisture, causing this plant to become spongy and to turn from almost white to a deeper shade of light grayish-green. Individual plants grow densely together and are from 2 to 6 inches tall.

Dicranums are very common, forming thick yellowish-green or dark-green cushions on the ground, decaying logs, and rocks, typically in moist woods. The leaves are characteristically curved—often all sweeping in one direction, as if blown by the wind. **Broom Moss** (*Dicranum scoparium*) is a conspicuous yellowish-green species, with 2- to 4-inch-tall stems. The glossy scythe-like leaves sweep in one direction. The long curved and cylindrical spore-

capsule is held not quite erect; and the veil is beaked and split along one side. Others in Acadia include *D. rugosum* and *D. spurium*.

Curly-leaved (or **Crisped**) **Ulota** (*Ulota crispa*) is a very common moss that forms small thick yellowish-green mats on the trunks of living trees, often in the company of the flat gray Parmelia lichen. When the moss is dry, its small narrow lance-shaped leaves curl tightly, to conserve moisture. The spore-capsule, which is borne on a short stalk, has striated markings along the sides and a wide mouth-like opening. The yellowish bell-shaped veil is covered with minute hairs.

Plume Moss (*Hypnum crista-castrensis*) is one of Acadia's more elegant mosses, forming thick light-green cushions on decaying logs in cool damp ravines. The individual plant looks much like a miniature feather or fern with pinnate fronds. Stems measure 3 to 5 inches tall, with the upper end held upright. Long-tapering leaves curl tightly to one side.

Red-stemmed Feather Moss (*Hypnum* [or *Calliergonella*] *schreberi*) is a common fern-like moss that forms extensive dense mats on rocks and the ground, in damp shady habitat, such as spruce forests. The 4- to 6-inch-tall reddish stems branch into branchlets; and the bright yellowish-green leaves are relatively broad, with margins that curve inward toward the apex.

Mountain Fern Moss (*Hylo-*

comium proliferum or *Hypnum splendens*) is a really beautiful large olive-green fern-like moss that forms rich carpets on boulders and decaying logs, in cool damp ravines and swampy habitat. Its most obvious characteristic is that each year's new arched frond-like shoot or branch grows from the *middle of the upper side* of the previous year's branch. The individual plant is 4 to 8 inches tall and is delicately branched once or twice.

Shaggy Moss (*Hypnum* [or *Hylocomium*] *triquetrum*) is another large, branching species. It has relatively wide, abruptly narrowing leaves that reach out from reddish stems that are sometimes as much as 5 or 6 inches long, especially in favorably moist woods.

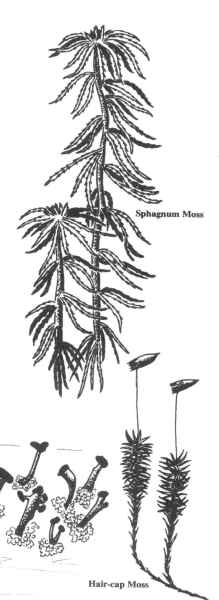

Sphagnum Moss

"British Soldiers" Cladonia

Hair-cap Moss

Fungi

There are many species of mushrooms and other fungi in Acadia. They grow in virtually every conceivable shape, texture, and color. Some are poisonous and some are edible. **(Please Note**: It is highly advisable not to experiment with eating wild mushrooms, unless you really know what you are doing.) Although a few species can be found in the spring and early summer, the best time to look for mushrooms is from mid-summer through early autumn. Their abundance varies greatly from year to year, depending on weather conditions. The best growths typically occur during and following periods of generous rainfall. They reproduce by microscopic-sized spores.

Fungi were previously considered part of the kingdom Plantae (plants). Since 1969, however, most biologists have classified them separately, along with Lichens, as kingdom Fungi.

Fungi include a tremendous variety of mushrooms, shelf fungi, and puffballs—all lacking chlorophyll and thus unable to produce their own food. Instead, they must act either as parasites, deriving food from other living organisms; or as saprophytes, obtaining it from dead organic matter. Fungi are vital in helping to break down and release nutrients, in the cycle toward new life.

The study of mushrooms and other fungi can be a very complex undertaking—with many confusing species that can make identifying them extremely frustrating. In Acadia, there are some relatively distinctive species, or at least some genera that the casual visitor can fairly easily enjoy learning to recognize. Among these are the following:

AGARICALES

Amanitas: This genus is best known for having among its species the most poisonous of Acadia's mushrooms. Its main characteristics are an outer veil around the button stage, which remains as a volva (cuplike enclosure) around the base of

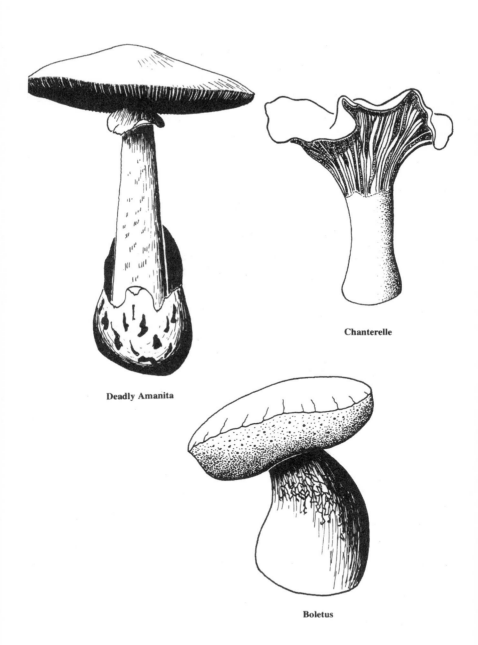

Deadly Amanita

Chanterelle

Boletus

the stem; a thin, membranous ring around the upper part of the stem; gills that do not attach to or fuse with the stem; and white spores.

Fly Amanita (*Amanita muscaria*) is a common poisonous summer species that has a bright orange (or sometimes yellow or white) 3- to 8-inch-wide cap, with a sprinkling of little splotchy white patches that are remnants of the outer veil covering the mushroom's early button stage. The volva, unlike other Amanitas, has two or more ragged scaly bands that circle around and above the bulbous base of the white 4- to 8-inch-tall stem. This species, which typically grows beneath spruces and pines, is somewhat similar to the poisonous **Panther Cap** (*A. pantherina*) that has a brownish cap sprinkled with white veil remnants and that has a striated and knobby margin.

Deadly Amanitas (*A. verna* and *A. virosa*) are similar species of a group of pure-white Amanitas, the toxicity of which is lethal. Their 3- to 5-inch-wide cap lacks any particles of the veil. A membranous ring hangs from near the top of the 4- to 8-inch-tall stem; and a membranous volva, which is frequently hidden underground, surrounds the base of the stem. A similar species, *A. phalloides*, may have either a white or pale-yellow cap. Deadly Amanitas, which can be found virtually any time during the summer and early autumn, typically grow in mixed deciduous-and-coniferous woods.

Leucoagaricuses: Some species of this genus, in superficial ways, resemble Amanitas: white gills that do not reach the stem, a ring around the stem, and the cap's scaly surface, which at first glance may resemble veil particles. These scales, however, are brown particles of a cap covering that breaks into a rough mottled surface as the cap expands. Unlike Amanitas, there is no volva around the bulbous base of the stem. The **Parasol Mushroom** (*Leucoagaricus* or *Lepiota procerus*) is a nonpoisonous species that grows 10 or 12 inches tall. From mid-summer to early autumn, it favors open woods, clearings, and brushy habitat.

Agaricuses: This is another genus with a thin ring around the stem, gills that do not reach the stem, and no volva around the base of the stem. Unlike Amanitas and Leucoagaricuses, the gills are pink or pinkish-red when young, maturing to chocolate-brown. The nonpoisonous 2- to 4-inch-tall **Meadow Mushroom** (*Agaricus campestris*) is probably the best known of this group. It is a late-summer to early-autumn species that grows in meadows and other grassy places.

Coprinuses: This is a genus that typically favors meadows and lawns. The most distinctive species is the **Shaggy Ink Cap** (or **Shaggy Mane**) (*Coprinus comatus*). It has no ring or volva, but the surface of the oblong or cylindrical cap is covered with scattered dark scales (similar to the

Parasol Mushroom). Its cap quickly expands to a bell shape, with whitish fluffy scales and dark striations that split inward from the margin. The gills then drip a black inky fluid that is created by the melting of its black spores—a process, known as autodigestion, which rapidly destroys the mushroom. Shaggy Ink Caps are nonpoisonous, usually grow 7 to 10 inches tall, and can be found in late summer or early autumn.

Cortinariuses: This genus has a vast number of species that are distinguished by having an unusual, cobweb-like veil that extends from the stem to the outer margin of the cap during the early stage of growth. The **Smeared Cortinarius** (*Cortinarius collinitus*) (*collino* means to besmear) is a yellowish-golden-brown mushroom, with a sticky and shiny glutinous coating resembling a thick coat of varnish. Mature gills are pale brown and the spores are ocherous-brown. The cap is 1.5 to 3 inches wide, and the stem is 2 to 4 inches tall. This species, which can be found from late summer to early autumn, typically grows in a mixed coniferous-and-deciduous forest.

Orange Clitocybe (or **Orange** or **False Chanterelle**) (*Clitocybe aurantiaca*) (or sometimes listed as *Cantharellus aurantiacus*) is a bright little mushroom that has narrow, regularly forked, decurrent and up-sweeping orange or yellowish gills and white spores. The 1- to 3-inch-wide cap, which is often brownish-orange, but sometimes grades outward

to pale yellow, is flat or barely concave, with a slightly de-curved margin. The 1- to 2-inch-tall stem is slightly darker than the gills. Although it somewhat resembles the true Chanterelles, the gills of the Orange Clitocybe are neither irregularly forked nor connected with interlacing veins. This species frequently grows on or near decaying conifer logs, and even rarely from a decaying spruce cone.

Tricholomas (*tricholoma* means hair or fringe): The caps of some of the difficult-to-identify species of this genus are covered with minute hairy or fibrous brown scales. There is no ring or volva. An important characteristic is that the gills are notched next to the stem; that is, they are sinuate: the lower edge of the gills suddenly curves upward, just before attaching to the stem. Spores are white. The **Earth-colored Tricholoma** (*Tricholoma terreum*) has a silvery grayish-brown cap that may be either flat or bell-shaped, with a knob (umbo) in the center. The surface of the 1- to 3-inch-wide cap appears to be thinly covered with minute downy scales. The 1- to 2-inch-long stem is whitish and has a fibrous texture. This species can be found even into October. It grows in mixed woods, sometimes beneath spruce trees.

Collybias: Among the species of this genus are some delicate brownish little mushrooms with a slender stem and an in-rolled margin of the cap. They typically grow in large dense clusters or tufts from decaying conifer wood. Such is the late-summer and early-autumn **Tufted Collybia** (*Collybia acervata*) that has a 1- to 2-inch-wide cap and a 2- to 3-inch-tall stem.

Mycenas: Many of the small, brownish species of this genus are similar to the Collybias, except that the margin of the cap is not in-rolled. Some appear like clusters of tiny rounded parasols—conical or bell-shaped, with a minutely toothed margin of the cap. The latter is usually about 0.5 to 1 inch wide. The stem is slender and delicate. In the autumn, many species typically grow on logs and other decaying wood.

Lactariuses and **Russulas** typically have short thick stems, which together with wide caps, give them a squat appearance. Both of these genera (genuses) are brittle and fragile. Species of the Lactarius genus have milky fluid that comes to the surface as tiny drops, if the gills of young plants are cut. Many Lactariuses and some Russulas have concave or even funnel-shaped caps, with upsweeping, decurrent gills and an incurving margin of the cap. **Emetic Russula** (*Russula emetica*) has a bright-red or pinkish-red cap and is one of Acadia's most striking mushrooms. Its cap is slightly furrowed around the margin, and the stem and gills are contrastingly pure white. This late-summer and early-autumn species grows beneath such conifers as the White Pine.

CANTHARELLACEAE

Chanterelles are part of this group, and the best known is the *Cantharellus cibarius*. Its characteristic vase shape is egg-yolk yellow, with an irregularly wavy margin of the cap. The long decurrent gills have thick blunt edges—more like folds than true gills; and they are interconnected with irregularly branched veins. The cap, which matures to a slightly concave shape, is 2 to 4 inches wide. The short thick stem is 2 to 3 inches tall. This mid- to late-summer, nonpoisonous species grows in clusters within open mixed deciduous-and-coniferous woods and clearings.

CLAVARIACEAE

(Branching Coral or Coral-like Fungi)
Clavarias are represented by a number of intricately branching species that vary from pure white to various shades of yellow. Some species, notably the yellowish-tan *Clavaria Formosa* and *C. stricta* of early autumn, are 3 to 4 inches tall, bushy, and contain numerous branches. There are also tiny bright-orange or yellow unbranched club-like species, such as *C. fusiformis*, that appear briefly in early autumn beneath spruce trees.

BOLETACEAE

(The Fleshy Pore Fungi)
Boletes, as a group, are easy to

identify from all other forms of mushrooms, but there are many confusing species that take an expert to tell one from another. There are two basic genera: the *Boletinus* (and *Suillus*)—the Boletus-like; and the true *Boletus*. They both have thick fleshy caps and stems, with a mass of tube openings (instead of gills) on the underside of the cap. Many species are dull colors of brown, yellow, orange, red, or olive. On some species of both genera, the tube openings are distinctly angled, rather than straight. Many species of Boletinus have sticky or slimy caps, but the dark-reddish *Boletinus pictus* is dry, with hairy scales on the cap and a yellowish undersurface of tubes. This latter species is typically found beneath the White Pine. Most Boletes appear from late summer to early autumn and most commonly after a period of rain. They grow under a wide variety of trees, with some species specifically associated with the larch, pine, oak, aspen, and birch.

POLYPORACEAE

(True Pore Fungi)

Shelf (or **Bracket**) **Fungi** are common in Acadia's woods, growing on decaying trees. Their undersurface has tiny pore holes, some of which are not visible without a magnifying lens. Bracket species vary from fleshy to tough and woody. One of the most attractive is the woody fan-shaped gray-and-brown-banded *Fomes fomentarius* that typically grows on decaying birch trees. It is somewhat similar to the **Artist's Fungus** (*F. applanatus*), which has a dark-gray or brown woody upper surface. Both of these prominent species have a clean whitish undersurface that consists of annual layers of spore tubes.

The smaller fan-shaped *Polyporus* (or *Piptoporus*) *betulinus* grows only on decaying birch trees. Its upper surface is light dusky gray, smoothly curving with in-rolled margins; and the undersurface is white. *Polystictus* (or *Corioles*) *versicolor* is a common fan-shaped tough little bracket that seems almost like cork. It has attractive, alternating zones of brown, gray, and yellow; and grows on tree stumps and other decaying wood—frequently forming cascades of sometimes fused, tiered clusters. Another species is a thickly tiered and fused bracket that consists of small creamy-white fans, some of which have a narrow brownish band around the margin. The latter grows on decaying beech trees.

HYDNACEAE

Hydnas (or **Hedgehog Fungi**) are easy to identify from all other fungi, because their undersurface consists of a mass of delicate spines or icicle-like "teeth." Some Hydnas have a cap and stem, such as the reddish-brown *Dentinum repandum*, which has creamy-colored spines and grows in mixed deciduous-and-coniferous woods; and *D. umbilicatum*, a brownish species found in bogs and cedar swamps. Two others of this group grow on deciduous tree trunks: the white and intricately branched **Bear's Head Hydnum** (*Hericium caput-ursi*) and *H. crinaceus*, a large impressive white fungus that has a dense mass of "icicles" hanging from its undersurface.

HELVELLACEAE

Morels (or **Morchellas**) are probably the best-known members of this group. They have unusual elongated brown heads that are variously pitted with a meshwork of holes, giving this mushroom the appearance of a sponge. Unlike so many fungi,

morels are almost always found during the spring, but reports of seeing them in Acadia are infrequent.

PUFFBALL FUNGI

There are various kinds of Puffball Fungi—those strange round or pear-shaped objects that explode in a powdery cloud of spores when they are squeezed. *Lycoperdons* and others are found during the summer and early autumn within a variety of habitats. A very young stage of an *Amanita* may resemble a Puffball, but a cross-section of the latter will reveal uniform flesh, rather than the outline of a developing Amanita mushroom.

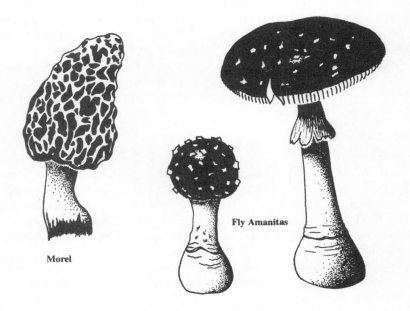

Morel

Fly Amanitas

Lichens

Lichens, which are classified as part of the kingdom Fungi, evolved a unique combination of a fungus and an alga—a symbiotic relationship, in which each performs certain vital functions for the success of the whole.

The fungus, which provides the lichen with its shape and anchors it to a rock, tree, or the ground, has tiny rootlets, which secrete an acid that dissolves minerals. The minerals and moisture are absorbed by the fungus for use by its partner, the alga, which in turn manufactures sugar and other food for the growth of the lichen.

There are three main groups of lichens, all of which are well represented in Acadia:

FRUTICOSE LICHENS

Fruticose (bushy) lichens rise on stalks and prominently include the **Cladonias**, which are coral-like and usually very branching. The scarlet-capped species, such as *Cladonia cristatella*, are often called **British Soldiers**, because their fruiting stalks have bright-red crests. This lichen is commonly found in somewhat sunny locations, growing on decaying logs and stumps. *C. bellidflora* is another red-cap—a striking species with greenish-gray scale-like "leaves" that cover one side of the tall fruiting stalk. There are a number of species of gray goblet-shaped Cladonias, such as *C. pyxidata* and *C. fimbriata*, the latter's "goblets" having fringed margins. The **Pixie-cups**, as they are popularly called, grow commonly in a variety of habitats, including decaying logs and stumps, typically in shady conifer forests.

A number of bushy lichens are called **Reindeer Lichen** (or Reindeer "moss") (*Cladina* and *Cladonia* spp.). They are beautifully branching, such as the prolific *Cladina rangiferina*; and the tall, slender, sparingly branched *Cladonia gracilis*. The more densely and finely branched *Cladina stellaris,* popularly known as **Cloud Lichen**, forms carpets of undulating rounded shapes

that resemble the upper billowy surface of cumulus clouds. Reindeer
and Cloud lichens form extensive
gray mats on many granite ledges of
Acadia's mountain ridges and summits. When they are damp after a period of rain, these lichens are soft
and pliable; but after drying out,
they are brittle and have a pleasant
faintly fragrant odor.

Fruticose lichens also include the
Usneas, also known as **Beard
Lichens**. These are the tangled pale
grayish-green wisps that hang, Span-
ish "moss"-like, from branches of
trees. *Usnea barbarda* is the prolific
pendent stringy-looking lichen that
thrives in spruce trees along such
coastal areas as Otter Point. In summer, the little Parula Warbler builds
its nest in the hair-like threads of
this lichen.

FOLIOSE LICHENS

Foliose (leaf-like) lichens are typically rather flat, forming greenish or
gray mats, with "leafy"-lobed edges.
Prominent among this group are the
following:

Other lichens form flat mats,
varying from gray, bluish-green,
grayish-green, and brownish-green
to dark brown. They are distinctly
branched and lobed. One of the
most common gray species is *Hyp-
ogymnia physodes*, which grows on
twigs and branches, sometimes completely encircling them. The fruiting
bodies in this species are brown or

reddish-brown shallow cups or
shields. *Xanthoparmelia conspersa*
forms beautiful flat rosettes on granite ledges and boulders of the mountains and seashore cliffs.

Umbilicarias are very leaf-like
and not much divided. They are
leathery when moist, but brittle and
crunchy when dry. **Rock Tripe**
(*Umbilicaria mammulata*) is a conspicuous species of lichen. Its single
smooth "leaf" is brown or black on
its upper surface, and hairy and
brownish-black beneath. It is frequently seen scattered across broad
expanses of granite on mountain
summits and ridges. A somewhat
similar-looking lichen, *Lobaria muh-
lenbergii,* differs from the latter
species by having an irregular pattern of shallow pits on its olive-green
upper surface. Both species resemble burnt corn flakes when dry.

Stictas (or **Lobarias**) include the
large **Spotted Lungwort** (*Sticta* [or
Lobarius] *pulmonaria*), which grows
in large mats on tree trunks and
rocks. It seems especially to favor
maple trees, in shady damp stream
valleys, such as along Little Harbor
Brook in The Amphitheater. The
long lobes are leathery, leaf-like, and
dark olive-green when wet; and papery brownish-green when dry. The
upper surface is netted and pock-
marked with shallow depressions;
and the undersurface varies from
pale green to a whitish color.

Xanthoria Lichen is conspicuously bright orange. It forms patches

on seashore rocks just above the spray zone, where it benefits from mineral salts in the air.

CRUSTOSE LICHENS

Crustose (encrusting) lichens are found on rocks and trees. Some of these are so thin that they are barely recognizable as lichens, except for their gray, green, or black color. The **Rhizocarpons** (notably *Rhizocarpon geographicum*), **Lecanoras**, and **Pertusarias** all form flat crusts on rocks and trees. **Cudbear Lichen** (*Ochrolechia tartarea*) forms a thick gray crust with a rough humpy surface and shallow pale-brown spore-bearing cups, with thick whitish margins.

Exploring Acadia's Trails and Carriage Roads

The following hikes provide a cross-section of the virtually limitless possibilities for exploring Acadia National Park. They range from short level walks and easy climbs to strenuous hikes—whatever is your preference. In most instances, loop routes are outlined, since many hikers prefer a different return route. The trail descriptions are divided into two groups: those on the East Side of Mount Desert Island (to the east of Somes Sound) and those on the West Side. All carriage roads are on the island's East Side.

Please Note: The National Park Service has indicated that, over the next 3 to 5 years (between 2007 and 2009), some trail names will likely be changed back to those originally given by the historic trail builders. It is also possible that from time to time in the future a few routing changes will occur.

For each hike, information is provided regarding where to begin and end, distance, average walking time (not including stops for such activities as photography, birdwatching,

and picnicking), and the approximate degree of difficulty—from easy to very steep. If you are a leisurely hiker, you may want to add to the estimates of walking time; or if you stride along at an especially rapid clip, you may find the estimates too high.

Please Note: The National Park Service and Friends of Acadia ask your help in keeping the trails, carriage roads, and mountain summits beautiful by not littering and by carrying out whatever you have carried in. Please stay on trails; and respect other hikers who may be below you, by not tossing rocks from mountain trails. If you take a pet on your walks, please observe the park's leash regulation (they are to be attended and leashed at all times). Removal of plants, animals, and other natural or historic features in the park is prohibited. Fires and camping are allowed only at designated sites; backcountry camping is not permitted. Feeding or approaching too close to wildlife is not only prohibited, but can be dangerous. Bicycles are not permitted on hiking trails or cross-country. Firearms are prohibited in the park (unless they are cased, broken down, or otherwise packed against their use).

EAST SIDE TRAILS

■ **GREAT HEAD LOOP TRAIL**
(map on page 169)

Begin and end: Sand Beach parking area, just off the Park Loop Road.

Distance: About 0.8 of a mile from parking area to highest point on Great Head; or about 1.4 miles around the entire loop.

Time: 20 to 40 minutes to highest point on Great Head; or 1 hour for the loop.

Difficulty: Mostly easy, with a few moderately steep stretches.

From the parking area, follow the flight of stone steps down to Sand Beach and walk across to the opposite end of the beach. There are, incidentally, only two sandy beaches on Mount Desert Island (the other is at Seal Harbor), and this one consists largely of tiny particles of shells.

A path leads up the steep slope from the beach, with a flight of stone steps. At the top of this slope, turn right (an abandoned driveway leads off to the left from an old millstone). The trail very quickly emerges onto the brink of a steeply sloping cliff, from which is an excellent view of Newport Cove, Sand Beach, and The Beehive beyond.

At a trail junction here, you can either go straight, continuing along the shore cliff; or turn left and scramble up to a pitch pine-dotted

rocky ridge. From here, you can look across this peninsula toward Frenchman Bay. The route now bears slightly to the right, descends through a young-growth woods of birches, aspens, and spruces (that has grown up since the 1947 wild-fire); and soon rejoins the shore cliff trail.

As the path continues around the southern end of Great Head, provid-ing views of the Ocean Drive shore and Otter Point, you will find a maze of trails, some leading along the brink of the cliffs, while others head slightly inland. The correct path, which is defined and blazed, leads up to the 145-foot-high summit of Great Head.

From the exposed summit, topped by the ruins of a stone tower, you can look far up Frenchman Bay, toward the clustered Porcupine Is-lands, and across to Egg Rock Light and the long low profile of mainland Schoodic Peninsula. The bedrock of this high point on Great Head is a finely speckled black-and-white vol-canic rock, called diorite. Much of the rock along the trail from the beach is a jumbled shatter-zone of variously intruded and reformed ma-terials (see the Rocks and Land-forms section).

The return trail leads westward from the summit, soon descending into a dense young-growth forest of birches and aspens. At a trail junc-tion, you can either continue straight to an abandoned driveway that will take you back to the millstone; or

turn left, scrambling steeply up and over the central rocky ridge of the peninsula. This latter route soon brings you back to junctions with the earlier outbound trails (turn right at both junctions) that return you to the path down to the beach.

■ THE BEEHIVE TRAIL
(map on page 169)

Begin and end: Sand Beach park-ing area, just off the Park Loop Road.

Distance: 0.5 of a mile by the ledges route; or 0.7 of a mile by the eas-ier route. The two trails provide a 1.2-mile loop.

Time: 30 to 45 minutes from the start of the trail to the summit.

Difficulty: Very steep up the ledges route; moderately steep, with sev-eral steep stretches, on the easier trail.

This trail begins on the opposite side of the Park Loop Road from Sand Beach parking area and heads into a young-growth woods of birches, maples, and aspens. At a junction, in 0.2 of a mile, you can either turn right and climb very steeply 0.3 of a mile up the precipitous pitch pine-dotted ledges of The Beehive (a route not recommended if you have a fear of sheer drop-offs); or you can bear to the left, following a much easier trail up a wooded little valley. At a junction on the latter route (a short distance to the left leads to a small shallow pond, The Bowl), turn

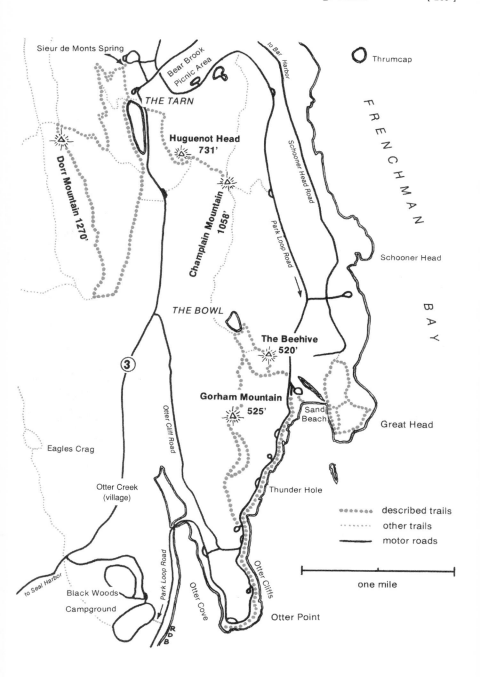

Sieur de Monts Spring

Bear Brook Picnic Area

Thrumcap

THE TARN

Huguenot Head 731'

Dorr Mountain 1270'

Champlain Mountain 1058'

to Bar Harbor

Schooner Head Road

Park Loop Road

F R E N C H M A N

Schooner Head

B A Y

THE BOWL

The Beehive 520'

Gorham Mountain 525'

Sand Beach

Great Head

③

Otter Cliff Road

Eagles Crag

Otter Creek (village)

Thunder Hole

⚫⚫⚫⚫⚫⚫ described trails
· · · · · · · · other trails
——— motor roads

to Seal Harbor

Black Woods Campground

Park Loop Road

P L R

Otter Cove

Otter Cliffs

Otter Point

one mile

right to the 540-foot-high summit of
The Beehive.

For such a short climb, the
panorama from here is extremely rewarding—down to Sand Beach,
Newport Cove, and Great Head; and
beyond to Frenchman Bay, the open
ocean, and along the granite shore
toward Otter Point.

■ OCEAN PATH
(map on page 169)

Begin and end: Sand Beach parking area or Otter Point parking
area. Several other parking areas
along Ocean Drive also offer access onto this trail.

Distance: 2.1 miles each way, between Sand Beach and Otter
Point.

Time: 30 to 45 minutes each way.

Difficulty: Easy.

Even though this trail runs most of
the way right beside the Ocean
Drive section of the Park Loop Road,
it provides one of Acadia's most scenic walks. Beginning at the upper
end of Sand Beach parking area, the
path offers a pitch pine-framed view
of Sand Beach, Newport Cove, and
Great Head. From there, the trail
leads southward just above the sloping fractured pink-granite cliffs and
ledges. Straight ahead, you can see
Otter Point, with its sheer dark cliffs.

About halfway along this shore,
you come to Thunder Hole—a narrow slot in the cliff, where the surf
often slams in with such tremendous

force that it causes a deep booming
sound that is felt as well as heard.
(Be careful to stay a safe distance
when a big sea is running.)

Opposite the Gorham Mountain
parking area, the path reaches a
darkly shaded old-growth forest of
pines and spruces (the 1947 wildfire
stopped at this point). You soon begin a gradual climb through tall
spruce trees, as the trail swings onto
the top of Otter Cliffs. At several
places, there are vistas back north,
along the shore toward Great Head,
with Gorham Mountain and The
Beehive to the left.

At the point where Ocean Drive
briefly divides into two levels, the
trail reaches a spectacular overlook
at the very brink of Otter Point's
high cliffs. The combined fragrances
of the sea, spruce trees, and crowberry often fill the air here. The
sound of crashing surf comes from
below; and a gonging bell-buoy offshore rings its warning to mariners
of a dangerous half-submerged
ledge. Small flocks of sea ducks,
such as eiders and scoters, can frequently be spotted as they ride the
ocean swells. In winter, eiders, most
of them from breeding grounds in
the Arctic, may number in the thousands, as they congregate just beyond the pounding surf.

The final 0.3 of a mile from here
to the tip of Otter Point is especially
beautiful and peaceful. As the path
swings around the curving shore,
Baker Island and the Cranberry Islands come into view. And then, as

you continue around the end of the point, tall spruces frame a magnificent view of Otter Cove, with Cadillac and Dorr mountains rising beyond.

Retracing the path to Sand Beach is hardly less exciting, for there are views and perspectives not noticed before, different lighting effects, and the constant activity at the edge of the sea.

■ GORHAM MOUNTAIN TRAIL
(map on page 169)

Begin and end: At Gorham Mountain parking area (just beyond Thunder Hole), along the Ocean Drive part of the Park Loop Road.

Distance: 1 mile from parking area to Gorham Mountain summit.

Time: 45 minutes to 1 hour to Gorham Mountain summit.

Difficulty: Easy to moderately steep; a few ledges to scramble over.

This trail climbs along the gradually sloping south ridge of Gorham Mountain. Because of the young forest that has grown up since the 1947 wildfire, you soon enjoy views of Frenchman Bay and the open ocean. Picturesque young pitch pines grow on many of the mountain's granite ledges. Other vegetation includes aspens, birches, maples, wild cherries, spruces, sheep laurel, sweetfern, meadowsweet, bracken fern, lowbush blueberry, wine-leaved cinquefoil, mosses, and lichens. In late summer and early autumn, various species of goldenrods and asters bloom along this area. This is likely habitat in which see and hear such birds as towhees, brown thrashers, and catbirds.

As you climb, the panorama widens to the south, across Otter Point with its dark old-growth spruce forest. Four miles beyond is Baker Island, with the low-lying Cranberry Islands to the right of Baker. On a very clear day, you may be able to see Mount Desert Rock on the horizon, about 20 miles at sea. To the east, beyond Newport Cove, Sand Beach, and Great Head, the broad expanse of Frenchman Bay extends across to mainland Schoodic Peninsula. Egg Rock Light is perched on a treeless rock about midway across the mouth of the bay.

At 0.2 of a mile, a trail branches to the right, leading to the base of Cadillac Cliffs, which are apparently ancient sea cliffs and caves (see the Rocks and Landforms section). This latter route rejoins the Gorham Mountain Trail at about 0.3 of a mile farther along. As you continue up Gorham Mountain, the village of Otter Creek comes into view in the valley to the west, with Cadillac Mountain beyond.

From the 525-foot summit of Gorham Mountain, you can continue northward 0.5 of a mile, to a trail junction, from which it is another 0.3 of a mile to the summit of The Beehive; or left from the latter junction to a small shallow pond, The Bowl. (From the pond, it is 1.5 miles up the ridge to the summit of 1,058-foot Champlain Mountain.)

The sound of crashing surf can sometimes be heard on the Gorham Mountain hike; and when a tongue of fog glides silently up Frenchman Bay, there is a special feeling of mystery, as you climb above the rocky shore. Not only is the Gorham trail one of the shorter, easier mountain hikes in Acadia; it can be one of the most rewarding.

■ **BEECHCROFT TRAIL, UP HUGUENOT HEAD AND CHAMPLAIN MOUNTAIN** *(map on page 169)*

Begin and end: Parking area near the north end of The Tarn, on State Route 3.

Distance: 1.2 miles to the summit of Champlain Mountain.

Time: 1 to 1.5 hours to the Champlain summit.

Difficulty: Easy to moderately steep up Huguenot Head; a steep climb on up to the Champlain summit.

The Beechcroft Trail begins on the opposite side (east side) of State Highway 3 from the parking area and enters a young-growth forest of birches, oaks, aspens, and maples. All of this hike is within the area of the 1947 wildfire and is still largely open, providing many views. The trail soon begins a series of switchbacks up the cliffs of Huguenot Head, where stands of picturesque young pitch pines cling to narrow ledges. The pathway itself is skillfully built of stone slabs and steps. There are frequent views of The Tarn below, Dorr Mountain rising steeply beyond, and Great Meadow to the north. In late May and early June, much of the flat marshy expanse of the meadow becomes a flaming pink carpet of rhodora flowers.

As the trail swings around eastward, along the brink of a cliff, you can see the village of Otter Creek to the south and Baker Island beyond. You are now at about the halfway point to the summit of Champlain Mountain. Continuing on the Beechcroft Trail, you soon descend into a small notch between the two summits; and then begin to climb up the steeply sloping granite. There are pitch pine-framed views nearly all the way. (The trail is not as well laid out here as it was on Huguenot Head.)

This approach to Champlain's 1,058-foot-high summit is a favorite because the unobstructed panorama from the summit suddenly confronts you at the climax of the climb. And what a sweeping panorama it is—extending from far up Frenchman Bay, southward across the Porcupine Islands, over to mainland Schoodic Peninsula, and around a broad sweep of the open sea to the Cranberry Islands. Dorr and Cadillac mountains rise boldly to the west.

From the summit, trails lead off to the north and south, along the ridge; the latter leading 1.5 miles down to The Bowl, and on to The Beehive and Gorham Mountain. The very steep Precipice Trail (not recommended if you fear heights and precipitous drop-offs) descends down the mountain's east face, reaching a parking area on the Park Loop Road in 1.4 miles.

■ DORR MOUNTAIN-TARN LOOP TRAIL
(map on page 169)

Begin and end: Sieur de Monts Spring parking area.

Distance: 1.6 miles from Sieur de Monts Spring to Dorr Mountain summit; or 4.9 miles around the entire loop.

Time: 1 to 1.75 hours from Sieur de Monts to the summit; 2.5 to 3.5 hours around the loop.

Difficulty: Very steep and strenuous from Sieur de Monts to the summit; south ridge trail is moderately steep, with a few steep places; the Tarn Trail is level and easy.

From the parking area at Sieur de Monts Spring, follow the paved path around the nature center building, cross a small brook, and turn right, straight by the spring house, onto the Dorr Mountain Trail. This is a beautifully built path that climbs very steeply on long flights of stone steps and slabs. Leaving the shaded woods, you switchback up the precipitous slope, following ledges that provide magnificent views. The

broad expanse of Great Meadow, cut through by a meandering stream, is directly below. Frenchman Bay and the Porcupine Islands become more impressive with every switchback of climbing. Opens stands of pitch pine and oak trees frame many of the views.

At 0.5 of a mile, bear right at a trail junction. (The trail to the left climbs up steeply from The Tarn.) Just beyond this point, views of The Tarn, directly below, begin to open up, as the trail follows pine-and-oak-bordered ledges.

At 1 mile from the start, bear right at another trail junction. (The trail to the left climbs very steeply from just south of The Tarn, by way of the Ladder Trail.) The final third of this route climbs steeply up expanses of sloping granite. At a trail junction just north of the Dorr Mountain summit, turn left. (Other trails lead off to Cadillac and Kebo mountains from the latter junction.)

From the highest point of 1,270-foot Dorr Mountain, the panorama is spectacular. Virtually all of Frenchman Bay is visible, with the mainland Gouldsboro Hills beyond to the northeast; mainland Schoodic Peninsula to the east, beyond the rounded summit of Champlain Mountain; Otter Cove, Baker Island, and the Cranberry Islands to the south and southwest; and the great mass of Cadillac Mountain rising just to the west. If you can spot people walking around on Cadillac's summit, they will help give you a sense of scale to

Acadia's highest mountain.

From the summit, the Dorr Mountain South Ridge Trail gradually descends along exposed lichen-covered granite ledges. Most of the way, you wind through an extremely beautiful open-grown stand of young pitch pines. Be careful, however, to watch for cairns and other trail markers. The village of Otter Creek is visible ahead to the south.

At 1.3 miles from the summit, at the end of the open granite ledges, the trail reaches a junction. (To the right, westward, Canon Brook Trail climbs up and over the south ridge of Cadillac Mountain.) Turn left, descending a short way to a left-hand turn in the trail. From here, the final 2 miles of the loop is level, as it leads north along the base of Dorr Mountain, passing through a long stretch of old-growth deciduous forest. A sluggish stream, to the right of the path, is likely to have been dammed at several places by beavers.

Continuing straight through two trail junctions, you soon come to the swampy southern end of The Tarn. There is then some fairly easy rock-hopping, as the trail follows the western edge of the pond and the base of the boulder-strewn talus slope. From The Tarn back to Sieur de Monts Spring, the path winds pleasantly through another stretch of deciduous woods.

■ CADILLAC MOUNTAIN SOUTH RIDGE TRAIL: SUMMIT TO THE FEATHERBED
(map on page 175)

Begin and end: At Cadillac Mountain summit parking area.
Distance: 1.2 miles each way.
Time: 2 to 2.5 hours round trip.
Difficulty: Mostly easy on gently sloping rock; moderately steep into a little notch, called The Featherbed.

To the east, south, and west, the open South Ridge of Mount Desert Island's highest mountain provides sweeping panoramas. The trail begins at the 1,530-foot-high Cadillac Mountain summit, among low-growing wind-swept balsam firs and red spruces, and soon comes to a sharp curve in the Cadillac Summit Road. (For a slightly shorter hike on the South Ridge trail, you can begin at the Sunset parking area, just across the road at this curve.)

The trail gradually descends from here, passing through a junction with the West Face Trail (the latter drops steeply 0.9 of a mile to Bubble Pond), and heads onto a broad and barren expanse of the South Ridge. Scattered here and there are granite boulders that are of a distinctly lighter color, with different and larger crystalline character, than the mountain ridge's bedrock. These boulders are known as glacial erratics—chunks of rock that were carried along for many miles by the gla-

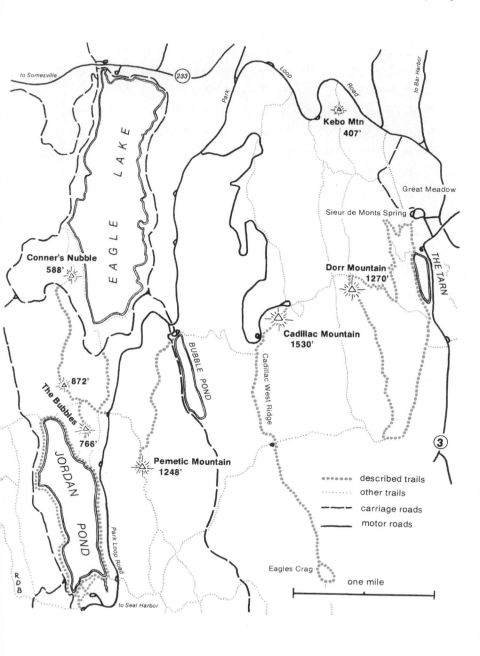

to Somesville

233

Park

Loop

Road

to Bar Harbor

Kebo Mtn
407'

Great Meadow

Sieur de Monts Spring

THE TARN

Conner's Nubble
588'

E A G L E   L A K E

Dorr Mountain
1270'

BUBBLE   POND

Cadillac Mountain
1530'

872'

Cadillac West Ridge

The Bubbles

JORDAN   POND

766'

Pemetic Mountain
1248'

3

••••••• described trails

············· other trails

– – – carriage roads

——— motor roads

Park Loop Road

R
D
B

Eagles Crag

one mile

to Seal Harbor

cial ice that covered this region thousands of years ago (see the Rocks and Landforms section).

In about a mile from the summit, the cairn-marked route reaches the brink of a cliff that drops into a notch in the ridge. Much of the year, the low part of this hidden valley, known as The Featherbed, is a reed-filled marsh; but after sufficient rainfall, the marsh becomes a little pond. A grove of pitch pines borders part of the pond's rocky shore. From here, you can return to the summit of Cadillac Mountain.

A trail junction is located at The Featherbed. (Canon Brook Trail leads to the eastward, dropping steeply along Canon Brook and joining the Dorr Mountain South Ridge Trail and The Tarn Trail; and the Pond Trail leads westward, ending at the south end of Jordan Pond, in just under 2 miles.) From this junction, the Cadillac Mountain South Ridge Trail continues southward, climbing out of The Featherbed notch and descending easily along a granite ridge that affords a sweeping view of the ocean. This route soon passes through a grove of the short-needled jack pines (rare on Mount Desert Island, but more common on mainland Schoodic Peninsula) and then an extensive picturesque open stand of pitch pines. At about 1.2 miles from the notch, a short loop trail branches to the left and leads to Eagle Crag. This rocky promontory overlooks the village of Otter Creek. From this point, it is another mile through a mixed coniferous-and-deciduous forest to State Highway 3, and then a short way to the national park's Blackwoods Campground. Many summer campers enjoy an exhilarating day's round trip on this 3.5-mile-long trail up to the Cadillac Mountain summit, taking anywhere from 4 to 6 hours up and back.

■ **BUBBLE POND-PEMETIC MOUNTAIN TRAIL**
(map on page 175)

Begin and end: Parking area near the north end of Bubble Pond.

Distance: 1.2 miles from the pond to Pemetic Mountain summit; 4.4 miles for the loop.

Time: 1 to 1.5 hours from the pond to the summit.

Difficulty: Some steep, rocky stretches; mostly moderately steep.

This trail almost immediately enters a dark cathedral-like red spruce forest, and begins a steep climb up the north end of Pemetic Mountain. Be especially careful to watch for trail markers along this part of the trail. In late May and June, this is a likely area in which to hear the flute-like song of the Hermit Thrush.

After a rapid rise in elevation, an opening in the forest affords a glimpse northward toward Eagle Lake and Aunt Betty Pond. The trail soon emerges onto open granite ledges, along the eastern brink of the mountain. Far below lies the narrow ribbon of Bubble Pond, hemmed in between Cadillac and Pemetic mountains. To the south is the first view of the open ocean.

The trail continues upward less steeply, dipping occasionally into a secluded shady little ravine, where the quiet hiker may happen to see a deer. Where the route emerges onto the open rocky summit, the Bubbles-Pemetic Trail branches to the right and plunges very steeply down to the Bubbles-Pemetic parking area, on the Park Loop Road. From this trail junction, it is only a short way to the highest point of 1,248-foot-high Pemetic Mountain. The view far down to Jordan Pond, across to the Jordan Cliffs and Penobscot Mountain, and southward to the island-dotted sea is a great reward for this invigorating climb.

From the summit, a trail descends along Pemetic's south ridge. Although it is a long way around, you can follow this route, instead of returning the way you have climbed. At 0.9 of a mile from the summit, just before the trail enters the forest, turn left at the junction and follow this trail down a steep route that quickly descends to its junction with the Pond Trail. Turn left and follow this route that descends eastward a short distance through a dense forest, until you come to a carriage road. Turn left and follow this road northward through an old-growth deciduous forest and along the west shore of Bubble Pond, until you

reach the starting point of this hike, near the north end of the pond.

■ SOUTH BUBBLE TRAIL AND NORTH BUBBLE LOOP
(map on page 175)

Begin and end: The second of two Bubbles parking areas, as you drive toward Bar Harbor, at 1.6 miles north of the Jordan Pond House, on the Park Loop Road; or 1 mile from Bubble Pond, driving from Bar Harbor.

Distance: About 0.7 of a mile from the parking area to the South Bubble summit; or about 2.7 miles around the North Bubble Loop, excluding the short South Bubble spur trail.

Time: 15 to 25 minutes to the South Bubble summit; or 1 to 1.5 hours around the North Bubble Loop.

Difficulty: Except for a couple of steep places, these two routes are only moderately steep.

The trail to the Bubbles heads into a heavily forested valley between Pemetic Mountain and the Bubbles and soon crosses the Jordan Pond Carry Trail that runs between Eagle Lake and Jordan Pond. Continue straight, climbing gradually through the forest of old-growth beeches, birches, and maples. Partway up a short steep slope, the trail comes to a junction: South Bubble to the left; North Bubble to the right.

If you are heading for the South Bubble, continue up the short steep slope, soon reaching another trail junction in the low saddle between the Bubbles. Straight ahead is a trail that descends steeply to the north shore of Jordan Pond; and to the left is a gradual moderately steep climb that will take you in 0.3 of a mile to the exposed rocky summit of 766-foot-high South Bubble. Just a few yards to the left of the summit, as you face toward Jordan Pond, rests a huge boulder, known as a glacial erratic, which appears to be precariously perched on the east shoulder of the mountain. A marked, blazed path leads to the erratic, which was transported here thousands of years ago by the continental glacier that spread over this region of North America (see the Rocks and Landforms section).

Follow the trail a few yards south of the high point of the South Bubble for a spectacular view down the length of Jordan Pond, with the ocean and the Cranberry Islands beyond. Pemetic Mountain rises to the left; and the Jordan Cliffs of Penobscot Mountain rise to the right. This trail drops off the steep south end of the South Bubble and joins the Jordan Pond Shore Path.

To reach the North Bubble, retrace your steps to the junction in the saddle and then continue partway down the steep slope to the North Bubble Trail junction. Turn left, passing first through a short stretch of young-growth birch woods and then climbing up a briefly steep rocky section. As this path winds up the exposed ledges, grand views open in nearly every direction: Penobscot and Sargent mountains to the west; Cadillac and Pemetic mountains to the east; Jordan Pond and the island-dotted ocean to the south; and Eagle Lake to the north.

From the 872-foot-high North Bubble summit, the trail continues northward, descending gradually along the mountain's northern ridge. Along some stretches of the trail (watch for trail markers) you follow exposed granite ledges near the brink of sheer bluffs on the east side of the ridge. The views down the length of Eagle Lake and across to Cadillac Mountain are very impressive from here.

In about 0.8 of a mile (20 to 25 minutes) from the North Bubble summit, the trail drops into a short stretch of dense deciduous woods and reaches a carriage road. (The North Bubble Trail continues across the road, climbs the 588-foot-high summit of Conner's Nubble, from which there are additional sweeping views of Eagle Lake, and descends to the lakeshore.) To proceed on the North Bubble Loop, turn right onto the carriage road and follow it down a long grade and into a deep forest. In 0.7 of a mile (10 to 15 minutes) the carriage road reaches the Jordan Pond Carry Trail. Turn right onto the trail and follow this shaded (and sometimes muddy) route, as it climbs gradually through a forest of hemlocks and beeches, and brings you back to the initial trail junction of the loop hike. Turn left to return to the parking area.

■ JORDAN POND TRAIL
(map on page 175)

Begin and end: Penobscot parking area, just beyond the Jordan Pond House, on the Park Loop Road, driving toward Bar Harbor.
Distance: 3.3 miles.
Time: 1 to 2 hours.
Difficulty: Easy and level.

This delightful path closely follows the shore of Jordan Pond and is one of the favorite hikes for many park visitors. Circling clockwise and beginning near the Jordan Pond House: After crossing over Jordan Stream that flows from the pond, you follow the winding west shore along the edge of a dense spruce forest and then beneath the Penobscot Mountain's Jordan Cliffs and the talus slope of boulders that have fallen from the cliffs. There are beautiful views across the pond of Pemetic Mountain, rising steeply from the opposite shore, and the Bubbles at the north end. In late spring and early summer, thrushes, warblers, and the winter wren typically fill the dark forest with melodious songs. You may be fortunate to spot a common loon or family of mergansers on the pond.

Around the north end, the path crosses the mouth of a stream. From here you enter a stretch of young-growth forest along a boulder-strewn talus at the base of the Bubbles. The 1947 wildfire burned over the Bubbles and stopped at the north end of Jordan Pond. Along the east side of the pond, the path again enters a stretch of old-growth forest, with birches, oaks, maples, and spruces. The view across the pond of Jordan Cliffs is a fitting climax to this hike. Shortly before returning to the parking area, a series of stepping stones carries the path across a small cove where sweetgale and other bog plants can be seen. This path is equally enjoyable when taken counter-clockwise around the pond.

■ PENOBSCOT AND SARGENT MOUNTAIN SUMMITS, BY WAY OF JORDAN RIDGE
(map on page 180)

Begin and end: Parking area, just northeast of the Jordan Pond House.
Distance: 1.5 miles from the Jordan Pond House to Penobscot Mountain summit; and about 1 mile farther to Sargent Mountain summit.
Time: 1 to 1.5 hours to Penobscot summit; and about 2 hours from the parking area to Sargent summit.
Difficulty: Easy to moderately steep, with one very steep section up the cliffs of Jordan Ridge.

From the west side of the Jordan Pond House (opposite the front entrance), the recently renamed Spring

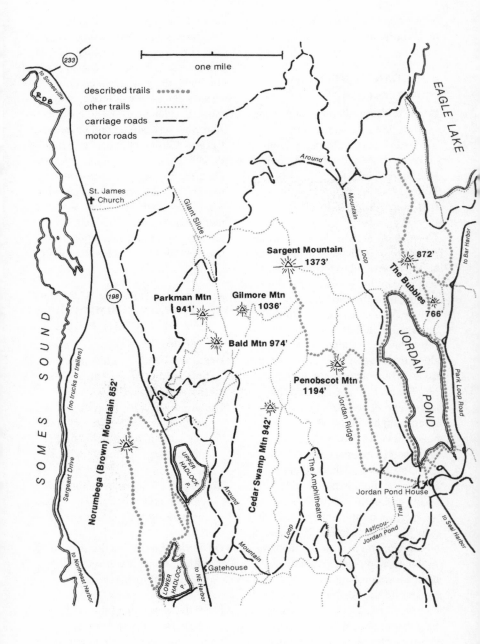

Trail (formerly Penobscot Mountain Trail) leads down the slope, crosses a carriage road and Jordan Stream, and enters a stretch of forest where thrushes, warblers, and the winter wren often sing in late spring and early summer. At about 0.4 of a mile, bear left at a junction (Jordan Cliffs Trail branches to the right). After the Spring Trail climbs a steep rocky embankment and crosses another carriage road, it begins to switch-back steeply up the cliffs of Jordan Ridge, following ledges and squeez-ing through a narrow slot. Beautiful tree-framed views immediately open eastward toward Jordan Pond and Pemetic Mountain.

After this steep stretch, the trail suddenly emerges onto the top of Jordan Ridge and joins the Penob-scot Mountain Trail. The latter trail, which runs the entire length of Jor-dan Ridge, climbs gradually north-ward across expanses of exposed granite. Shallow depressions in the rock are filled with miniature natural gardens of such plants as Labrador tea, sheep laurel, chokeberry, moun-tain sandwort, wine-leaved cinque-foil, lowbush blueberry, huckle-berry, ground juniper, and low-growing birches, alders, and spruces. There are unobstructed views: eastward to Jordan Pond, the Bubbles, and Pemetic Mountain; southward to little Long Pond and the island-dotted ocean; and west-ward to The Amphitheater (a small valley below Jordan Ridge) and mountains beyond. Near Penobscot

summit, the cairn-marked route passes a small pond nestled beneath a fractured granite wall. A species of sedge, called cotton grass, with long, silky white bristles, grows around the edge of this pool.

From Penobscot's 1,194-foot-high summit, Eagle Lake, Cadillac Moun-tain, and the nearby summit of Sar-gent Mountain are included in the spectacular panorama. From this rocky height, a trail descends to a forested saddle between Penobscot and Sargent mountains. Just before the trail climbs back out of the trees toward Sargent's summit, it passes Sargent Mountain Pond (about 0.25 of a mile from Penobscot's summit). This little wilderness lake is ringed around with spruce trees and partly covered with water lily pads. From this tranquil spot, the trail gradually climbs for about 0.75 of a mile, crossing open granite ledges to the 1,373-foot-high summit of Sargent Mountain—the island's second high-est point.

■ **JORDAN CLIFFS TRAIL**
(map on page 180)

Begin and end: Parking area, just northeast of the Jordan Pond House.
Distance: Just under 1.7 miles to Penobscot Mountain summit.
Time: 1.5 to 2 hours.
Difficulty: Moderately steep, with tricky footing along narrow ledges. *Please Note:* Jordan Cliffs Trail has been closed during the

spring and summer for the past few years, because of nesting peregrine falcons. Also, if you do not like precipitous places, you may wish to avoid this trail and take the previously scribed route instead.

As in the previous description, begin on the Spring Trail just west of the Jordan Pond House, cross Jordan Stream, and proceed into the forest. At 0.4 of a mile, turn right at the trail junction. After crossing a carriage road, Jordan Cliffs Trail climbs gradually among spruces and across lichen-covered granite.

In just under a mile from the start, the trail takes you along the sheer cliffs. At times, it follows narrow ledges that afford an exciting panorama of Jordan Pond directly below, and Pemetic Mountain and the Bubbles rising beyond. Delicate blue harebell flowers may be blooming from narrow crevices in the cliffs. Or you may find a handful of ripe blueberries, as you carefully maneuver from ledge to ledge.

Toward the end of this trail, iron ladders and handrails, set in the rock, help you up a steep stretch of cliff. A bit more of a climb leads to Penobscot Mountain's 1,194-foot-high summit. From here you may continue a mile farther to the summit of Sargent Mountain and/or return southward by way of the Penobscot Mountain Trail atop Jordan Ridge, enjoying unobstructed views

as you gradually descend; and returning by way of the Spring Trail.

■ NORUMBEGA (BROWN) MOUNTAIN TRAIL; OR NORUMBEGA-LOWER HADLOCK POND LOOP TRAIL
(map on page 180)

Begin and end: At Route 198 parking area, just up the hill from and on the opposite side of State Highway 198 from Upper Hadlock Pond.

Distance: 0.5 of a mile from parking area to Norumbega summit; or a 2.5-mile loop, continuing down the south ridge to Lower Hadlock Pond, upstream along Hadlock Brook, and back to the parking area.

Time: 25 to 45 minutes up the trail to the summit; or 1.5 to 2 hours for the complete loop.

Difficulty: The Norumbega Mountain Trail is very steep, until you reach the upper, more gently sloping ledges. The rest of the loop trail is only moderately steep.

The Norumbega (Brown) Mountain Trail leads into a dark spruce forest and immediately begins a very steep climb, with switchbacks up the cliffs and steep ledges. Soon there are a few spruce-framed vistas back down to Upper Hadlock Pond. In 15 to 25 minutes, this challenging climb levels off to an easier route. From here to the highest point of the 852-foot-high summit of Norumbega Mountain, the trail winds through delightful, open groves of pitch pines, red spruces, and an occasional jack pine. Low growths of Labrador tea, rhodora, lowbush blueberry, and ground juniper border expanses of lichen-covered granite.

It is difficult to find good views from the mostly forested summit of Norumbega, but there are a few open ledges, from which you have impressive views to the west, down to Valley Cove of Somes Sound, with Acadia, St. Sauveur, and Western Mountain rising beyond; to the northwest, up Somes Sound to Somesville; to the northeast, toward Sargent Mountain; and southward, to boat-filled Northeast Harbor and the island-dotted ocean beyond. Some of the best of these views can be enjoyed from rocky outcrops a short way south of the summit marker.

If you hike the whole loop trail, rather than returning down the Norumbega Mountain Trail, continue by way of the mountain's south ridge. This 1.1-mile stretch, from the summit to the shore of Lower Hadlock Pond, descends gradually through a beautiful, fragrant mixed conifer forest of red spruces and red, white, and pitch pines.

Turn left at the trail junction near the lakeshore and follow the shore path to where Hadlock Brook cascades down the rocks into the pond.

From here, follow the brook upstream (a loop trail around Lower Hadlock Pond crosses the brook, but keep straight along the stream), until you reach Highway 198. Turn left, following the shoulder of the road for a short distance to a trail sign. From here, the trail winds a short way through the forest, bringing you back to the Route 198 parking area.

CARRIAGE ROADS

■ WITCH HOLE CARRIAGE ROAD LOOP
(map on page 185)

Begin and end: Duck Brook Bridge (between Duck Brook Road and the Witch Hole Loop Carriage Road).
Distance: just under 3.5 miles.
Time: 1.25 to 2 hours.
Difficulty: Easy.

This mostly level loop (with only two or three easy grades) circles through a young-growth deciduous forest of oaks, maples, birches, and aspens. If you go counterclockwise around this loop, keep bearing left at all the road junctions, until you return to Duck Brook Bridge. Witch Hole Pond, at the northwest corner of this route, is the largest expanse of water along the way; and there are also several beaver ponds. (At Halfmoon Pond, a spur road leads a short distance to the Breakneck

Ponds and reaches the north end of Eagle Lake and State Highway 233 in 1.2 miles.)

Witch Hole loop and the adjoining shorter Paradise Hill loop, to the north, are among the best maintained stretches of carriage road for bicycling. The Paradise Hill loop can also be reached by way of a short trail that begins at the north end of the parking area at Acadia National Park's visitor center.

■ BREAKNECK PONDS CARRIAGE ROAD
(map on page 185)

Begin and end: Parking area at the north end of Eagle Lake, on the north side (right side from Bar Harbor) of State Highway 233.

Distance: About 0.7 of a mile from parking area to the ponds.

Time: 15 to 25 minutes from parking area to the ponds.

Difficulty: Easy and level.

This short, level walk, northward from where State Highway 233 spans the carriage road on a Gothic-arch stone bridge, leads you through a stretch of young-growth forest. After a short walk, the ponds (which are end-to-end and at high water become virtually a single pond) are on the left side of the road. From here, you can continue on to the Witch Hole carriage road loop (see the previous description) or return to the parking area. This route is well maintained for bicycling.

■ EAGLE LAKE (AROUND LAKE) CARRIAGE ROAD LOOP
(map on page 175)

Begin and end: A parking area on the north side (right side from Bar Harbor) of State Highway 233, across from the north end of Eagle Lake.

Distance: 6 miles.

Time: 2 to 3 hours.

Difficulty: Easy, with only one moderate upgrade where the road swings around Conner's Nubble.

This loop is equally delightful in either direction, but the following description begins at the north end of Eagle Lake and runs counterclockwise. From the parking area, follow the carriage road under the Gothic-arch stone bridge and keep straight (south) at two carriage road junctions (the first forks to the left and loops clockwise around the lake; the second forks to the right and goes to Aunt Betty Pond). The road soon leads through a long stretch of oak forest, with Eagle Lake visible to the left through the screen of trees.

The carriage road next swings away from the lake and winds on a gradual upgrade through an extensive forest of beech trees. At a junction, after this climb, bear to the left. After curving around Conner's Nubble and crossing the North Bubble Trail (North Bubble to the right and Conner's Nubble to the left), you begin a long downgrade and shortly

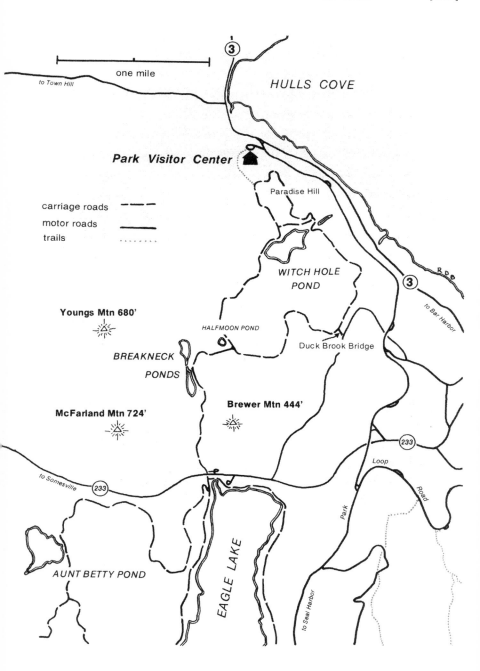

cross the Jordan Pond Carry Trail, which runs between Eagle Lake and Jordan Pond. As you wind through an old-growth deciduous-and-coniferous forest, the south end of the lake is just a few hundreds yards to the left.

Keep to the left at the next road junction (the carriage road forking to the right leads 0.6 of a mile up to Bubble Pond). The loop road now goes north along but mostly out of sight of Eagle Lake's east shore. This long stretch takes you through a variety of habitat—tall pines, spruces, and hemlocks; shady beech, birch, and maple woods; and open blueberry clearings.

As the carriage road curves around the northeast corner of the lake and follows its north shore, there are frequent views across and southward up the length of the lake. My personal favorite vista is from a small cove at the northwest corner of Eagle Lake, where a small grove of pines on a point frames the view of Pemetic Mountain in the distance.

The Eagle Lake loop is a popular stretch of carriage road for bicycling. The roadbed is well maintained. *Note:* You can also hike or bicycle this loop, beginning at the Bubble Pond parking area. Total distance: 7.5 miles.

■ BUBBLE POND CARRIAGE ROAD
(map on page 175)

Begin and end: Parking area near the north end of Bubble Pond, just off the Park Loop Road.
Distance: About 0.7 of a mile each way, along the pond shore.
Time: 15 to 20 minutes each way.
Difficulty: Easy.

This is a delightful short walk on the carriage road that follows the west shore of Bubble Pond. The west face of Cadillac Mountain rises steeply from the opposite shore of this narrow pond; and Pemetic Mountain, to the west, rises abruptly above the carriage road. At both the north and south ends of the pond, you can see the U-shaped valley that was sculpted thousands of years ago by glacial ice (see the Rocks and Landforms section).

Beyond this short walk to the south end of Bubble Pond, the carriage road leads through old-growth deciduous forest (predominantly of beech and birch trees); and continues on south toward Day Mountain. It eventually winds around Wildwood Stables and crosses the Park Loop Road at the gatehouse, just south of the Jordan Pond House.

Also from the parking area near the north end of Bubble Pond, you can follow the carriage road northward, as it descends through a stand of old-growth hemlock trees. In 0.6 of a mile, this road reaches the southeast corner of the Eagle Lake (Around Lake) Carriage Road Loop (see the previous description).

■ AUNT BETTY POND
CARRIAGE ROAD LOOP
(map on page 185)

Begin and end: Parking area on the north side (right side from Bar Harbor), across from the north end of Eagle Lake.
Distance: 6.4 miles.
Time: 2.25 to 3 hours.
Difficulty: Easy, with a moderate upgrade in one stretch.

From the parking area, follow the carriage road under the Gothic-arch stone bridge and keep straight (south) at the first junction. At the second junction, you can decide whether to go counterclockwise or clockwise around the Aunt Betty Pond Loop. For the shortest route to the pond from here and the counterclockwise direction of this description, turn right.

This pleasant route winds first through a stretch of old-growth mixed forest and then emerges into more open young-growth, where birches and aspens are predominant. In roughly 45 minutes to an hour from the start, you round a bend to Aunt Betty Pond—an attractive shallow body of water that is framed by pines and spruces. Marshy borders provide habitat for frogs, painted turtles, red-winged blackbirds, and marsh wrens. To the south rises the rounded form of Sargent Mountain.

From the pond, the carriage road leads southward, soon reaching a road junction. (The right fork leads through the gap between Parkman and Norumbega mountains.) To continue on the Aunt Betty Pond loop, bear left. You will soon begin a gradual climb that ends by crossing a moss-bordered brook a half-dozen times, on a series of small bridges.

At the junction with the Around Mountain Carriage Road Loop (see description below), turn left and then immediately left again, as you pass through a dark cathedral-like grove of tall red spruces. A short distance farther brings you to the junction with the Eagle Lake (Around Lake) Carriage Road Loop (see previous description). Turn left (north) and you will soon enter a long stretch of beech forest, as the road gradually descends and nears the west shore of Eagle Lake. For much of the distance northward along the lakeshore, the road passes through a semi-open stretch of red oaks, before returning to the original Aunt Betty Pond loop junction. This is a delightful loop, with its long gradual grades, for bicycle touring; and is also popular for cross-country skiing in winter.

■ AROUND MOUNTAIN
CARRIAGE ROAD LOOP
(map on page 180)

Begin and end: Parking area, just beyond the Jordan Pond House, to the left of the Park Loop Road as you drive toward Bar Harbor.
Distance: just under 12 miles.
Time: 4 to 5.5 hours.
Difficulty: Generally easy, except for

a moderate upgrade around the northern flank of Sargent Mountain.

From the parking area, just to the northeast of the Jordan Pond House, walk to the west side of the Jordan Pond House and follow a signed trail that leads down to the carriage road, where it crosses Jordan Stream on a small stone bridge. Turn right (north) and continue a short distance to a junction with the Around Mountain Carriage Road Loop. At this point, you can hike either clockwise or counterclockwise. Either way is outstanding. The following description proceeds counterclockwise.

Continuing straight ahead (north), you pass through a long stretch of old-growth spruce forest and then emerge onto a steep boulder-covered talus slope beneath Jordan Cliffs. Below, the broad expanse of Jordan Pond extends across to the base of Pemetic Mountain and the Bubbles. From this beautiful panorama, the carriage road proceeds northward, crosses Deer Brook, which produces an impressive cascade after sufficiently heavy recent rainfall, and passes through a mixed deciduous-and-coniferous forest.

Bearing left at each of two road junctions, the Around Mountain route begins its gradual climb through young-growth forest, as it ascends the northern flank of Sargent Mountain. After crossing a stone bridge that spans Chasm Brook, the road begins a series of switchbacks that provide increasingly broad views of the northern part of Mount Desert Island; Aunt Betty Pond below; Cadillac Mountain and Eagle Lake to the east; and Somes Sound to the west.

As this highest part of the carriage road system swings southward around Sargent Mountain, it soon brings you to a spectacularly scenic stretch, where the road was carved into the steep northwestern slope of Parkman Mountain. At a few places here, pines frame the view of Somes Sound and Norumbega (Brown) Mountain.

After the road curves between Parkman and Norumbega mountains, you reach a road junction. (The sharp-right turn leads down to the lower carriage road in Upper Hadlock valley.) To continue on the Around Mountain loop, go straight at this junction. You will soon get a glimpse now and then of Upper Hadlock Pond, as the road swings into the head of Upper Hadlock valley and crosses two tributaries of Hadlock Brook, on a pair of stone bridges. From one of these bridges, you can pause and enjoy the sight and sound of Acadia's highest waterfall (assuming there has been sufficiently heavy recent rainfall), as it plunges about 30 feet from the brink of a sheer cliff and tumbles in spray below.

From here, the Around Mountain route leads south, bears left at a road junction (to the right, it is a short way to the Brown Mountain Gatehouse, adjacent to State Highway 198), then swings around the end of Cedar Swamp Mountain and leads northward into The Amphitheater. At the head of this sheltered little valley, the carriage road crosses Little Harbor Brook on a curving stone bridge. This bridge affords a view of the hemlock-shaded stream and a waterfall that is especially beautiful after a period of sufficiently heavy rainfall. As the road curves and heads southward, there is a stretch of sloping granite ledges, where stately red pines and white pines grow, along with lowbush blueberry, sheep laurel, and ground juniper. At a junction, bear left, as the road swings around the southern end of Penobscot Mountain's Jordan Ridge. In a few more minutes, you will return to the first road junction of the loop hike. Turn right, returning to the south end of Jordan Pond.

Note: The entire Around Mountain Carriage Road Loop can be a really long, tiring excursion, especially if you not in condition. There are segments of this loop, however, that make very enjoyable shorter walks—two of which are the following:

■ **AMPHITHEATER CARRIAGE ROAD LOOP**
(map on page 180)

Begin and end: Parking area, just northeast of the Jordan Pond House. (You can also access this

loop from the Brown Mountain Gatehouse, just south of Upper Hadlock Pond, on State Highway 198. Distance and time would be slightly less.)

Distance: 5.3 miles; or 4.8 miles, returning by way of the Asticou-Jordan Pond Trail.
Time: 1.75 to 2.5 hours.
Difficulty: Easy.

Begin, as on the Around Mountain loop (see above), but at the first carriage road junction, turn left. In about half an hour, you will swing around the south end of Penobscot Mountain's Jordan Ridge and reach a road junction, where you begin the Amphitheater Carriage Road Loop. The clockwise direction of this 2.8-mile loop, takes you first through the lower and more heavily forested part of the valley. The following description proceeds counterclockwise, heading straight into The Amphitheater.

The carriage road passes a stretch of sloping granite ledges, where stately red pines and white pines grow, along with lowbush blueberry, sheep laurel, and ground juniper. At the head of the sheltered valley, a curving stone bridge, spanning Little Harbor Brook, affords a view of the hemlock-shaded stream and a waterfall that is especially beautiful following a period of sufficiently heavy rainfall. The road now swings around southward and soon reaches a junction. (Brown Mountain Gatehouse and Upper Hadlock

Pond are to the right.) To continue on The Amphitheater loop, turn left and follow a winding woodland route through the lower part of The Amphitheater valley. Not far beyond a small stone bridge over Little Harbor Brook, the road crosses the Asticou-Jordan Pond Trail. This delightful path, following mostly level ground through the spruce forest, is a short-cut of just over a mile back to the Jordan Pond House. To return by way of the carriage road, however, bear left at the next carriage road junction, cross the Asticou-Jordan Pond Trail farther on, and return to the original Amphitheater loop junction. From there, turn right and retrace your original route back to the parking area near the Jordan Pond House. This loop can be delightful for cross-country skiing in winter.

■ HADLOCK VALLEY CARRIAGE ROAD LOOP
(map on page 180)

Begin and end: Brown Mountain Gate parking area. (You can also access this loop by way of the trailhead leading east from State Highway 198, just north of Upper Hadlock Pond.)

Distance: 4.2 miles.

Time: 1.5 to 2 hours.

Difficulty: Easy, but with moderate switchback grades, if the route is taken in a clockwise direction.

At a road junction, just in from the gatehouse, you can proceed in either direction around the Hadlock Valley Carriage Road Loop. The following description is clockwise. Turn left and follow the road through the forest. After passing a small opening in the trees, which offers a view of Upper Hadlock Pond and Norumbega (Brown) Mountain, the road enters a dark forest, crosses Hadlock Brook, where tall white pines grow, and gradually ascends toward the gap between Norumbega and Parkman mountains. The road soon crosses Parkman Mountain Trail, and here you can turn right, for a short-cut to a higher stretch of this carriage road loop; or you can continue on the carriage road, bearing right at the next junction.

Emerging into more open terrain on the southern flank of Parkman Mountain, you come to the junction with the Around Mountain Carriage Road Loop (see previous description). Continue straight, following the Hadlock loop into the head of Upper Hadlock valley. Two stone bridges span adjacent tributaries of Hadlock Brook. At one of these is Acadia's highest waterfall. It is spectacular following periods of sufficiently heavy rainfall.

From here, the carriage road turns southward and gradually descends along the west side of Cedar Swamp Mountain. At a road junction, bear right; then left at a second junction, returning to the Brown Mountain Gate parking area. This is a popular cross-country skiing route in winter.

WEST SIDE TRAILS

■ ACADIA MOUNTAIN-MAN O' WAR LOOP TRAIL
(map on page 192)

Begin and end: The entrance to Man o' War Road (Robinson Road), on the east side (to the left, driving south) of State Highway 102, about 3 miles south of Somesville or about 3 miles north of Southwest Harbor. (Since there is limited space at the gate, you may have to use a larger parking area on the opposite side of the highway, about 0.1 of a mile to the south.)

Distance: 0.4 of a mile to Acadia Mountain's west summit; 0.2 of a mile on to the east summit (not marked with a park sign); and 2.5 miles around the loop.

Time: 30 to 45 minutes to the west summit; 1.25 to 2 hours around the loop.

Difficulty: Some steep sections.

From the locked gate, follow the gravel road through the dark forest for less than 0.1 of a mile. Turn left onto the Acadia Mountain Trail. You climb quickly out of the lower forest, scramble up steep granite ledges, and wind through delightful groves of red and pitch pines and small clumps of the rare bear oak. Soon there are pine-framed vistas westward across Echo Lake, toward Beech Cliff and Beech Mountain.

Just before reaching Acadia Mountain's west summit, an expanse of open ledges provides a beautiful view southward toward the mouth of Somes Sound, and the ocean and islands beyond. The granite ledges of the 681-foot-high west summit are covered with a scattering of picturesque pitch pines. From here, the mostly level stretch of the trail soon reaches the east summit. The panorama from there takes in the entire length of Somes Sound, with Norumbega (Brown) Mountain rising from its east shore.

If you wish to avoid returning by the same route, the trail (watch for cairns and other trail markers) descends *very* steeply off the south end of the mountain, crosses Man o' War Brook, and connects with the Man o' War Road in 0.6 of a mile. As you drop from ledge to ledge, there are some really magnificent pitch pine-framed views down to Valley Cove, Flying Mountain, the mouth of Somes Sound, and the island-dotted ocean beyond.

Shortly after crossing Man o' War Brook and within a dark grove of northern white cedars, a short spur trail branches to the left and leads to a view of the stream descending into Somes Sound. Just beyond the spur, the main trail reaches a junction with trails to St. Sauveur Mountain and Valley Cove. Turn right here to continue the loop, coming immediately to the end of the Man o' War Road. This pleasant mile-long route then climbs gradually out of the valley between the mountains, passes

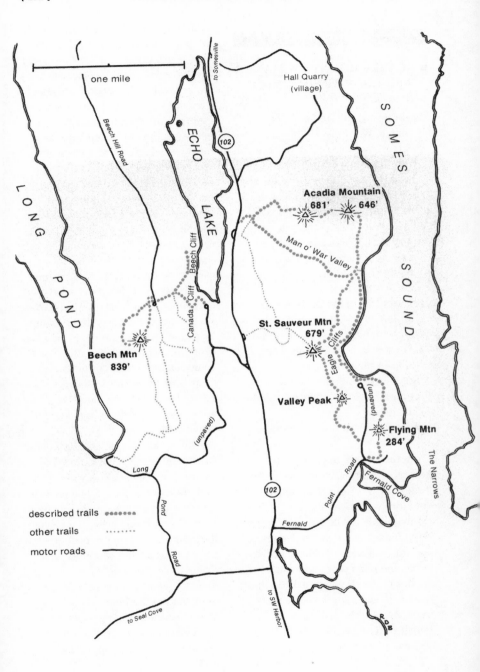

through an old-growth coniferous-and-deciduous forest, and brings you back to Highway 102.

■ VALLEY PEAK-ST. SAUVEUR MOUNTAIN-VALLEY COVE LOOP TRAIL
(map on page 192)

Begin and end: The entrance to the Valley Cove Road, branching left (north) from Fernald Point Road.
Distance: 3 miles.
Time: 1.75 to 2.50 hours.
Difficulty: There are some moderately steep to steep sections, especially a few places on the climb up Valley Peak, on the descent from St. Sauveur Mountain, and zigzagging across the steep slope and jumble of boulders around the shore of Valley Cove.

The start of the Valley Peak Trail leads into a spruce forest, branching left (west) at 0.1 of a mile from the entrance of the Valley Cove Road. After crossing a brook, the path begins climbing the forested lower slope of Valley Peak. After a few steep spots, the route soon emerges onto open sloping ledges. From here to the summit, you climb through open groves of picturesque pitch pines that frame views southward of Fernald Cove, Greening Island (near the mouth of Somes Sound), and the Cranberry Islands beyond. Close to the summit, there is a junction (the trail to the left leads 1.1 miles to the

St. Sauveur Mountain parking area on State Highway 102).

From Valley Peak's 520-foot-high summit, you have the first glimpse down to Valley Cove, with Acadia Mountain to the north and Norumbega (Brown) Mountain to the east across Somes Sound. From here, the trail leads into a slight saddle and climbs quickly to the 679-foot-high summit of St. Sauveur Mountain and to the brink of sheer Eagle Cliff, high above Valley Cove. (A trail junction here meets a 0.9 of a mile trail to St. Sauveur Mountain parking area, on Highway 102.)

The loop trail continues along the open juniper-and-lichen-covered ledges atop Eagle Cliff. A magnificent unobstructed panorama spreads out before you, with (right to left, as you face Somes Sound) Flying Mountain, Valley Cove, Norumbega Mountain across Somes Sound, and Acadia Mountain. The route soon descends rather steeply, at first running along open, sloping granite ledges and then descending into a dense forest.

The final northward section of this loop trail leads through the level valley between St. Sauveur and Acadia mountains. In a semi-open area, you come to a trail junction (1.6 miles and 1 to 1.5 hours from the start). The end of the Man o' War Road (Robinson Road) is 0.1 of a mile to the left; and the mouth of Man o' War Brook, where it dashes down rocks and plunges into Somes Sound, is 0.2 of a mile straight

ahead. To reach the latter, walk
briefly on the Acadia Mountain Trail
and then turn right on a short spur
to an overlook above the shore.

After backtracking on the spur
and left (south) onto the south end
of the Acadia Mountain Trail, bear
left at the next junction. This trail,
which leads southward along the
shore of Somes Sound and Valley
Cove, passes through dark groves of
old-growth cedars and open stands
of ash and birch trees, and rounds a
bend to the cove. From here, you
scramble up and down some steep
tricky stretches, along the talus
slope below Eagle Cliff. As you start
into this area, the massive fractured
wall of the cliff's escarpment is especially impressive.

After some rock-hopping across
this boulder-strewn slope, the trail
enters a dark spruce forest, which is
at the end of the Valley Cove Road—
just up the slope from the trail. It is
0.4 of a mile on this road back to the
starting point of the loop. Or you can
continue on the trail another 0.3 of a
mile to the summit of 284-foot-high
Flying Mountain, and from there
proceed down to the parking area at
the entrance to Valley Cove Road.

■ **FLYING MOUNTAIN
LOOP TRAIL**
(map on page 192)

Begin and end: Parking area at the
entrance to the Valley Cove Road,
which branches left (north) from
Fernald Point Road.

Distance: 0.3 of a mile to Flying
Mountain summit; 1.1 miles for
the loop.
Time: 15 to 20 minutes to the summit; 45 minutes to 1 hour for the
loop.
Difficulty: Easy to moderately steep,
with several steep spots.

Flying Mountain is only 284 feet
high, but for a short climb, it offers
some exciting views of the mouth of
Somes Sound. In summer, it is often
fun to watch numerous sailboats
coming and going through the Narrows.

The trail climbs through a spruce
forest for a short distance, before
quickly reaching granite ledges to
the exposed summit. From here, you
can look across the mouth of Somes
Sound toward the village of Northeast Harbor, and out to Greening Island and the Cranberry Islands clustered on the sea beyond.

From the highest point, the trail
leads on northward through spruce
trees. Before it descends to the
shore of Valley Cove, this route provides a couple of glimpses northward along Somes Sound, where it
extends between Acadia Mountain,
to the left, and Norumbega (Brown)
Mountain, to the right. In an old-
growth spruce forest, along the
shore of Valley Cove, the trail
reaches a junction. Walk up the
slope to the end of the Valley Cove
Road. From here, it is an easy half
mile back southward to the parking
area.

■ BEECH CLIFF TRAIL
(map on page 192)

Begin and end: Echo Lake beach parking area.

Distance: 0.4 of a mile to the top of the cliff.

Time: 20 to 40 minutes to the top of the cliff.

Difficulty: Moderately steep, with some very steep stretches, including iron ladders. If you are uncomfortable climbing sheer cliffs, you will likely prefer to hike an easier access (see next trail description).

This well-designed trail begins the climb through an old-growth birch-and-maple forest. It then switchbacks more steeply, climbing stone steps, following stretches of level and shaded ledges, and finally scaling 4 iron ladders, just before emerging onto the top of the cliff. During the climb, there are only a few glimpses of the view outward, when the deciduous trees are leafed out. But as the trail emerges onto the open ledges at the top, you suddenly have a view of the southern part of Echo Lake, with Acadia and St. Sauveur mountains rising beyond.

(*Please Note:* As you climb to the top of the cliff, watch carefully for trail markers. At one point, a well-worn spur confusingly leaves the main trail at a sharp turn and leads onto a dead-end ledge that affords a view of Echo Lake.)

From the brink of the cliff, a short stretch of trail leads north to a 4-way trail junction and the 0.4 mile Beech Cliff Loop Trail (a 4-way junction). By bearing to the right (counterclockwise around the loop), you will first follow the brink of Beech Cliff, from which you can enjoy an even more sweeping view of Echo Lake. By returning to the first trail junction at the top of Beech Cliff, you can continue south (straight ahead) 0.2 of a mile to the 0.6 mile Canada Cliff Trail loop. Please see the next trail description for the latter hike and for an easier access to both loop trails.

■ CANADA CLIFF TRAIL
(map on page 192)

Begin and end: Parking area at the south end of Beech Hill Road, taking the trail to the left (east) of the road, signed "Beech Cliff Loop Trail."

Distance: 0.2 of a mile to a 4-way trail junction: right to the Canada Cliff Trail (straight or left onto the Beech Cliff Loop Trail).

Time: 15 to 20 minutes to the brink of the cliff.

Difficulty: Easy.

This hike climbs gradually through a shady old-growth spruce forest, where thrushes frequently sing in late spring and early summer. At 0.2 of a mile, the trail comes to a 4-way junction. To the left (north) is the Beech Cliff Loop Trail, described above. To reach the Canada Cliff Trail, turn right (south), keep straight ahead at the next trail junction, and continue southward 0.2 of a mile to the 0.6 mile Canada Cliff Trail loop. After completing the loop, you can return by the same route to the parking area at the end of Beech Hill Road. Or you can branch left from the loop (after 0.4 of a mile, if you hike the loop clockwise), proceeding 0.2 of a mile to the junction with the Valley Trail and bearing right (north) for the final 0.2 of a mile back to the parking area.

■ **BEECH MOUNTAIN LOOP TRAIL**
(map on page 192)

Begin and end: Parking area at the south end of Beech Hill Road, taking the trail to the right (west) of the road.
Distance: just under 0.4 of a mile by the shortest route to the summit.
Time: 30 to 40 minutes by the shortest route.
Difficulty: Easy to moderately steep.

This trail climbs up a short fairly steep stretch, quickly emerging onto open granite ledges. At a junction, you can go either to the left on the most direct trail to the summit or to the right. The latter route swings around the mostly exposed western side of the mountain, providing spectacular views of Long (Great) Pond, as it extends to the north. The final stretch of this trail swings up to the 839-foot-high summit of Beech Mountain. (The fire tower atop the summit is normally used only during periods of extreme fire danger.)

From here, you can return by whichever trail you did not take coming up, thereby making a pleasant short loop. (Beech Mountain's South Ridge Trail leads southward from here, reaching the south end of Long Pond in 1.5 miles.)

■ **GREAT POND TRAIL**
(map on page 199)

Begin and end: At the south end of Long (Great) Pond.
Distance: 1.5 miles from the parking area to the point where the trail turns westward, away from the lakeshore.
Time: 40 to 50 minutes each way.
Difficulty: Easy and level.

This exceptionally pleasant level path, beginning just beyond the pump station, curves around the end of the pond and follows the west shore, along the base of Mansell Peak. (At 0.2 of a mile, the Perpendicular Trail, to the summit of Mansell Peak, branches off to the left.) At many places, deer-browsed cedar trees frame the view up the long expanse of water, with Beech Mountain rising from the opposite lakeshore. At other places, the path winds through stands of birches and maples, follows the shore of intimate little coves, and leads by ledges shelving into the clear water.

Where the trail finally swings away from the shore, you can retrace your steps 1.5 miles on the same route. (If you continue westward away from the lake, the trail winds through a wild stretch of forest. In 1.4 miles from the lakeshore, you reach a junction with the Western Mountain Trail: to the right, leading to the Long Pond Road; to the left, climbing into Great Notch and connecting with the Western Mountain trails.)

■ MANSELL PEAK LOOP TRAIL
(map on page 199)

Begin and end: Either at the south end of Long (Great) Pond or at Gilley Field, on the Western Mountain Road. The following description begins and ends at the pond's end.

Distance: 3 miles.

Time: 2 to 3 hours.

Difficulty: Some very steep sections. It is strongly recommended that the Perpendicular Trail be hiked up, not down; thus, following the loop counterclockwise. Those who dislike sheer dropoffs and/or long, steep climbs may wish to avoid this hike.

From the parking area at the south end of Long (Great) Pond, the trail begins just beyond the pump station. This level path, called Great Pond Trail (see description above), swings around to the pond's west shore and in 0.2 of a mile reaches a junction with the Perpendicular Trail to

Mansell Peak. This path switchbacks upward through a spruce forest; then suddenly emerges onto a steep talus expanse of huge boulders that have fallen from the cliffs and ledges above. For a long stretch, the trail consists of beautifully laid stone steps that take you abruptly up the mountainside and afford views now and then of Long Pond.

The steep, stair-stepping climb finally ends and a more level stretch of the trail follows the base of a great slanting expanse of cliff, before scrambling up a small ravine. Especially in spring and early summer, ravens nest on cliffs along the way, and you may hear their varied musical croaks, as they communicate with each other in what appears to be an amicable tone of call. You may be startled, as several of these large black birds suddenly leave their perches and flap noisily away.

After the climb up the ravine, an open expanse of gently sloping granite, to the right of the trail, offers a welcome resting place, from which to enjoy a limited view of Long Pond far below. There is now only a short gradual climb, through a more open spruce forest and areas of exposed granite to the 949-foot-high Mansell Peak summit, from which there is no view because of the trees. At this point, you have come 1.4 miles from the start of the hike.

Mansell Peak Trail leads southward from here, soon reaching a junction. (The 0.8 of a mile trail, to the right, leads westward across

Western Mountain to the summit of Bernard Peak.) Continuing straight ahead at this junction, the Mansell Peak loop descends steadily along an open granite ridge that is dotted with spruces and ground juniper. The trail then drops very steeply from the end of this ridge into a dark spruce forest. The route continues a sloping descent into a mixed deciduous-and-coniferous forest, coming finally to Gilley Field on the Western Mountain Road, at 1.1 miles from Mansell Peak summit. From here, a fairly level, pleasant woodland path, the Cold Brook Trail, leads 0.5 of a mile back to the south end of Long Pond.

■ BERNARD PEAK LOOP TRAIL
(map on page 199)

Begin and end: At Mill Field, on the Western Mountain Road.
Distance: 3.2 miles.
Time: 2 to 2.5 hours.
Difficulty: Moderately steep, with a few short steep places.

This loop trail offers a unique hike through one of the wildest parts of Acadia National Park. If you especially enjoy wilderness solitude and a feeling of remoteness from civilization, this route should appeal to you.

Beginning at Mill Field, much of the moderately steep 1.2-mile climb on the Sluiceway Trail to Great Notch winds through a dark spruce forest, following a brook much of the way. At a junction in the notch, turn left onto the 0.6 of a mile trail to Bernard Peak. After scrambling up several steep places, the Bernard Peak trail reaches Knight Nubble, where a small overlook, just to the left of the trail, provides a view southeast toward Norwood Cove, Southwest Harbor, and the island-dotted ocean. There is no view from the actual summit of the 930-foot-high Knight Nubble. Much of this route winds through picturesque dense stands of red spruce trees, where the ground is thickly carpeted with moss.

The path next drops quickly into Little Notch, from which a 1.3-mile trail (very steep and tricky walking for a stretch) reaches a junction. Continuing straight for 0.2 of a mile from this junction, the Bernard Peak trail now climbs for the final time. It passes through an area that provides a view northward toward the upper reaches of Blue Hill Bay and the northern end of Long Pond. Because of trees, there is no view from the actual 1,071-foot-high summit of Bernard Peak.

On the return stretch of the loop, the trail leads to a junction less than 0.2 of a mile beyond the summit. To the left is the most direct route— joining the Sluiceway Trail directly down to Mill Field. The longer route, to the right, swings an arc around the western side of the mountain, by way of the South Face Trail. The lat-

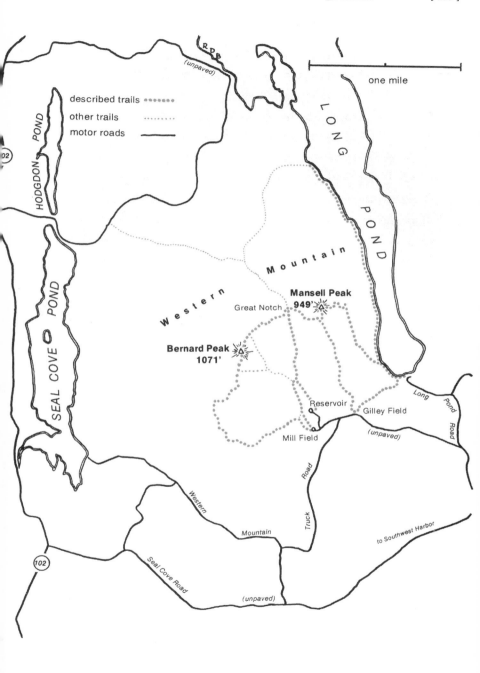

ter is beautiful; but the name seems misleading, since there are few views and no south-facing cliffs. This 1.2-mile trail initially meanders through some dense little stands of red spruce trees, beneath which the ground is deeply carpeted with moss. This delightful intimate forest conveys a feeling of hushed primeval mystery, completely isolated from the outside world.

The trail soon swings out to a couple of open ledges that offer views down to Seal Cove Pond and across the broad expanse of Blue Hill Bay. Once beyond this point, the trail turns eastward and begins a long angling descent through an old-growth deciduous-and-coniferous forest, bringing you back to Mill Field.

■ WONDERLAND TRAIL
(map on page 201)

Begin and end: Parking area 1 mile south of Seawall Campground, on the east (left) side of State Highway 102A.

Distance: About 0.6 of a mile to the shore.

Time: 15 to 20 minutes to the shore.

Difficulty: Easy and level.

This wide level path leads first through a mixed deciduous-and-coniferous woods and then through an open grove of pitch pines, before entering a stand of tall spruces along the seashore. The path encircles a small peninsula, on each side of which is a beautiful little cove with pebble beaches, cobblestone seawalls, and ledges of granite shelving into the sea. Great Cranberry Island is to the east, with Great and Little Duck Islands farther across the ocean. This a peaceful place to enjoy the sounds and fragrance of the ocean. The waters offshore are often dotted with flocks of sea ducks—most commonly eiders and scoters.

■ SHIP HARBOR TRAIL
(map on page 201)

Begin and end: Ship Harbor parking area, 1.3 miles south of Seawall Campground, on the east (left) side of Highway 102A.

Distance: 0.6 of a mile to the mouth of Ship Harbor; or 1.6 miles around the loop.

Time: 40 minutes to 1 hour.

Difficulty: Easy and level.

This pleasant loop begins with a view from above the head of Ship Harbor—a sheltered little cove that drains nearly dry at low tide. A short stretch through a wooded area and a right turn at a trail junction will bring you onto a rocky ledge that overlooks the harbor. The path then leads through a stand of spruces, provides frequent vistas, and soon reaches the pink granite ledges at the narrow mouth of the harbor, where you can often smell the com-

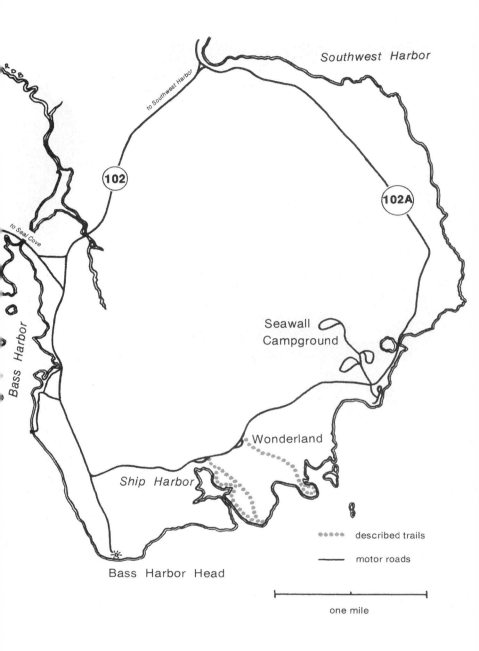

Southwest Harbor

to Southwest Harbor

102

102A

to Seal Cove

Bass Harbor

Seawall
Campground

Wonderland

Ship Harbor

Bass Harbor Head

••••• described trails

—— motor roads

one mile

bined fragrances of the sea, spruce trees, and crowberry.

On a clear day, you can see to the southeast the Great Duck and Little Duck islands, the latter protected as a sanctuary for breeding colonies of eiders, petrels, cormorants, and gulls. From this viewpoint, the trail winds back to the parking area.

SCHOODIC PENINSULA TRAILS

A short trail invites exploration of the two summits on mainland Schoodic Peninsula. At about 2.5 miles from the park unit's entrance, a narrow mile-long gravel road branches to the left, climbs steeply, and ends near the top of Schoodic Head. The 440-foot-high summit is only 0.2 of a mile by trail. From the summit, a mile-long trail descends through the forest and climbs the smaller summit, known as The Anvil. This trail ends 0.3 of a mile farther, at the main park road.

Note: In planning an excursion from Mount Desert Island to Schoodic Peninsula, you should anticipate devoting most or all of a day for a leisurely visit. Acadia National Park's Schoodic Peninsula unit is reached most directly (about 33 miles) by driving 5 miles north from the Mount Desert Narrows bridge, and turning right onto State Highway 204. In nearly 2 miles, turn left at a T junction and then immediately

right, continuing on Highway 204. At 1.5 miles farther, in the midst of open fields, bear left onto an unsigned paved road, proceeding 3 miles to the junction with U.S. Highway 1. (You can also reach this junction by way of U.S. Highway 1 from Ellsworth.) Turn right and head eastward for about 13 miles on U.S. 1. Turn right at the junction of Route 1 and State Highway 186, where there is a directional sign to Acadia National Park. Proceed for about 6 miles. At a junction in the village of Winter Harbor, turn left, continuing on Route 186 for another 0.5 of a mile. At a park-signed junction, turn right and go the final 1.5 miles to the park entrance.

ISLE AU HAUT TRAILS

Access to Isle au Haut (High Island) is necessarily very limited, with thrice-daily 45-minute mail boat trips during the summer (once daily in winter, weather permitting) from the village of Stonington, on nearby Deer Isle. Visitors may walk or bicycle the 14-mile loop road that circles around part of the island. There are trails along Jerusalem Mountain; to the top of Duck Harbor Mountain, from which there are good views of the surrounding island-dotted ocean; and along the shore from Duck Harbor to Western Head.

Simple overnight camping facilities (*by reservation only*) are provided by the park at Duck Harbor, toward the southwestern end of Isle au Haut. There are no other overnight accommodations; so, if you arrive without a camping reservation, you will not be permitted to remain overnight. In the summer, a park ranger meets the mail boat to offer information. *Note:* Visitors should make every effort to respect the private property and privacy of island residents.

Historical Highlights

Prior to European discovery, Native Americans, who were possible ancestors of the present Penobscot and Passamaquoddy tribes, had encampments on the coast of Maine. They lived off the land—hunting, fishing, clamming, and gathering berries and other plant materials. Although archaeological evidence is sparse, large shell heaps and a few Carbon-dated artifacts, such as spearheads and simple tools, suggest that the earliest of these settlements dated from around 4000 B.C.

1524 Giovanni da Verrazano, a Florentine mariner on an expedition for France, named the New England coastal region "Arcadia," in memory of a scenic part of Greece.

1529 Diego Ribero, a Portuguese mariner, named Somes Sound "Rio de las Montañas"—the first known written mention of Mount Desert Island.

1603 King Henry IV of France granted all of French-claimed northeastern North America, called "La Cadie" or Acadia, to Pierre du Guast, Sieur de Monts (or Pierre Dugua, Sieur de Mons), a Huguenot nobleman.

1604 Samuel Champlain, cartographer-recorder on de Monts's expedition, described and accurately identified Mount Desert as an island, naming it "l'Isle des Monts-déserts."

1613 The first attempted permanent settlement, St. Sauveur, on Mount Desert Island was founded by a colony of French Jesuits somewhere near the mouth of Somes Sound. The colonists were welcomed by the local Indians, but their colony was subsequently destroyed by the British. Thus began a long period of conflict between the French and British for control of northeastern North America.

1688 Mount Desert Island and

vicinity were granted to Antoine de la Mothe Cadillac, by the governor of French Canada—an act later approved by France's King Louis XIV. (Cadillac subsequently founded the city of Detroit and became France's governor of the vast Louisiana Territory.)

1759 British forces defeated the French at Québec, thus giving undisputed control of Maine to Great Britain.

1761 Abraham Somes, of Gloucester, was encouraged by Governor Francis Bernard of the Massachusetts Bay Colony to settle with his wife and daughters at the head of Somes Sound, thereby founding Somesville, the oldest community on Mount Desert Island.

1762 In gratitude for Gov. Bernard's efforts to promote the settlement of Maine (then part of the Massachusetts Bay Colony), he was granted the West Side of Mount Desert Island by the colony's General Court—an act later officially approved by England's King George III.

1768 John Hamor and his family founded the village of Hulls Cove, the first English settlement on the island's East Side.

1783 After years of conflicting claims between Canada and the United States of America, the international boundary between Maine and New Brunswick was set along the St. Croix River, instead of the Penobscot River or even farther to the west.

1809 John Clement founded the village of Seal Harbor.

1837 First bridge connected Mount Desert Island to the mainland.

1840s–1850s First summer visitors came to Mount Desert Island—mostly writers, painters, and scientists.

1868 Steamboat service began between Boston and the island; and the first rustic hotel, the Island House, was built near the first steamboat wharf, in Southwest Harbor. Many other small hotels were soon built in Bar Harbor and other island villages.

1880s A land-speculation boom, caused by the demands of wealthy summer "rusticators," vacationing from the major East Coast cities, resulted in the building of many summer "cottages." Hiking, buckboard excursions, canoeing, sailing, and berry-picking were popular.

1883 A sightseeing cog railway began a 7-year operation, running from the eastern shore of Eagle Lake to the summit of Cadillac (then called Green) Mountain.

1890   Roughly 25,000 summer visitors reached the island, either by coastal steamer or railroad.

1890s   Bar Harbor became the undisputed major summer resort for many of America's wealthiest and most influential families. Numerous large elaborate mansion-sized "cottages" were built in the vicinity of Bar Harbor. The harbor was filled with elegant yachts, and the streets and roads were busy with horse-drawn carriages and buckboards.

1895   Jordan Pond House was founded by Mr. and Mrs. Thomas A. McIntire, becoming one of many popular island tea houses.

1901   The first meeting of a few of the island's leading summer people, establishing the Hancock County Trustees of Public Reservations for the purpose of acquiring and preserving some of the island's most beautiful landscapes. George B. Dorr was named its executive officer.

1903   The State Legislature granted a charter to the Trustees, whereby the tax-exempt corporation could "acquire, by devise, gift, or purchase, and to own, arrange, hold, maintain, or improve for public use

lands . . . which by reason of scenic beauty, historical interest, sanitary advantage . . . may become available. . . ." A small tract on a summit overlooking Jordan Pond and a site near Seal Harbor (to commemorate Champlain's visit) were the first two small parcels given to the Trustees.

1908   The Beehive and The Bowl (a small mountain and pond near Sand Beach) were given to the Trustees. Cadillac Mountain and Sieur de Monts Spring soon followed.

1913   Legislative lobbyists attacked the tax-exempt status of the Trustees, a move causing Mr. Dorr to begin efforts toward the establishment of a national reserve. The Trustees now owned about 5,000 acres. The first automobile came onto the island—an event that led summer resident John D. Rockefeller Jr. to construct a separate network of carriage roads.

1916   Sieur de Monts National Monument was signed into law by President Woodrow Wilson, thereby accepting the Trustees' gift to the nation. Mr. Dorr was named custodian. More than 100,000 visitors toured the island.

1919   Congress established Lafayette National Park (redesignating the former national monument)—the first national park east of the Mississippi. Mr. Dorr was named its first superintendent.

1929   Congress renamed the reserve Acadia National Park.

1932   Cadillac Mountain summit road was completed.

1933   Mr. Rockefeller completed construction of a 57-mile carriage road network (44 miles of which are now within the park) and he generously donated more than 11,000 acres of land to the park.

1947   A horrendous October wildfire, pushed at times by powerful northwesterly winds after a dry summer, burned 8,750 acres of the park's east side, plus more than 8,400 acres of private lands, including much of the village of Bar Harbor and many of the large summer mansions.

1954   The park recorded one million visitors.

1966   The park recorded two million visitors.

1970   The Maine Coast Heritage Trust was established to conserve coastal and other lands that define Maine's distinct landscape, protect its environment, sustain its outdoor traditions, and promote the well-being of its people. Since its founding, MCHT has

helped protect more than 117,000 acres, including 270 entire coastal islands. In partnership with Acadia National Park, the organization, by means of conservation easements and fee acquisition, has enabled the protection of 137 properties totaling more than 11,000 acres, within the park's congressionally authorized master boundary. The MCHT can be reached at: P.O. Box 669, Mount Desert, ME 05660; telephone: (207) 244-5100; website: www.mcht.org.

1986   Friends of Acadia, a nonprofit membership organization, was founded to help ensure the protection and appreciation of the national park. The Friends of Acadia can be reached at: P.O. Box 725, Bar Harbor, ME 04609; telephone: (207) 288-3340; and website: www.friendsofacadia.org. (Please see the section on Volunteers.)

2003   The park recorded 3 million visitors.

2004   Acadia National Park comprised more than 46,800 acres: 30,300 acres on Mount Desert Island, 2,728 acres on Isle au Haut, 2,266 acres on Schoodic Peninsula, 1,110 other acres, and more than 10,450 acres under conservation easements.

Activities

Information on Acadia National Park is available from late spring through early autumn at the Visitor Center, which is located just off State Highway 3, immediately south of the village of Hulls Cove. Maps, books, interpretive brochures, and information on interpretive walks, cruises, and evening campground programs are available. The park's winter information center is at park headquarters, located 3 miles west of the village of Bar Harbor on the Eagle Lake Road (State Route 233). Mailing address: Acadia National Park, P.O. Box 177, Bar Harbor, ME 04609; telephone: (207) 288-3338; and website: www.nps.gov/acad.

Interpretive programs, during the late spring, summer, and early autumn, feature bird and seashore walks, ecology and geology hikes, mountain-climbing excursions, astronomy watches, introductory nature walks for children, interpreter-led cruises on Frenchman Bay and elsewhere, and evening programs at Blackwoods and Seawall campgrounds. Schedules of these and other events are available at the Visitor Center and the campgrounds.

Natural history exhibits, in the **Nature Center** building; Native American artifacts, at the **Abbe Museum at Sieur de Monts Spring** (admission fee; open daily from Memorial Day weekend to mid-October); and **Wild Gardens of Acadia** are all part of the interpretive center at Sieur de Monts Spring, located just off the Park Loop Road, about 6 miles from the Visitor Center.

Abbe Museum Downtown is located at 26 Mount Desert Street, in downtown Bar Harbor (admission fee; open daily from Memorial Day weekend to mid-October; open Thursday through Sunday from mid-October to Memorial Day weekend; and closed Thanksgiving, Christmas, and January). This new museum on Native American cultures of Maine includes its permanent exhibition, "Wabanaki: People of the Dawn." This privately operated museum also sponsors workshops and demonstrations by Native Americans, as well as offering a variety of other educational programs and a gift shop. For further information: Abbe Museum, P.O. Box 286, Bar Harbor, ME 04609; telephone: (207) 288-3519; website: www.abbemuseum.org.

Islesford Historical Museum, located on Little Cranberry Island, is a National Park facility that offers interpretive exhibits of 19th-century life on the Cranberry Islands, when schooners were the primary means of transportation on the seas. For further information: telephone: (207) 288-3338; website: www.nps.gov/acad/home.html.

Park campgrounds: Blackwoods Campground, which is open all year (reservations for May-October), is located in a spruce forest near the seashore, just off State Highway 3 (near the village of Otter Creek) on the island's East Side. Seawall Campground is open from late May through September (first-come, first-served). It is located just off State Highway 102A, about 4 miles south of the junction of Highways 102 and 102A in Southwest Harbor.

Privately operated campgrounds, outside the park, are located at many places around Mount Desert Island, including near the Mount Desert Narrows bridge from the mainland, near the villages of Town Hill and Salisbury Cove, at the head of Somes Sound, and near Southwest Harbor.

Park picnic areas: Bear Brook Picnic Area, along the Park Loop Road, just beyond the Sieur de Monts Spring turnoff, adjacent to the Park Loop Road; Fabbri Picnic Area, overlooking Otter Cove, after rounding the end of Otter Point on the Park Loop Road; Seawall Picnic Area, along the shore, on the opposite side of Highway 102A from Seawall Campground; Pretty Marsh Picnic Area, on the shore of Blue Hill Bay, just off Highway 102 (midway between Somesville and Seal Cove); Thompson Island Picnic Area, on the east side of Highway 3 at Mount Desert Narrows; and Frazer Point Picnic Area, at the entrance to the Schoodic Peninsula unit of the park.

Automobile touring of the park is highlighted, on the East Side of the island, by the 20-mile Park Loop Road. This scenic route leads south 3.5 miles from the Visitor Center to the junction with the loop. To drive the entire loop in a clockwise direction, by way of scenic Ocean Drive, turn left and begin an 11-mile one-way stretch. (A right turn at this junction will lead you directly to the Jordan Pond House and the park's Stanley Brook entrance at Seal Harbor.) Along the way are Sieur de Monts Spring, Bear Brook Picnic Area, views overlooking Frenchman Bay, Sand Beach, Thunder Hole, Otter Cliffs and Otter Point, Fabbri Picnic Area, Wildwood Stables, Jordan Pond House (luncheons, afternoon tea-and-popovers, and dinners; and a gift shop), views of Jordan Pond and Bubble Pond, and the 3.5-mile spur road to the 1,530-foot-high summit of Cadillac Mountain. *Please Note:* A fee is collected at a half-mile north of (before) Sand Beach.

Other scenic roads include Sargeant Drive, along the eastern shore of Somes Sound (no large trucks, motor homes, or trailers are permitted along this narrow road); unpaved roads (sometimes closed) between Southwest Harbor and Seal Cove; and the Long Pond Fire Road (sometimes closed) that loops eastward from State Highway 102, between Pretty Marsh and Seal Cove.

There are other scenic stretches of highway on the island, such as State Route 233, between Bar Harbor and the junction with State Route 198, which passes the north end of Eagle Lake and the nearby park Headquarters; Route 198, where it passes Upper Hadlock Pond, just north of Northeast Harbor; Route 102 along the east shore of Echo Lake, between Somesville and Southwest Harbor; and Route 102A, where it passes Seawall, Ship Harbor, Bass Harbor Head, and Bass Harbor.

Island Explorer shuttle bus system: An excellent alternative to driving the park's loop road and other roads during the summer months on Mount Desert Island is to board an Island Explorer shuttle bus. These quiet, wheelchair-accessible buses, which are powered by clean-burning propane, offer convenient shuttle stops along more than a half-dozen routes on Mount Desert Island. This transportation service began in 1999 and by August 2003 had recorded its millionth rider. Is-

land Explorer receives major funding from private sources, such as L.L. Bean, Inc., Friends of Acadia, and Eastern National. For further information: telephone: (207) 288-4573; website: www.exploreacadia.com.

Hiking is one of the most rewarding and popular ways to explore and come to know Acadia. There are more than 120 miles of maintained trails. In addition, there are 44 miles of "broken-stone" carriage roads in the park, plus another 13 miles on adjacent private land. (See the section on suggested hikes.)

Bicycling is a popular pleasure on the national park's 44-mile carriage-road network—notably the Paradise Hill and Witch Hole Pond loops and the Eagle Lake loop. *Please note:* Bicycling is *not* permitted on the 13 miles of carriage roads on private land to the south of the park boundary (in the general vicinity of Little Long Pond); and bicycles are not allowed on hiking trails or off road. The National Park Service asks that bicyclists "remember to yield to all carriage road users." When approaching walkers from behind, please offer a greeting and pass slowly to the left; and be extremely cautious when approaching horseback riders or horse-drawn carriages. Speeding is not an appropriate use of these unique park roadways.

On the island's West Side, there are several other good routes for bicycling, including the Western Mountain Road, Seal Cove Road, and

Long Pond Fire Road. Bikes can be rented and purchased at a number of businesses on the island. A handy reference for carriage-road bicycling is Audrey Minutolo's *A Pocket Guide to Biking on Mount Desert Island* (Down East Books, 1997).

Carriage tours are seasonally offered from the park's Wildwood Stables. Tours range from one to two hours. Reservations are advised by contacting Carriages in the Park, P.O. Box 241, Seal Harbor, ME 04675; telephone: (207) 276-3622. Reservations are required for wheelchair-accessible carriage tours.

Horseback riding is permitted on some stretches of carriage road in the vicinity of Wildwood Stables, located just off the Park Loop Road, near Seal Harbor. There are no horse rentals, but horse stalls are offered for rent at the stables (reservations are required by contacting Carriages in the Park).

Canoeing is a delightful peaceful way to enjoy the lakes and ponds. You can rent or purchase a canoe from several businesses on the island.

Kayaking is an increasingly popular way to explore the waters around Mount Desert Island—notably Somes Sound, Frenchman Bay, Blue Hill Bay, and the Cranberry Islands. An excellent reference is Jennifer Alisa Paigen's *The Sea Kayaker's Guide to Mount Desert Island* (Down East Books, 1997).

Swimming facilities are provided at the south end of Echo Lake, just off State Route 102. Because of municipal water supplies, swimming is not permitted in Eagle Lake, Bubble Pond, Jordan Pond, Upper and Lower Hadlock ponds, and the southern end of Long (Great) Pond. If you can tolerate the cold ocean, swimming is also possible at Sand Beach, but you should be extremely careful of the dangerous pull of the surf's undertow.

Sailing the bays and harbors and around the outer islands is one of the ultimate thrills. You can rent, charter, or purchase a sailboat (or motorboat) from a number of businesses on the island.

Boat cruises and ferry services are a great way to get out on the ocean. They are offered by a number of boat operators. During the summer, passenger ferry service runs from Northeast Harbor and Southwest Harbor out to Great Cranberry and Little Cranberry islands several times a day. The park's Islesford Historical Museum is located on Little Cranberry Island. And there is year-round passenger ferry service from Stonington, on nearby Deer Isle, out to Isle au Haut, where there is a unit of the park.

Cross-country skiing can be ideal on the carriage roads, when there is sufficient snowfall. Some favorite routes include the Paradise Hill and Witch Hole loops, the stretch north from near the Jordan Pond House above the west shore of Jordan Pond, and the stretch along the west shore of Eagle Lake.

Longer, more challenging routes encircle Sargent and Penobscot mountains.

Snowmobiling is permitted, as conditions allow, on the unplowed Park Loop Road and on only one stretch of carriage road: from State Route 233, south along the east side of Eagle Lake and up to the Park Loop Road.

Ice skating is only occasionally excellent on the lakes and ponds, if the surface has initially frozen over smoothly under calm conditions and has been followed by a long and really cold spell, with no rain or snow to rough up the surface. Before venturing out, you should be certain that the ice is sufficiently thick; and beware of thin places, such as along shallow marshy edges or where there is upwelling of warmer water.

Mount Desert Oceanarium has facilities at two locations: Oceanarium Southwest Harbor is adjacent to the U.S. Coast Guard station, on Clark Point Road in Southwest Harbor. It provides an excellent introduction to a wide variety of marine animals, as well as exhibits by fishermen and boat builders, and current information on fishing. Open 9 a.m. to 5 p.m. (except Sundays) from mid-May to late October. Information: (207) 244-7330. Oceanarium Bar Harbor is adjacent to State Route 3, just east of Mount Desert Narrows at Thomas Bay. Open 9 a.m. to 5 p.m. (except Sundays) from mid-May to mid-October. It includes a Maine lobster museum, a lobster

hatchery, and a Thomas Bay marsh walk. Information: (207) 288-5005. There is an admission fee to these privately operated facilities, with a discount for combination tickets.

George B. Dorr Museum of Natural History, College of the Atlantic, in Bar Harbor, interprets the natural history of Maine through a "human ecological perspective" and includes exhibits of Maine's plant and animal life. Further information: telephone: (207) 288-5395; website: www.coa.edu/nhm.

William Otis Sawtelle Collections & Research Center contains collections relating to the Cranberry Islands and Acadia National Park. For further information: (207) 288-5463.

Mount Desert Island Biological Laboratory, at Salisbury Cove, sponsors research on marine life. For further information: telephone: (207) 288-3605.

Asticou Azalea Garden, located across State Route 3 from the Asticou Inn, at the head of Northeast Harbor, is a 1.5-acre exquisitely landscaped Oriental garden that was designed by the late Charles K. Savage. Many varieties of azaleas bloom in the spring and early summer, especially in June. A pathway winds along the shore of two ponds and passes a Zen Sand Garden. The garden is open from May through October. The Asticou garden is maintained by The Island Foundation and its volunteers. For further information: The Island Foundation, P.O.

Box 208, Seal Harbor, ME 04675; telephone: (207) 276-3727.

Thuya Gardens and Lodge at the Asticou Terraces, overlooking the east side of Northeast Harbor, is a peaceful place where the natural beauty of cedars (*Thuja occidentalis*) and other trees blend with a carefully landscaped flower garden and lawn. The gardens, which were originally designed by the late Charles K. Savage, are open daily from 7 a.m. to 7 p.m. from May through October. The property is managed by The Island Foundation. For further information: The Island Foundation, P.O. Box 208, Seal Harbor, ME 04675; telephone: (207) 276-3727.

Hotels, motels, and other lodgings are located in the villages of Bar Harbor, Northeast Harbor, Seal Harbor, Southwest Harbor, and at a few other places on Mount Desert Island. Especially for the months of June through September, reservations are advised as far in advance as possible.

Restaurants are located in Bar Harbor, Northeast Harbor, Seal Harbor, Southwest Harbor, and at a few other places, including the Jordan Pond House in Acadia National Park.

Jordan Pond House offers luncheon, afternoon tea-and-popovers, and dinner overlooking mountain-framed Jordan Pond. It is open daily from mid-May to October. This restaurant is operated by The Acadia Corporation, a National Park Service concessionaire. For information and reservations, telephone: (207) 276-3316; website: www.jordanpond.com.

The Acadia Corporation also operates gift shops (featuring books, maps, and interpretive gifts) from May to late October at the Jordan Pond House, telephone: (207) 276-3244, at Thunder Hole, and atop Cadillac Mountain; and year-round: The Acadia Shop, 85 Main Street, Bar Harbor, telephone: (207) 288-5600; and the Acadia Country Store, 128 Main Street, Bar Harbor, telephone: (207) 288-2426. Gift shops website: www.acadiashops.com.

Checklist of Birds

Common Loon .... *resident*
Red-throated Loon .... *winter*
Red-necked Grebe .... *winter*
Horned Grebe .... *winter*
Pied-billed Grebe .... *summer*
Fulmar .... *summer offshore*
Greater Shearwater ..... *summer offshore*
Sooty Shearwater .... *summer offshore*
Manx Shearwater .... *summer offshore*
Leach's Storm-Petrel .... *summer offshore*
Wilson's Storm-Petrel ... *summer offshore*
Gannet .... *rare offshore*
Great Cormorant .... *winter*
Double-crested Cormorant ..... *summer*
Great Blue Heron .... *summer*
Green Heron .... *summer*
Little Blue Heron .... *rare summer*
Cattle Egret .... *rare summer*
Common Egret .... *rare summer*
Snowy Egret .... *rare summer*
Black-crowned Night-Heron *rare summer*
Least Bittern .... *rare summer*
American Bittern .... *summer*
Glossy Ibis .... *rare summer*
Canada Goose .... *transient*
Brant .... *rare transient*
Snow Goose .... *rare transient*
Mallard .... *transient and resident*
Black Duck .... *resident*
Pintail .... *uncommon transient*
Green-winged Teal .... *transient*

Blue-winged Teal .... *transient*
Wood Duck .... *summer and transient*
Ring-necked Duck .... *summer*
Greater Scaup .... *winter*
Lesser Scaup .... *rare transient*
Common Goldeneye .... *winter*
Barrow's Goldeneye ... *uncommon winter*
Bufflehead .... *winter*
Long-tailed Duck .... *winter*
Harlequin Duck .... *winter uncommon*
Common Eider .... *winter resident*
King Eider winter ..... *uncommon winter*
White-winged Scoter ..... *winter resident*
Surf Scoter .... *winter; rare summer*
Common Scoter ..... *winter; rare summer*
Ruddy Duck .... *rare transient*
Hooded Merganser .... *rare*
Common Merganser .... *resident*
Red-breasted Merganser .. *resident; rare summer*
Goshawk .... *resident*
Sharp-shinned Hawk .... *rare*
Cooper's Hawk .... *rare*
Red-tailed Hawk .... *summer*
Red-shouldered Hawk .... *rare*
Broad-winged Hawk .... *summer*
Rough-legged Hawk .... *rare winter*
Bald Eagle .... *resident; rare winter*
Northern Harrier .... *summer*
Osprey .... *summer*

Gyrfalcon .... *rare winter*
Peregrine Falcon .... *spring–summer*
Merlin .... *rare transient*
American Kestrel .... *summer*
Ruffed Grouse .... *resident*
Clapper Rail .... *rare summer*
Virginia Rail .... *rare transient*
Sora Rail .... *rare transient*
Common Moorhen .... *rare summer*
American Coot .... *rare transient*
Semipalmated Plover .... *transient*
Piping Plover .... *rare transient*
Killdeer .... *summer*
American Golden-Plover ... *rare transient*
Black-bellied Plover .... *transient*
Ruddy Turnstone .... *transient*
American Woodcock .... *summer*
Common Snipe .... *transient*
Whimbrel .... *transient*
Upland Sandpiper .... *rare transient*
Spotted Sandpiper .... *summer*
Solitary Sandpiper .... *rare transient*
Greater Yellowlegs .... *transient*
Lesser Yellowlegs .... *transient*
Knot .... *transient*
Purple Sandpiper .... *winter*
Pectoral Sandpiper .... *transient*
White-rumped Sandpiper .. *rare transient*
Baird's Sandpiper .... *rare transient*
Least Sandpiper .... *transient*
Dunlin .... *transient*
Short-billed Dowitcher .... *transient*
Stilt Sandpiper .... *rare transient*
Semipalmated Sandpiper ...... *transient*
Sanderling .... *transient*
Red Phalarope .... *rare offshore*
Northern Phalarope .... *transient*
Pomarine Jaeger .... *rare offshore*
Parasitic Jaeger .... *rare offshore*
Long-tailed Jaeger .... *rare offshore*
Skua .... *rare offshore*
Glaucous Gull .... *rare winter*
Iceland Gull .... *rare winter*
Great Black-backed Gull .... *resident*

Herring Gull .... *resident*
Ring-billed Gull ..... *uncommon transient*
Black-headed Gull .... *rare winter*
Little Gull .... *rare winter*
Laughing Gull .... *rare summer*
Bonaparte's Gull ...... *transient or winter*
Black-legged Kittiwake ...... *uncommon*
Sabine's Gull .... *rare offshore*
Common Tern .... *summer*
Arctic Tern .... *summer*
Roseate Tern .... *rare summer*
Least Tern .... *rare summer*
Caspian Tern .... *uncommon summer*
Black Tern .... *uncommon transient*
Razorbill .... *rare winter offshore*
Common Murre ..... *rare winter offshore*
Thick-billed Murre ... *rare winter offshore*
Dovekie .... *uncommon winter
offshore*
Black Guillemot .... *resident*
Atlantic Puffin .... *rare offshore*
Mourning Dove .... *resident*
Yellow-billed Cuckoo .... *rare summer*
Black-billed Cuckoo .... *summer*
Great Horned Owl .... *uncommon*
Snowy Owl .... *uncommon winter*
Northern Hawk Owl .... *rare winter*
Barred Owl .... *resident*
Long-eared Owl .... *rare*
Short-eared Owl .... *rare*
Boreal Owl .... *rare winter*
Northern Saw-whet Owl .... *rare*
Whip-poor-will .... *summer*
Common Nighthawk .... *summer*
Chimney Swift .... *summer*
Ruby-thr. Hummingbird .... *summer*
Belted Kingfisher .... *summer*
Northern Flicker .... *summer*
Pileated Woodpecker .... *resident*
Red-bellied Woodpecker .... *rare*
Red-headed Woodpecker .... *rare*
Yellow-bellied Sapsucker .... *summer*
Hairy Woodpecker .... *resident*
Downy Woodpecker .... *resident*

Black-backed Woodpecker ... *rare winter*
Three-toed Woodpecker ..... *rare winter*
Eastern Kingbird .... *summer*
Great Crested Flycatcher .... *uncommon summer*
Eastern Phoebe .... *summer*
Yellow-bellied Flycatcher ..... *uncommon summer*
Traill's Flycatcher .... *summer*
Least Flycatcher .... *summer*
Eastern Wood-Pewee .... *summer*
Olive-sided Flycatcher .... *summer*
Northern Shrike ...... *uncommon winter*
Loggerhead Shrike .... *rare*
Yellow-throated Vireo ...... *rare summer*
Solitary Vireo .... *summer*
Red-eyed Vireo .... *summer*
Philadelphia Vireo .... *transient*
Warbling Vireo ...... *uncommon summer*
Gray Jay .... *uncommon*
Blue Jay .... *resident*
Common Raven .... *resident*
American Crow .... *resident*
Horned Lark .... *uncommon winter*
Tree Swallow .... *summer*
Bank Swallow .... *summer*
Rough-winged Swallow ...... *uncommon summer*
Barn Swallow .... *summer*
Cliff Swallow .... *summer*
Purple Martin .... *rare transient*
Black-capped Chickadee .... *resident*
Boreal Chickadee .... *uncommon*
White-breasted Nuthatch .... *resident*
Red-breasted Nuthatch .... *resident*
Brown Creeper .... *resident*
House Wren .... *uncommon summer*
Winter Wren .... *summer*
Carolina Wren .... *rare*
Marsh Wren .... *rare summer*
Sedge Wren .... *uncommon summer*
Golden-crowned Kinglet .... *resident*
Ruby-crowned Kinglet .... *summer*
Blue-gray Gnatcatcher ..... *rare summer*
Eastern Bluebird .... *rare summer*

Wood Thrush .... *summer*
Hermit Thrush .... *summer*
Swainson's Thrush .... *summer*
Gray-cheeked Thrush ..... *rare transient*
Veery .... *summer*
American Robin .... *resident*
Northern Mockingbird ...... *uncommon*
Gray Catbird .... *summer*
Brown Thrasher .... *summer*
American Pipit .... *transient*
Bohemian Waxwing .... *rare*
Cedar Waxwing .... *summer*
Black-and-white Warbler .... *summer*
Prothonotary Warbler ...... *rare summer*
Worm-eating Warbler ...... *rare summer*
Golden-winged Warbler .... *rare summer*
Blue-winged Warbler .... *rare summer*
Tennessee Warbler .... *summer*
Nashville Warbler .... *summer*
Northern Parula Warbler .... *summer*
Yellow Warbler .... *summer*
Magnolia Warbler .... *summer*
Cape May Warbler .... *transient*
Black-throated Blue .... *summer*
Yellow-rumped Warbler .... *summer*
Black-throated Green .... *summer*
Cerulean Warbler .... *rare summer*
Blackburnian Warbler .... *summer*
Chestnut-sided Warbler .... *summer*
Bay-breasted Warbler .... *summer*
Blackpoll Warbler .... *summer*
Pine Warbler .... *uncommon summer*
Prairie Warbler .... *rare summer*
Palm Warbler .... *uncommon summer*
Ovenbird .... *summer*
Northern Waterthrush ...... *uncommon*
Connecticut Warbler .... *rare summer*
Mourning Warbler .... *transient*
Common Yellowthroat .... *summer*
Yellow-breasted Chat .... *rare*
Hooded Warbler .... *rare summer*
Wilson's Warbler .... *summer*
Canada Warbler .... *summer*
American Redstart .... *summer*
Scarlet Tanager .... *summer*

Summer Tanager . . . . *rare summer*
Eastern Towhee . . . . *summer*
Savannah Sparrow . . . . *summer*
Grasshopper Sparrow . . . . *uncommon summer*
Sharp-tailed Sparrow . . . . *summer*
Vesper Sparrow . . . . . . *uncommon summer*
Tree Sparrow . . . . *winter*
Chipping Sparrow . . . . *summer*
Clay-colored Sparrow . . . . *uncommon summer*
Field Sparrow . . . . *summer*
White-crowned Sparrow . . . . *transient*
White-throated Sparrow . . . . *resident*
Fox Sparrow . . . . *transient*
Lincoln's Sparrow . . . . *rare summer*
Swamp Sparrow . . . . *summer*
Song Sparrow . . . . *resident*
Dark-eyed Junco . . . . *resident*
Lapland Longspur . . . . *rare winter*
Snow Bunting . . . . *uncommon winter*
Rose-breasted Grosbeak . . . . *summer*

Blue Grosbeak . . . . *rare*
Northern Cardinal . . . . *uncommon*
Dickcissel . . . . *uncommon winter*
Bobolink . . . . *summer*
Eastern Meadowlark . . . . *summer*
Yellow-headed Blackbird . . . . *rare*
Red-winged Blackbird . . . . *summer*
Rusty Blackbird . . . . *transient*
Common Grackle . . . . *summer*
Brown-headed Cowbird . . . . *summer*
Orchard Oriole . . . . *rare summer*
Baltimore Oriole . . . . . *uncommon summer*
Purple Finch . . . . *summer or resident*
Pine Grosbeak . . . . *winter*
Evening Grosbeak . . . . . *winter or resident*
Common Redpoll . . . . *winter or absent*
Hoary Redpoll . . . . *rare winter*
Pine Siskin . . . . *resident or absent*
American Goldfinch . . . . *resident*
Red Crossbill . . . . *resident or absent*
White-winged Crossbill . . . . *resident or absent*

Further Reading and References

Abrell, Diana F. *A Pocket Guide to the Carriage Roads of Acadia National Park* (2nd Edition). Camden, Maine: Down East Books, 1995.

A.M.C. Trail Guide to Mount Desert Island and Acadia National Park. Boston: Appalachian Mountain Club, 1975.

Bond, James. *Native Birds of Mount Desert Island and Acadia National Park.* Philadelphia: The Academy of Natural Sciences of Philadelphia, 1971.

Brechlin, Earl. *A Pocket Guide to Hiking on Mount Desert Island.* Camden, Maine: Down East Books, 1996.

Butcher, Russell D. *Maine Paradise: Mount Desert Island and Acadia National Park.* New York: The Viking Press 1973 and 1975, Penguin Books, 1976 and 1987.

Carson, Rachel. *The Edge of the Sea.* Boston: Houghton Mifflin Company, 1955; New York: The New American Library, Inc., 1971.

Chapman, Carleton A. *The Geology of Acadia National Park.* Old Greenwich, Conn.: The Chatham Press, Inc., 1962, 1970.

Collier, Sargent F. *Acadia National Park: George B. Dorr's Triumph.* Privately published, 1965.

————. *Mt. Desert Island and Acadia National Park: An Informal History.* Camden, Maine: Down East Magazine, 1978.

Coman, Dale Rex. *The Native Mammals, Reptiles and Amphibians of Mount Desert Island, Maine.* Privately published, 1972.

Dorr, George B. *Acadia National Park: Its Origin and Background.* Bangor, Maine: Burr Printing Company, 1942.

————. *Acadia National Park: Its Growth and Development.* Bangor, Maine: Burr Printing Company, 1948.

Eliot, Charles W. *John Gilley of Baker's Island.* The Century Magazine, 1899; Philadelphia: Eastern National Park and Monument Association, 1967.

Favour, Paul G., Jr. (amended by William C. Townsend). *Checklist of the Birds of Acadia National Park.* Bar Harbor, Maine: Acadia National Park, 1969, 1974.

Hale, Richard W., Jr. *The Story of Bar Harbor.* New York: Ives Washburn, Inc., 1949.

Katona, Steven, David Richardson, and Robin Hazard. *A Field Guide to the Whales and Seals of the Gulf of Maine.* Rockland, Maine: Maine Coast Printers, 1975.

Kingsbury, John M. *Seaweeds of Cape Cod and the Islands* [and the Maine coast]. Old Greenwich, Conn.: The Chatham Press, Inc., 1969.

———. *The Rocky Shore*. Old Greenwich, Conn.: The Chatham Press, Inc., 1970.

Long, Ralph. *Native Birds of Mount Desert Island and Acadia National Park*. Mount Desert Island, Maine: Beech Hill Publishing Company, 1982.

Minutolo, Audrey Shelton. *A Pocket Guide to Biking on Mount Desert Island*. Camden, Maine: Down East Books, 1996.

Moore, Barrington, and Norman Taylor. *Vegetation of Mount Desert Island, Maine, and Its Environment*. Brooklyn, N.Y.: Brooklyn Botanic Garden, Brooklyn Institute of Arts and Sciences, 1927.

Morison, Samuel Eliot. *Samuel de Champlain: Father of New France*. Boston: Little, Brown & Company, Inc., 1972.

———. *Spring Tides*. Boston: Houghton Mifflin Company, 1965.

———. *The Story of Mount Desert Island*. Boston: Little, Brown & Co., Inc., 1960.

Paigen, Jennifer Alisa. *The Sea Kayaker's Guide to Mount Desert Island*. Camden, Maine: Down East Books, 1997.

Perrin, Steve. *Acadia's Native Flowers, Fruits, and Wildlife*. Fort Washington, Pa.: Eastern National, 2001.

Rand, Edward L., and John H. Redfield. *Flora of Mount Desert Island,*

Maine: A Preliminary Catalogue of the Plants Growing on Mount Desert and the Adjacent Islands. Cambridge, Mass.: John Wilson & Son, University Press, 1894.

Rich, Louise Dickinson. *The Peninsula* [Schoodic Peninsula]. Philadelphia: J.B. Lippincott Company, Inc., 1958; Old Greenwich, Conn.: The Chatham Press, Inc., 1971.

Sharpe, Grant W. *A Guide to Acadia National Park*. New York: Golden Press, 1968.

Sharpe, Grant, and Wenonah Sharpe. *101 Wildflowers of Acadia National Park*. Seattle: University of Washington Press, 1963, 1970.

Street, George E. *Mount Desert: A History*. Boston: Houghton Mifflin Company, 1905.

Thayer, Robert A. (text and photographs) *Acadia's Carriage Roads: A Passage into the Heart of the National Park*. Camden, Maine: Down East Books, 2002.

———. (text and photographs) *Beyond the Park Loop Road: Continuing the Exploration of Acadia National Park*. Camden, Maine: Down East Books, 2001.

———. (text and photographs) *The Park Loop Road: A Guide to Acadia National Park's Scenic Byway*. Camden, Maine: Down East Books, 1999.

Wherry, Edgar T. *Wild Flowers of Mount Desert Island, Maine*. Bar Harbor, Maine: Garden Club of Mount Desert, 1928.

Index

Maine Paradise: Mount Desert Island and Acadia National Park

New Mexico: Gift of the Earth

The Desert

Exploring Our National Parks and Monuments, Ninth Edition

Exploring Our National Historic Parks and Sites

Guide to National Parks (regional guides)

America's National Wildlife Refuges: A Complete Guide

Russell D. Butcher is a lifelong conservationist who has worked for such organizations as Save-the-Redwoods League, National Audubon Society, and most recently as Pacific Southwest regional director for the National Parks Conservation Association. He has written numerous articles and editorials for publications including *National Parks, Audubon, Down East,* and *The New York Times.* Russ has served as president of the Maine Audubon Society's Down East Chapter and as a conservation zoning consultant for the Town of Mount Desert, Maine. His books include *Maine Paradise,* a portrait of Mount Desert Island and Acadia National Park; *The Desert,* with text and photographs highlighting some of the most spectacular and interesting places in the American West's desert regions; *Exploring Our National Historic Parks and Sites;* and the ninth edition of his parents' long popular *Exploring Our National Parks and Monuments* (written by Devereux and Mary Butcher). Russ has traveled extensively throughout the United States and Europe, visiting numerous national parks and wildlife refuges.